P9-EAI-680

George Christian

STEPS DOWN

THE TRANSFER OF POWER

The Macmillan Company

LIBRARY

SEP 24 1970

UNIVERSITY OF THE PACIFIC

221621

Copyright © 1970 by *George Christian*

All rights reserved. No part of this book may
be reproduced or transmitted in any form or
by any means, electronic or mechanical, including photocopying, recording or by any
information storage and retrieval system,
without permission in writing from the
Publisher.

The Macmillan Company
866 Third Avenue, New York, N.Y. 10022
Collier-Macmillan Canada Ltd., Toronto, Ontario

Library of Congress Catalog Card Number: 75–110985

First Printing

PRINTED IN THE UNITED STATES OF AMERICA

TO THE MAGNIFICENT SEVEN:

Jo Anne
Elizabeth
Susan
George Scott
Bruce
John
and *Brian*

PROLOGUE

Any person fortunate enough to see history from an unusual vantage point still has only limited vision of what is unfolding. It is colored by his own perspective, philosophy, prejudice, and personality.

This book does not seek to interpret what is commonly called "the grand sweep" of Lyndon Johnson's years in the White House. That should be left to the scholars and to the former President himself. What it does seek to do is to telescope one critical period in the Johnson Presidency—the final months of his Administration, when major decisions were still required but freedom of action became more restricted.

The term "lame duck" is an unhappy one. Lyndon Johnson did not like to be compared with a crippled waterfowl, and he should not be. After his announcement on March 31, 1968, that he would retire from office, Johnson did not relinquish the reins of leadership overnight. There was much unfinished business, and, if anything, he attacked it with more fervor than before. But while he remained an activist to the end, the disappointments became more frequent and the decision-making process more complicated. As the summer waned, so did Presidential power. It is remarkable to me how much of it he managed to pull back, by sheer will and obstinance. Lyndon Johnson's demise as a political leader was not mellow and quiet but was more in the character of his thirty-year career. Frank Reynolds, the American Broadcasting Company's top newscaster, predicted on the air one evening that Johnson would be a "screaming eagle," not a lame duck, right up to the moment his successor put his hand on the Bible. This proved to be true, although it might be more accurate to picture Johnson as a somewhat lame eagle by the time Richard Nixon took his oath.

Lyndon Johnson's favorite story in his latter days was the one about Winston Churchill and his brandy. This is the hoary account of Churchill's challenge by the temperance lady—"a little old lady in tennis shoes," as Johnson embellished it—who accused the Prime Minister of drinking enough brandy to "fill this room up to here." To which complaint Churchill allegedly replied, looking at the halfway point and then at the ceiling: "My dear lady, so much have I done; so much yet to be done."

Though the White House press grimaced en masse at the third or fourth telling of the joke at public gatherings, it always brought a howl of approval from the President's audiences. And to Johnson it was more than a good story.

He wanted much to be done, even as his days in office dwindled. He wanted Vietnam peace talks to begin in earnest. He wanted freedom for the crew of the Pueblo. He wanted a treaty to stop the spread of nuclear weapons. He wanted peace in the Middle East. He wanted to begin talks with the Russians on halting the arms race. And he wanted to see man fly to the moon, fulfilling an objective of the space program he had fostered in the Senate ten years before.

Above all, he wanted to leave the office of the Presidency in proper shape for his successor and the state of the Union as strong as he could make it in the limited time left to him.

This is one account of how he tried. His successes and his failures are not merely history, for their effect has been felt in the Nixon Administration and will be felt for years to come.

The transition from one President to another actually began with the selection of the Democratic nominee in late August, which gave the party in power a second spokesman, so my account will meander back and forth to that time. But for purpose of focus I have chosen to begin with the crowded events of a single day— October 11, 1968—because they set the pattern for so much that followed in those last hundred days.

George Christian
Austin, Texas
January 20, 1970

ONE

I · *The Dawn Patrol*

Two hours before dawn Art McCafferty set out from his home in McLean, Virginia, for the West Basement of the White House, as he had done on a thousand other mornings during Lyndon Johnson's Administration. Awaiting him in the Situation Room were the cables reporting the battle action in Vietnam during the previous twenty-four hours. McCafferty, a National Security Council staffer, collected the cables from the duty officer, edited them, and turned them over to a secretary for typing. Before seven o'clock McCafferty's handiwork was delivered to the President's bedroom by messenger.

Above all else, Lyndon Johnson's first thoughts of the day came from the summary of the fighting and the casualties which McCafferty compiled in the darkness before dawn.

Across the Potomac in Alexandria, a black Mercury from the

White House garage drove up to the apartment of Bill Blackburn, a young lawyer on the President's legislative staff. Blackburn climbed into the back seat, turned on the reading lamp, and began thumbing through the *Congressional Record* which was fresh off the press. On his way to the White House, Blackburn read pertinent passages and marked them with paper clips and a yellow wax pencil. At the office he quickly prepared a summary, attached it to the *Record,* and sent the package to the bedroom. By eight o'clock the President had a head count on praise or criticism for any facet of his program, foreign or domestic, and a ready reference to comments inserted into the *Record* by friendly or hostile congressmen.

The *Record* was the President's bible, his compendium of current events, his window into the inner workings of the legislative body which was ever on his mind. No man knew the Congress as well as Lyndon Johnson. And no man was as adept at reading the *Record* and understanding its finer points. Here was a thermometer measuring Congressional temperatures while most people were still sleeping or relaxing with their first cup of coffee and the *Washington Post.*

Johnson was already ahead of them on reading the *Post.* He had seen the bulldog edition at eleven o'clock last night. So he gave the city edition this morning only a cursory reading and turned to the other four papers he always rummaged through in bed—the *New York Times, Baltimore Sun, Wall Street Journal, Christian Science Monitor.* News stories and editorials were first, followed by the columns and the business page. The society section of the *Post* was always good for a few Washington gossip items and a "hard" news story or two. The sports section was ignored as too unrelated to business. Between newspaper items, he listened to network radio news on the push-button set the Signal Corps had devised for him. Three coordinated television sets were on at seven o'clock, each tuned to a network. The sound was on Channel 4, NBC, for a Presidential favorite, the *Today* show. If something interested him on Channel 7 or Channel 9, he changed the sound by remote control.

Lyndon Johnson absorbed news and current events like a blotter. During the day he listened to as many radio newscasts as he could. And in the Oval Office the Associated Press and United Press International teletypes clacked away until he retired to the Mansion late at night. Whenever he entered his office, morning or afternoon, he walked straight to the tickers. And he monitored them regularly during the day. The telephone on his desk had a long cord so he could stand at the tickers and talk to a staffer or cabinet officer on an item that interested him—pleased or distressed him. Almost always, he was well ahead of his staff on fast-breaking news. When he rang you on the phone, the conversation usually began, "AP 34 . . . who's been talking too much in Saigon?" You scribbled down the log number, listened to what he had to say, and then sought out AP 34 to see about the problem.

There was little doubt that the President was the best informed man in Washington. No one had to give him a tidy little summary of the news. He knew what was going on, he reacted quickly, and sometimes he was able to stamp out fires with both feet. His habits also made his staff and other colleagues somewhat more conscious of the world around them. We could never keep up with him, but we were forced to try.

The bedroom was an integral part of the business of the Presidency. Like Winston Churchill and Mark Twain, Lyndon Johnson did a great deal of serious thinking on his back. He was a born early riser—early waker would be more accurate. The news, including McCafferty's battle report, was always the first item on his agenda. He paused from his reading only long enough to eat breakfast at bedside.

Morning in the bedroom was also memo time. When the President prepared to retire at night, the *Washington Post* and two or three stacks of "night reading," bound by rubber bands, always rested on the folded-back covers. There might be eighty or a hundred pieces of reading material—memos, reports, analyses, correspondence, position papers. If he didn't finish this at night, the leftovers stared at him in the morning, and he dutifully resumed his reading. Most of the memoranda came from his two "program" assistants—Walt Rostow (foreign policy) and Joe Califano (domestic policy). The staff tried to make his task easier by ending their memos with suggested courses of action, then a "yes, no, call me" multiple-choice entry. The President often added a few earthy comments with a number one pencil.

Shortly after eight o'clock the first of the "bedroom regulars" arrived. In the latter days this was Jim Jones, the appointments secretary. He was soon followed by Larry Temple, whose title was special counsel and whose duties were catholic. Both were young lawyers—Jones from Oklahoma and Temple from Texas. They were also durable, calm by nature, good humored, and able to function on six hours' sleep. For the next hour or two they went over the day's business with Johnson, interrupted frequently by telephone calls, and collected assignments for other staff members.

At ten o'clock or later I usually arrived, often accompanied by the deputy press secretary, Tom Johnson. We would relieve the others and take up our own problems with the Boss, staying with him until he had showered and dressed for his first office appointment. Frequently, we walked with him to the Oval Office, still getting instructions en route.

The bedroom itself was rather ordinary, except that few bedrooms have three television sets, a bullet-proof window, and a full view of the Washington Monument. The canopied bed was ample, with many large pillows to make reading easier. A stuffed chair and a rocker were handy for bedside conferences. Across the room, next to the fireplace, were two more stuffed chairs facing each other with an ottoman wedged in between. They were strictly for emergency use. The pictures varied from time to time, except for family photographs and a watercolor of a Negro woman sewing an American flag. The total effect of the room was bland; bright colors were sparse. This was a workroom first, living quarters second.

Remarkably, Mrs. Lady Bird Johnson shared this room with her husband much of the time, although she had an adjoining bedroom available when things got too disturbing. But as often as not, she was still with the President when the daily troupe of White House aides invaded the sanctuary.*

Johnson's morning habits varied little from year to year. The cast of "bedroom regulars" changed, of course, as assistants came and went. Formal breakfasts were rare; the only one scheduled regularly was the Democratic leadership breakfast once or twice a month when Congress was in session. And it was held at the civilized hour of 8:30 a.m., allowing the President time for his chores before dressing for his guests.

There was a distinct purpose in the bedroom routine. Always mindful of his health, Johnson diligently conserved his strength by spending part of the day relatively immobile. This entailed a long morning in bed and then a nap in midafternoon, after which he began his "second day" at five o'clock. He believed that the time spent before going to the office was his most productive period; he could think, he could read, he could talk, he could decide. His body might be reclining, but his mind was moving like a meteor.

The press jeered when Jack Valenti said Johnson had "extra glands." But that was Valenti's way of explaining that the President knew how to shepherd his energies and remain a long-distance runner despite the wear and tear of the years.

II · *The Palace Guard*

In the early part of his Presidency, Lyndon Johnson's habits were crushing to hapless staff members. Later, many found ways to adjust. Although events frequently dictated long days, the Johnson staff over the years learned the secret of separating public and private life with at least partial success. Their jobs were not supposed to be easy. The President had no tolerance for sloth and very little for blatant mistakes and inefficiency. He knew the bear-

* Over the fireplaces in both bedrooms were the little silver plaques placed by Mrs. John F. Kennedy after the assassination of her husband, signifying that President Kennedy had occupied one of the rooms and Mrs. Kennedy the other during the period 1961–63. Other than this, historical references were absent in the bedroom suite.

pit technique of playing men off against each other, usually with some objective in mind. He knew how to extract every ounce of stamina from a staff, and the taxpayers never got half-measure from the White House while he was President. He could be rough, he could terrify, he could explain himself in terms no one could forget. He could also be generous to a fault and exceptionally kind to those around him.

Most politicians place a premium on loyalty. Johnson did this in spades. He felt that a President, of all people, was entitled to the single-minded loyalty of his associates. As Vice President he had given this type of fidelity to John Kennedy; he expected it now from the Cabinet, the Presidential appointees, the staff. For some, the challenge was too great.

Johnson's thirst was for ideas, even as his Presidential years moved inevitably toward an end, and he was attracted to those with imagination and the boldness to innovate. He did not necessarily demand that the idea men be overly blessed with political judgment. He would be the check and balance in that regard. And though he might put the stamp of idiocy on someone's scheme, it did not necessarily mean he wanted no more ideas from that individual. A staffer who could not bounce back from temporary defeat had no business working for Johnson. But when anyone in government submitted too many suggestions of little merit, or talked too freely to the press about maneuvers "the Johnson Administration" was considering (whether Johnson knew about them or not), or ran too frequently with the wrong political crowd, woe unto that man insofar as retaining any influence with the President. The usual fate was to be consigned to limbo, to perform meaningless tasks or none at all, until some twist of fate or changed events might restore him to favor. Dismissal from government was exceedingly rare, although a downtrodden outcast might ultimately resign receiving a letter of acceptance from the President praising him for patriotic service.

The Johnson staff in late 1968 bore little resemblance to the two-layer staff of the post-assassination months, when Kennedy and Johnson aides both occupied key spots, or even to the staff of the halcyon days of 1965–66 when the Johnson touch was still magic and the chill caused by the war was only beginning to set in. There was only a handful of veterans who were there when Lyndon Johnson became President. Bill Hopkins, a career civil servant who had been at the White House since Herbert Hoover was President, kept the administrative functions well oiled. Mike Manatos, a politically astute Greek-American from Wyoming, was on Kennedy's legislative liaison staff and was retained by Johnson to work the Senate; one of his lieutenants, Chuck Roche, was also a Kennedy original. George Reedy, a big and wise warrior of many skirmishes during the Johnson's Senate, Vice Presidential, and Presidential years, had been recalled to the White House from private life in 1968 after an unhappy stint as press secretary in 1964–65. Reedy now handled labor matters and gave experienced advice in other areas. Few men at the White House were his peer in understanding the complexities of government.

The other originals and near-originals were long gone—Horace Busby, Bill Moyers, Jack Valenti, Walter Jenkins, Larry O'Brien, McGeorge Bundy, Henry Hall Wilson. Some had come, lent their talents for a while, and then moved on. Bob Kintner, hard-nosed former president of NBC, was one. Jake Jacobsen of Texas, Johnson's closest aide for a long period, was another. Marvin Watson had been promoted to Postmaster General. John Roche, an Irish firebrand, once national chairman of the super-liberal Americans for Democratic Action, was a more recent departee. Roche fascinated Johnson. The President had genuine affection for him, but tried to restrain his alley fighter instincts and probably never achieved full use of his intellectual talents. Another to leave late was Douglass Cater, a soft-spoken Alabamian who was surely one of the three or four men most responsible for the health and education program Johnson pushed through Congress. Cater had quit to help Hubert Humphrey. Colonel Jim Cross, military aide and Presidential pilot, had volunteered for Vietnam.

A White House staff does not have to be static to be competent. New blood brings new ideas, and equally important, new perspectives to a staff which might suffer from the isolation so common in the Executive Branch. Of all the staff losses, the most difficult to replace was Walter Jenkins. When he departed in 1964, no one was able to succeed him as chief of staff, though some tried. Different aides were able to assume pieces of his responsibilities, but none totally replaced this tireless, loyal, terribly pressured administrator of the Presidency.

Two of the staff's earlier strong men, Marvin Watson and Bill Moyers, were of immense value to Johnson in entirely different ways. For three years Watson was the President's alter ego and Jenkins-like administrator; Johnson ordered a tight ship at the White House and Watson took him at his word, often crossing swords with Moyers and others in his single-minded intent to carry out his orders as he saw them. Watson was also a deft operative in Congressional relations; when the going got tough on the Hill he always seemed to be able to pull a few badly needed votes out of his pocket.

Moyers, like Watson, was a Texas Baptist. But his outlook was definitely not fundamentalist, and during his three years at the White House he consumed himself in everything the President himself touched, a daring young quarterback who learned from the coach and added a few plays of his own. Around him he built a loyal staff which was virtually a White House within the White House, and this was bound to cause conflicts in the tightly structured environment of 1600 Pennsylvania Avenue. After he became press secretary in 1965, Moyers and his staff continued to dabble in foreign policy, domestic programs, speech writing, and assorted other fields, and his imprint on the White House was far greater than his detractors liked to concede.

By 1966 Moyers' once-close personal relationship with Lyndon Johnson was crumbling and he finally decided late in the year to accept the position of publisher of *Newsday*. Later someone in the press coined the term "the Moyers Gap" to explain what the writer considered flaws in the President's handling of Vietnam and the racial disturbances. Be that as it may, Moyers' unique talents most certainly were missed after he departed for a quieter life on Long Island.

His old adversary, Watson, remained Johnson's key staffer until 1968 when the President made him Postmaster General. Watson was always an enigma to the press, partly because he did not like to return telephone calls. ("I'm not paid to talk to the press," he would say, much to the President's admiration.) His conservatism, his religious code, his facade of unbending sternness were not readily adaptable to the Washington circles in which Great Society liberals moved. But as appointments secretary, White Housekeeper, and ramrod of a sometimes undisciplined executive office, he had one of the tougher jobs in Washington, and Lyndon Johnson would not have exchanged him for any other.

Walt Rostow and Joe Califano both arrived after the course of the Johnson Administration, foreign and domestic, had been set. They were essentially shirtsleeves operators, buried in paperwork and attempting to keep a variety of ideas and programs cooking at the same time. Of his piled-up desk in his basement office, Rostow commented, "Someday one piece of paper will fall through the cracks and NATO will collapse." Rostow was a hard-muscled tennis player who thrived on competition and dreamed of a well-ordered world based upon sound economies and national pride. He actually seemed more fascinated with the future of South America than Southeast Asia, but it fell his lot to draw continuous fire from many in the press for his dogged optimism on Vietnam and from many of his intellectual colleagues for the U.S.'s being there in the first place.

Califano handled the domestic program with the exuberance of a kid who finally made railroad engineer. The young staff he gathered around him quite possibly topped anything the White House had ever seen. Writers, composers, lawyers, economists, dreamers, slaves—each of them was a little of all. Larry Levinson, an exceptionally talented lawyer from New York, played first violin. Jim Gaither from California was right behind. Others came and went, contributing their bit to President Johnson's appetite for new schemes to abolish domestic devils wherever they were found.

Like Moyers, Califano collected enemies within the staff and out. But he understood the need for a "power base" in the Administration and fed it constantly, enduring the complaints of those whose duties he encroached upon and answering their jabs with a sort of "who, me?" expression that belied his motives. He could also be crafty. Once he enlisted my aid in a lengthy but unsuccessful conspiracy to get a Cabinet officer appointed Ambassador to India, believing this would get the man sufficiently distant from White House policy.

Harry McPherson, like Moyers and Watson, sprang from the East Texas pine woods and knew what he wanted in life. But for McPherson it was not power, but peace of mind. He dodged the power struggles as best he could and concentrated on influencing the President with the written word; his hand was in virtually every Presidential utterance on major policy. He was one of the more successful aides when it came to living a private life of his own, and the only one I knew who occasionally left home with his family without telling the White House switchboard where he was going. More importantly, he was the only one who got away with it.

Most of the others on the latter-day staff were relative newcomers. Ernest Goldstein, a former law professor, was on leave from a lucrative international practice in Paris. Larry Temple had come up from Texas only a few months before Johnson announced he would not run again. He was much respected for his legal ability, as was DeVier Pierson of Oklahoma. Jim Jones, who came to the White House as an Army lieutenant, had replaced Marvin Watson as appointments secretary. Ervin Duggan, native of South Carolina and still in his twenties, had subbed for Douglass Cater. Barefoot Sanders had come from the Justice Department to handle legislative chores along with Mike Manatos and a small staff. Charles Murphy was an old salt from the Truman days; he would be the staff man on transition problems. Harry Middleton and Bob Hardesty led a team of writers and researchers; Charles Maguire was Cabinet secretary and also a writer. The military staff was now led by Marine Colonel Haywood Smith. Another

Smith, Bromley, had headed the National Security Council staff since Eisenhower's time, and held Rostow's operation together.

Of course, others played roles of equal importance in Lyndon Johnson's life: his secretaries like Marie Fehmer, Juanita Roberts, and Mary Rather; his doctor, Admiral George Burkley; his valets and companions, Ken Gaddis and Paul Glynn; Mrs. Johnson's veteran aides, Liz Carpenter, Ashton Gonella, and Bess Abell; and others whose names will crop up in this narrative.

So now a few of us manned the battlements until our White House days would end in glory, and relief, on January 20, 1969.

It was part of the Johnson legend that he was a man who drove his employees mercilessly, abused them without cause or limitation, and cast them aside when he had wrung all he could from their shattered psyches. This was a careless interpretation, at best. I am confident that nearly every member of the Johnson staff thought himself overworked or abused at one time or another, but only a few allowed such sensitivities to get the better of them. Any large organization working under immense pressure might tread on an individual's rights to a tranquil life, reasonable liberty, and the occasional pursuit of happiness. But the excuse of working late at the office has also been used since the invention of the white collar as a means of escaping a shrewish wife, covering a love affair, or merely fulfilling one's personal ambition to get ahead.

Johnson's staff was reasonably cosmopolitan and represented a cross-section of American political thought. The President may not have been liberal enough for some nor conservative enough for others, but most were intensely loyal to him and his program. The staff was Texanized to an extent, just as many of John Kennedy's people were New England born or New England educated. But there was no cabal of Texans, bent upon making the White House an extension of the Lone Star State. Harry McPherson was far more oriented to the Eastern Seaboard, where he had lived for years, rather than to Texas where he was reared. Ernie Goldstein was proud to call himself a Texan because he had taught law there for a time, but the East was his birthplace and Paris was his love. Barefoot Sanders had served a hitch in the Texas Legislature, as an outspoken liberal, but was less provincial than many of the non-Texans on the staff.

Larry Temple and I were the only Texans in top positions who considered ourselves to be on leave from our state. We came because we were asked to come, and we were anxious to return home when we could. As soon as Johnson made his March 31 decision, my wife and I began making plans to return to Texas. By the end of the summer she and the children were home in Austin, leaving me to "batch" it in Washington with the Temples and the Johnsons.

The Texans were often called "cronies" of the President, and we became overly sensitive about it. The more we tried to avoid the label, naturally, the more firmly the press fastened it to us. Goldstein was even commissioned a Presidential appointee as a resident of the District of Columbia, although he hadn't lived in Washington for at least fifteen years. Defensive maneuvers such as this did little to dispel the notion that Johnson had surrounded himself with Texas cronies to the exclusion of the rest of the country. Of course, three Texans sat in the last Johnson Cabinet—Attorney General Ramsey Clark, Postmaster General Marvin Watson, and Commerce Secretary C. R. Smith. But none of the Texans on Johnson's staff had a long-term relationship with him except for McPherson, a former Senate employee. We came to know him only after arriving at 1600 Pennsylvania Avenue in fear and trepidation of what we were getting into.

It should be added as a postscript that some of the Texas cadre overreacted to reporters' needling. This helped blow the issue out of proportion and stimulate the desire of those in Washington who wanted to get rid of the damned Texans.

The President's efforts to maintain a balanced staff created a sometime luncheon topic in the White House Mess. We joked among ourselves that Marvin Watson was the resident conservative, Ernie Goldstein the resident liberal, Cliff Alexander the resident Negro, Joe Califano the resident Italian, Larry Levinson the resident Jew, Mike Manatos the resident Greek, John Roche the resident intellectual, George Christian the resident Texan, Walt Rostow the resident hawk, Harry McPherson the resident dove, Tom Johnson the resident youth. Other backgrounds and persuasions were also available, such as Boston Irishman Chuck Roche (no relation to John Roche) and Scottish-born John Gonella on the legislative staff, but the game had to stop somewhere.

Late in Johnson's Administration, as always, there was the ever-present struggle for power within the palace guard, but it had diminished as the need for position became less important. Because there was no chief of staff, lines of communication from staff to President were direct. It was fairly easy for an aide to see the Boss if he had something important to discuss, but in many instances Johnson preferred memos. There was a direct telephone line to each of the special assistants and some of the junior staff, which the President could activate by simply picking up the phone and pushing a button. The red button on the assistant's phone was marked POTUS (President of the United States). No matter what an aide was doing, a loud and steady ring on the POTUS line caused a scramble for the telephone. Tales abound in print about the President's telephoning habits, so I feel compelled to add another to the lore.

Once after a rugged several hours in the office I decided to take a walk around the perimeter of the White House with Ray Scherer of NBC, who also liked to escape the confines of the building occasionally. I had no sooner left than my POTUS line rang and was picked up by one of my secretaries. "He's not here now, Mr. President," she said. "Where is he?" the President asked. "He's outside and away from the phone for a few minutes, Mr. President," she replied. There was a pause, and then Johnson said sweetly, "Honey, I want you to get this phone fixed so it will ring *wherever* he is."

There were several small indicators in the Johnson White House of a staffer's alleged importance. One, of course, was the POTUS line, or the number of telephone lines on your console.

Another was access to the Presidential bedroom. Another seemed to be how many memos one could add to the stack of night reading, and how many "yeses" came back on suggestions. Aides with the largest staffs and the biggest problems (Rostow and Califano) naturally added the most to the ocean of paper funnelled into Johnson. But some staff members with few specific assignments were prone to long memos and dissertations of a quality which required many man-hours of labor. I always envied anyone with the time to compose such documents. Much of this, of course, was valuable to Johnson in terms of ideas, criticisms, and studied conclusions. However, he frequently sent memos back unread if they were too long and involved, leaving the aide miserably in doubt as to what Johnson thought of the idea. Or he might send one to another aide with the scribbled note: "Read this and tell me what he's talking about." The President was leery of staff members he thought to be overly ambitious or too impressed with their own importance and enjoyed taking them down a peg or two.

One of Johnson's real talents—obscured by other aspects of his Presidency—was his aptitude for administration. He knew how to keep the paper flowing. If he could be criticized for devoting too much time to details, he could likewise be praised for his knowledge of the issues requiring decisions. He did his homework. He would study the pros and cons of a subject with something akin to fascination, and if he did not have all of the information he wanted he would call a meeting of everyone connected with the problem and discuss it at length. He would plunge deeply into complicated issues such as the European Common Market, the balance of payments, the monetary crisis. His first love was the budget. Like a mathematics teacher, he relished applying the pencil to the knotty problems of taxes and expenditures. He could brief the press on the Executive Budget with more clarity and precision than the budget officers themselves, and he seldom had to refer to notes when it came to figures.

His office habits were ritual. Rarely did a letter prepared for his signature wait on his signing table more than one day. No matter how large the stacks were, he would bear down in the late evening and get the job behind him. He read a high proportion of his mail, especially the letters from servicemen in Vietnam, and frequently dictated replies to important correspondence. He fulfilled requests for autographed pictures as quickly as he could sign his name, and spent part of each evening signing the bookmarks and other small items he and Mrs. Johnson mailed as gifts to high school graduates who had sent them commencement invitations.

Johnson was not adverse to delegating authority when he had to, but he left little doubt as to who was to make the important decisions. In brief, he ruled.

III · *Banning the Bomb*

On Friday, October 11, the President cut short his morning in the sanctuary of the bedroom and headed for the Oval Office at ten o'clock.

I met him at the elevator on the ground floor of the Mansion when he got off with Jim Jones and Tom Johnson. He was more cheerful than I thought he would be, because the day was already shaping up as one of those in which we would scratch for every extra minute.

"Well, there's Georgie," he said. "I'll bet you don't want to go to Texas." He knew very well I wanted to go to Texas at every opportunity since moving my family home to Austin. I picked up his loping pace through the hallway, past the towering portrait of the lovely Mrs. Grover Cleveland and out onto the colonnade separating the Mansion from the West Wing of the White House, with Jim and Tom trailing slightly behind. Jones was loaded with the morning business—everything the President had read and acted upon in the last ten hours.

"We might go to Texas tonight," he told me as we walked. "We could stop in Kansas City and see President Truman. I want to sign the United Nations Day proclamation with him. We might do that and then decide whether we can go on to the ranch."

I knew from experience that it would take a major crisis to

keep the President away from Texas this weekend now that he was giving it serious thought. He had received the weather reports from home—mild weekend, warm enough for swimming. He was being stifled by the weight of events, a heavy office schedule, and the restrictions of the White House. Autumn was the right time of year in Washington, but it was also the right time of year in the Texas hill country. There the sun would still be hot in midday, and if Johnson had a special craving it was for bright sunshine.

But the President rarely made a final, firm decision on travel away from the White House until he was completely satisfied he could go. This always exasperated the press and frustrated Presidential assistants, especially press secretaries. The newsmen never accepted any of our explanations for this, contending that other Presidents scheduled trips ahead of time and were far less secretive about them. Johnson was unimpressed. He said he would not base such decisions on the convenience of the reporters but on his own determination of when he should or should not travel. When advance notice was possible, he gave it; when not: Follow the Boy Scout slogan.

All of Johnson's press chieftains—Pierre Salinger, George Reedy, Bill Moyers, George Christian—tried to be sure the travelling press at least had enough notice to pack a bag, and on trips to Texas there was usually some warning. But short notice was the rule, and it required playing the game called "Second Guessing the President on Travel Arrangements." We won a few, lost a few, and broke even sometimes, meaning we incurred the anger of both the press and the President.

This time I felt like a winner. I had cautioned the White House press the afternoon before that a trip to Texas was a possibility: "A prudent man will bring a bag." I had asked Jiggs Fauver, our transportation chief, to put an airplane on standby for Friday afternoon. The Tropicano Motor Hotel in San Antonio blocked out enough rooms for us. The Secret Service and White House Communications Agency (nicknamed "WHOCKA") were alerted and had their men prepared.

All we needed was word from the President.

What we had was the usually hesitant "might go." And for good reason, when the situation was analyzed.

Today, the Ninetieth Congress was in a frenetic countdown to adjournment, with two or three important bills hanging. The Republicans had staged a successful stalling maneuver to kill a proposal permitting debates on television between Richard Nixon and Hubert Humphrey. Both the House and Senate were beset by partisanship, dimming an otherwise good record on many Administration programs. The Senate had rejected by acrimonious filibuster the President's nomination of Abe Fortas to be Chief Justice of the United States. Then came the Republican effort to delay ratification of the treaty designed to curb the spread of nuclear weapons. This treaty was one of President Johnson's foremost objectives, hammered out over the years with a suspicious Soviet Union and several equally suspicious allies of America.

Nixon had urged that the treaty not be ratified until the next session of Congress—ostensibly to punish the Russians for invading Czechoslovakia. Most Senate Republicans reacted accordingly, with sympathetic help from some Democrats. Johnson thought Nixon was chiefly interested in seeing the treaty ratified during a Nixon Administration rather than the Johnson Administration. But the President himself had been reluctant to push ratification too hard after the invasion of Czechoslovakia. The last thing he wanted was a negative vote. However, the more Hubert Humphrey advocated the treaty and the more Nixon demurred, the more Johnson became convinced he had to lay the blame for delay where it belonged: on the Republicans.

The President was worried that the longer the treaty lacked American ratification, the less leverage the United States had on countries like West Germany, India, and Israel which were already balking at signing the pledge not to enter the nuclear arms race. Western Europe was again fearful of Russian pressures, and there was a growing belief—nurtured by Charles de Gaulle—that the United States, no matter what it said, would not go to nuclear war in defense of Europe.

With congressmen now eager to go home, Johnson was faced

with the decision of demanding speedy action on the treaty, threatening a special session, or letting the issue hold over until the new Congress convened in January.

Senate Majority Leader Mike Mansfield, who favored postponement of the issue until January, was on the President's schedule this morning. Johnson would talk with Mansfield and then decide what to do. He had in his hands a tough statement which several advisers had recommended he make on television and radio. Yesterday he had leaned away from the statement; this morning he was leaning toward.

Other matters shared Johnson's attention this day.

At eleven o'clock, the Apollo 7 space shot would be launched from Cape Kennedy. It was America's first manned venture in outer space since the tragic fire in January 1967 that killed three astronauts. This had been a rough twenty months for the space program, for which Johnson felt considerable pride. The space budget had been trimmed, NASA and its contractors had been bumped around in Congress and the press, and—most importantly—the Apollo program had to prove itself again and three more men were staking their lives on it. This was no ordinary space shot, but none ever was.

On the purely domestic front, Johnson was roundly displeased with the 1968 Farm Act, recently sent to his desk by the Congress. He was especially irritated that huge subsidy payments would continue for large-scale farmers after he had recommended reforms in this area, where 80 per cent of the subsidies are paid to only 20 per cent of the farmers. This was his last day to sign or veto the bill. "Fix me a veto message," he had ordered Harry McPherson and DeVier Pierson, who prudently prepared a signing statement as well.

The word was out that the President was contemplating a veto. Agriculture Secretary Orville Freeman made a strong recommendation that the bill be signed. Democratic leaders in the Congress thought a veto would be politically harmful. And Hubert Humphrey, scrapping hard for the Midwestern states in an uphill battle, thought a veto would be a blow to his cause.

On touch-and-go matters of this kind, it was the President's habit to delay the decision until the deadline pressed close. It was obvious the farm bill would not be signed or vetoed until well after dark, since he had until midnight to act. The proponents would have to sweat all day.

The President's schedule included three important meetings with foreign visitors. Foreign Ministers Michel Debré of France, Michael Stewart of Britain, and Giuseppe Medici of Italy had successive appointments beginning at ten-thirty. They had been attending the United Nations General Assembly in New York, a session faced with the simmering questions of Czechoslovakia and the Middle East.

Mixed reports were coming from Central Europe on Soviet intentions, and Czech acquiescence, in the crisis there. Czech leaders had been in Moscow, but our intelligence reports were murky as to what had transpired. The communique seemed to say the Czechs had been made to pay the price for dissent, but there were also hints that they had balked again and might soon face further repression and new arrests.

The news from Vietnam was also muddled. The Associated Press had quoted a "reliable source" in Saigon as saying a coup against President Thieu had been thwarted. This prompted our Ambassador, Ellsworth Bunker, to cable that the Thieu government was jumpy, but there were no real signs of an attempted takeover. Finally, Thieu went on the air to deny there was an attempted coup—contradicting officials on his own staff who had reported the threat to the press. Just to make sure nothing was afoot, Bunker issued a statement that "any deviations from the normal constitutional processes which the Vietnamese people have established for themselves would be a matter of the gravest concern. We cannot envisage a situation in which changes brought about by extralegal means could obtain the approval or support of the American people and government."

In nondiplomatic terms, Bunker was saying a coup might be the beginning of the end of U.S. support for Saigon. The fear of a government upheaval in South Vietnam haunted the President.

No matter how strongly one believed in turning back the "war of liberation" in Vietnam, no one could envisage a worse predicament for the U.S. than a coup in Saigon. All of the painstaking work of building even a semblance of democratic institutions there would go up in the smoke of political and military jealousies among South Vietnam's leaders. The Communist offensive at Tet had been a psychological blow to American public opinion, regardless of the Allied military success. A coup would be even harder to endure.

All of these assorted troubles and opportunities were compartmentalized somewhere in Lyndon Johnson's mind as he walked to his office on that mild October morning. But all shrank in immediate significance when matched against yet another development involving the omnipresent Asian war. There had been a hint of movement in the Paris peace talks for the first time since they began, and he was anxious to receive further news from the American negotiators.

Before we reached the West Wing, I handed the President a suggested statement on a subject far removed from the war. Congress had passed a gun control bill falling considerably short of the President's demands. He had swum upstream on this issue from the beginning. Hopeful that a great public outcry would finally bring workable legislation to curb firearms, he had discovered that crime, violence in the streets, and political assassination combined could not offset organized opposition to gun control. The bill just passed was only a shell of his original proposal.

"That statement doesn't say anything," Johnson told me impatiently. "I want to say I'm glad the bill passed but mad as hell the gun lobby ruined it. Who wrote this thing? Get with Larry Levinson and beef it up."

The President had stopped on the colonnade, at the door to the Cabinet Room where the House and Senate Democratic leaders had gathered to present him with an end-of-the-session gift. I had a carbon copy of a statement he had been sent on the nuclear nonproliferation treaty and handed this to him in hopes of obtaining a decision. "I've read this," he said, but looked it over again. "Okay, I think I'll do it. But I've got to talk to Mansfield again after this ceremony. Don't do anything till you hear from me."

"Will you do it for the cameras?" I ventured.

"You always tell me I'm overexposed."

"I wish you would do this one on camera."

"We'll see after I decide what I want to say."

He pushed through the French doors into the Cabinet Room, where he greeted Mansfield, Senator Robert Byrd of West Virginia, Speaker John McCormack, and House Majority Leader Carl Albert. This was the first of many farewells, ceremonial and otherwise, which the outgoing President would have in the final three months of his Administration. At the President's last Democratic leaders' breakfast of the session, Senator Russell Long had collected twenty dollars or so from each of his colleagues to purchase Johnson a going-away gift. There had been considerable sentiment and nostalgia at the breakfast, held as always in the Presidential Family Dining Room, because the House and Senate leaders thought this would be the final business session with Lyndon Johnson. But they underestimated their lame duck. In January the President would be calling leadership meetings again, still struggling to help Congress reach crucial decisions before yielding his power.

At the presentation ceremony today two of the leaders, Long and House Majority Whip Hale Boggs, could not come. But after hearty formalities, the other four grouped around the Cabinet table with the President. Then Mansfield rose to read a speech. The Senior Senator from Montana, reserved as always, said in part:

> We have had our differences, always in the open. . . . You have never crossed the line of demarcation that divides the Executive from the Legislative but you have scrupulously observed the rights of your office as we have observed ours. Because of our feelings toward you personally, because of the mutual respect which has been the norm in the relationship between

the Leadership and the Chief Executive, because of the awareness of the difficulties which have confronted you down through the years and have multiplied lately, and because of the respect that we have for you and the office of the Presidency, we would like to take this occasion to present you with this token of our esteem.

The Speaker of the House handed the gold-wrapped gift to the President while the White House photographer Yoichi Okamoto snapped pictures. Then old John McCormack said simply:

You will go down as one of the great Presidents of the United States. I have admired you intensely, especially for your firmness. I've wanted a man in the White House with the courage to make his own decisions. This has been a wonderful relationship. It is not the end; it is only the beginning.

The press photographers were invited in to take pictures of the President holding a new set of Florentine cufflinks, inscribed "LBJ," while the Democratic leaders smiled and crowded around.

Afterward, the President conferred privately with Mansfield on the nonproliferation treaty. The Senator had said all along he did not think it wise to bring up the treaty at this session. He reinforced that view today in the waning hours of the Ninetieth Congress. He said he was planning to make a statement on the matter, but had no serious objection if the President wanted to voice his support of the treaty again and criticize those responsible for the delay.

Satisfied, the President passed the word to shape up a final draft of the statement. Several on the staff who had favored a Presidential blast—both as a statement of principle and possible help for Vice President Humphrey—were delighted. I called one of them, Harry McPherson, on the staff intercom and reported: "Victory." McPherson replied: "Great!"

Foreign Minister Debré, meeting Johnson for the first time, told him how much he was going to be missed by the French government when he retired from office in January. This bit of Franco-American diplomacy surprised and flattered the President.

France had been an estranged ally of late. However, Johnson had always refrained from quarreling publicly with President de Gaulle, even when the Frenchman twitted the Americans on everything from NATO to Vietnam. At eleven o'clock Johnson and Debré paused to watch the launching of Apollo 7 on television.

The photographers were allowed in again to record Johnson's observation of the space shot. He sat beside his three color television sets in the Oval Office, eyes riveted to the scene. Debré, standing next to him, bent down to say something, but the President acknowledge his comment without moving his eyes from the blazing Saturn rocket.

Later in the day the President sent one of those strangely stilted formal messages to Apollo crewman Walter Schirra, Walter Cunningham, and Donn Eisele:

> Everything in the President's Office came to a halt as Foreign Minister Debré of France and I watched with mounting excitement the magnificent launch of the Saturn 1B. You can well imagine the great pleasure which filled the room as word came of your successful insertion into orbit. The path to the moon takes courage, ability, and devotion to our goals. You are making a major stride on this star-studded way.

His feelings were probably more accurately interpreted by his grandson Lyn Nugent, who toddled into the office during a brief interlude between appointments. By this time the television networks were rerunning the tape of the launch. As the Saturn rocket rose in the sky, Lyn marched to the middle set and kissed the glass.

The President's meetings with Britain's Michael Stewart and Italy's Giuseppe Medici were brief but full. The British Foreign Secretary had Vietnam on his mind; Johnson told him there would be no bombing halt in the panhandle of North Vietnam unless the danger to Allied troops was removed. One of the topics for Johnson and Medici was the nuclear nonproliferation treaty. The Italian Foreign Minister caused a brief flurry when he walked out through the press lobby and was interviewed closely by the reporters on the treaty. Misunderstanding a question, he left the impression he thought the United States should delay further consideration of the treaty—which sounded like a direct poke at Johnson. His intent was to say that Italy would refrain from signing until the European crisis settled down.

Italian Ambassador Ortona, understanding English better than Medici, attempted to straighten out the confusion but only partly succeeded. When UPI sent out a story implicating Medici in the American political debate over the treaty, the President was thunderstruck. Carroll Kilpatrick of the *Washington Post*, who had understood Medici's confusion, had already warned me that some of the newsmen were misinterpreting the Foreign Minister's statements because of the language difficulties. I called the Italian press attaché and was assured a clarifying statement was being telephoned to the wire services.

The mishap, coincidentally, came just as the President had made up his mind to issue a strong statement on the nuclear treaty. The statement had been drafted by Rostow and McPherson and an expert on the National Security Council staff, Spurgeon Keeny. The President strengthened the language, and shortly after noon made the long walk to the White House theater in the East Wing to record it for radio and television.

Looking sternly into the cameras, Johnson pointed out that the United States had been trying for many years to reduce the threat that "someday, somewhere" a limited nuclear war would break out and eventually involve the major powers in a worldwide catastrophe. He noted that the lengthy negotiations had finally produced a treaty which was approved in the United Nations by a vote of ninety-five to four, and was designed to keep additional fingers from reaching nuclear triggers.

"We negotiated with the Soviet Union on the language of this treaty—not as a gift to the Soviet Union, nor as a matter of bridge building between us, but because we were seeking a result in our own interest which they happened to share for their own reasons," the President said.

"If we do not proceed to ratify this treaty promptly, the forces at work against it in other countries will quickly gather strength."

Then Johnson got to his main point, the Republican delays: "Those who now argue for postponing ratification of the treaty must assume the grave responsibility for its failure—and for presenting our country with that dilemma. . . ."

Johnson said he knew the pressures of the election were on the Senate, but hoped it would act responsibly without further delay. Since he was already certain this would not happen, his expression of hope was merely the predicate for a threat to "seriously consider" calling the Senate into special session.

"I consider the adoption of this treaty that important to the security of our nation and world peace."

Later, and for many days thereafter, the newsmen grilled me on the special session threat, until the subject became somewhat of a bore. It was only after Christmas—a few days before the Congress was due to come back in regular session—that I admitted the issue was dead.

While the logic of calling a special session for consideration of the treaty became thin after the November election, Johnson entertained the thought even after a negative reaction from President-elect Nixon. Characteristically, Johnson did not want to give up without a struggle, while there was even the slightest possibility of treaty ratification before he left office. Nixon's attitude remained constant; he was in no hurry. After November 5, a neutral Nixon was not enough for a successful "run" with the treaty. Without his active participation the Senate Republican leaders could hardly be expected to show enthusiasm.

It appeared for a time that a head-on public collision would come on this issue between Johnson and Nixon in the post-election period, even though Johnson was anxious to effect a gentlemanly transfer of power. But Vietnam was a strong factor in nullifying this possibility. A reconvened Congress would have provided a ready forum for all sorts of angry exchanges over difficulties with the Saigon government during November and December when the peace talks were stalled. Frustrations after the bombing cessation might have become even more complicated with a hundred Senators debating the issue before the world.

IV · *Message from Harvan*

The President had lunch in the Family Dining Room with Mrs. Johnson, Tom Johnson and me. Tom, a twenty-six-year-old Georgian who had come to Washington from Harvard Business School as a White House Fellow, worked on the sidelines for a couple of years and then moved into the mainstream both in responsibility and in Presidential esteem. When Bob Fleming, a veteran, scholarly ex-reporter, moved from deputy press secretary to the U.S. Information Agency, I put Tom Johnson—a man half his age—in the slot. Tom had become a regular at most Presidential conferences, no matter how sensitive. His primary assignment was to take notes and keep the President's mind fresh on the twists and turns of involved deliberations such as the Vietnam de-escalation proposals.

Over baked fish and cole slaw the President waxed mellow at the morning's events. He always showed great relief after reaching a decision that had been distressing him, such as what to do about the nuclear nonproliferation treaty.

Johnson talked about visiting former President Truman in Missouri. He saw both Truman and former President Eisenhower as often as he could, Truman less so because of his age. Johnson felt genuine affection for both and had given standing orders that they be kept up to date on crucial issues, especially Vietnam. Today he had a specific reason for wanting to see Truman: Congress had adopted a resolution recognizing the special role he played in creation of the United Nations. Johnson wanted to sign this resolution, along with the annual proclamation on United Nations Day, in Harry Truman's parlor.

From the dining room the President directed Jim Jones to call Mrs. Truman and ask if it would be convenient for him to drop in between four and six o'clock. The Trumans already expected Johnson from an earlier call.

The conversation at the table soon got around to Vietnam, as always, and to recent letters from the President's two sons-in-law in the battle zone. I told him I thought the public pressures for an unconditional bombing halt were less than they had been before the Democratic Convention. Some of the more outspoken doves—Bill Fulbright, Wayne Morse, George McGovern, Frank Church—were fighting for their political lives in their home states. Gene McCarthy's voice was also muted after his defeat in Chicago.

"I hope Morse comes through okay," the President said. "He gives me hell on Vietnam, but he's done everything else I ever asked him to do. I'd hate for him to lose. I think the Senate needs him."

The relationship between Johnson and Morse was one of those understandings between political men who can denounce each other and still remain friends. Johnson thought Morse's instincts were generally good. I think his regard for Morse was also the result of a similarity between them; they were both "Senate men," legislative warriors who knew the machinery of government and how to bend it to their will. Johnson held little brief for some of the other Senate "doves," but he seemed to have a special tolerance for Morse's barbs.

The President told me to advise the press he had discussed the nuclear nonproliferation treaty with both Mike Mansfield and Everett Dirksen. He gave Tom and me a discourse on why the Senate should not "piddle around" with the treaty, because there was no incentive for some of our friends to sign when our own Senate had not ratified it. He was afraid Nixon did not have a clear reading. Johnson seemed to hold the hope that the Republican nominee might come around to his thinking after a little "reasoning together." It should be noted that at this point the polls indicated a Nixon victory in November, and the White House sensed the same result. Hubert Humphrey had not yet fit together the pieces of his campaign for the final run that made the election close. Humphrey's dovish speeches on Vietnam had also stepped on some toes. But war was war and politics was politics. Johnson had no intention of letting Humphrey down, even if he looked like a loser, and the proposed trip to see President Truman was partly an effort to call attention to Democratic achievements and continuity.

After lunch Tom and I followed the President into his bedroom and waited until he was in his pajamas and under the covers. He said he would decide after seeing Mr. Truman whether to return to Washington that night or go on to Texas. "I've got a meeting in a little while," he said. "I just don't know whether we ought to go to Texas or not."

He tried to take a nap, but there was no rest this afternoon. By four o'clock Dean Rusk and Walt Rostow were in the Cabinet Room waiting for him; Rusk's briefcase and Rostow's manila folder held cable traffic from Paris that indicated a possible turning point in the war in Vietnam. A few minutes later the President joined them, and they dug into the questions at hand.

In recent hours the Harvan traffic—Harvan was the code name for the Averell Harriman-Cyrus Vance mission in Paris—contained intriguing evidence that North Vietnam was shifting its negotiating position for the first time. The Americans had sought three assurances in exchange for a bombing halt: sanctity of the demilitarized zone, an end to rocket and mortar attacks on South Vietnamese civilian population centers, and productive discussions at the conference table. The U.S. insisted there could be no productive discussions unless South Vietnam was represented in the talks. And it had no objection to the National Liberation Front also being present.

Now Harvan advised the President that at the eleventh private meeting of the negotiators, Ho Chi Minh's delegates had posed a question: Would an unconditional bombing halt follow on the heels of an agreement to admit the Saigon government to the Paris talks? Harvan pressed again on the American conditions and felt that the North Vietnamese clearly understood them even though they would be adamant against accepting them as "conditions." Earlier, the Soviet Union had insisted that positive results would emanate from a bombing cessation. Hanoi's move now convinced Harvan that the enemy was dead serious about accepting the "our side, your side" formula for talks after refusing for months to discuss anything with the "puppets" of South Vietnam.

Dean Rusk felt the implications of Hanoi's changed position might go far beyond that. He thought the North Vietnamese feeler could have the effect of a signal to the Viet Cong that the war was lost militarily. The enemy was already on the defensive, harassed and pummeled by General Creighton Abrams' forces. "Charlie" was becoming more difficult to find; more and more enemy troops were slipping across the frontiers into Cambodia, Laos, and North Vietnam. However, there was no clear evidence that the withdrawals meant anything more than a breather for the NVN-NLF troops. This had been their strategy before.

On March 31, the President had ended the bombardment of 78 per cent of the territory, containing 90 per cent of the population of North Vietnam. The last vestige of bombing—south of the nineteenth parallel—was his hammer to force some degree of restraint on Hanoi. He was reluctant to give it up on a hope and a prayer. He wanted more cold facts before he would even entertain the idea of a bombing cessation. The first thing he wanted was the reaction of Ellsworth Bunker and General Abrams.

Should he go to Honolulu and meet Bunker and Abrams to talk about it? Probably not. That would cause fanfare and a spate of press speculation that something was in the wind. Johnson disliked relying on the formalities of the printed word when major questions needed answers. He preferred to talk face to face—to probe, wheedle, argue, and brainstorm—until he felt he had drawn every ounce of information from the men upon whom he relied. But in this case he would have to be satisfied with cables.

He instructed Rusk to draft a message to Harvan, reiterating the importance of the DMZ and the shelling of the cities. He wanted it made clear to Hanoi that serious talks, once begun, could not continue in an atmosphere of shellings and DMZ violations. Hanoi had to show its good faith.

The instructions to Harvan were to be sent first to Bunker and Abrams for their comments. If they said the deal was a bad one, that was that. Johnson was not going to jeopardize Allied troops

along the DMZ who would have no defense against North Vietnamese guns across the line if he ordered an end to the bombing
and shelling of all North Vietnamese territory. If that was his
"hang-up" on the bombing, then so be it. No Commander-in-
Chief should put his men in that kind of jeopardy. If Bunker and
Abrams thought the arrangement might float, then we would
move at full speed.

Rusk had another base to touch: the Soviet Union. Johnson
wanted Kosygin and Brezhnev to understand our reluctance to
move without some understanding in regard to the DMZ and the
attacks on the cities.

Johnson ordered total secrecy on the developments. He was still
unsure whether this was a true breakthrough or a false alarm.
Earlier peace feelers had proved to be little more than wishful
thinking on the part of Americans anxious to see an end to the
war. Hanoi had never offered anything more than the possibility
of substantive talks when the bombing ended. It would give no
assurance of corresponding restraint on its part, no hint that its
forces would not take advantage of the reduced military pressure
against them. Johnson called that "trading a horse for a rabbit."

The meeting broke up with the President seeming to be both
skeptical and patient. Little could be done until Bunker and
Abrams were completely up to date on the Paris talks, so Johnson
put the subject in the back of his mind, to be moved up front
again when developments warranted. He rarely had trouble handling a number of sticky problems at one time; in fact, he seemed
to enjoy having several oranges in the air at once. It was a challenge to see if he could catch them all.

That deplorable farm bill would require his attention, and it
was already past the time that he had told the Trumans he would
be coming into Kansas City. Jim Jones packed up the bill to take
along on Air Force One. Jones also ordered a small jet to be
available at the Kansas City airport to fly the bill back to Washington before midnight in the event the President proceeded on
to Texas.

The Marine Corps helicopter was called into the South Lawn

and at five-thirty the President went aboard with Luci Nugent and her son Lyn. Mrs. Johnson and Lynda Robb were staying behind. Luci, with her husband in Vietnam, had been living at the White House. She was taking advantage of the President's probable trip to Texas as a means to check her home and see her friends in Austin.

At Andrews Air Force Base, the airplane chartered by the press took off for Kansas City. My assistants, Tom Johnson and Loyd Hackler, had been given the usual static by the newsmen who had waited on the plane for more than an hour, wondering why the President was running so late. By this time, the press did not look forward to Presidential travel, especially to Texas. My usual response was that they would appreciate San Antonio, Austin, and Johnson City after they had been to Waverly, Minnesota, a few times in the next Administration, especially in December.

Just before the chopper blades were to start whirling, the President spotted Harry McPherson and his tiny son Peter standing at the South Portico in position to observe the takeoff. McPherson had brought Peter by a few minutes earlier to see the Boss and receive a dole of candy and other small gifts. "Get Harry here a minute," the President ordered the nearest aide, and McPherson promptly rushed to the chopper, toting Peter under his arm like a watermelon.

The President told him he would act on the farm bill that evening, and he wanted all the bases touched again before he did. That would be the task of McPherson and DeVier Pierson.

McPherson nodded and departed, the motor whined and we were hoisted up over the South Lawn, the wind forcing the McPhersons and the ground crew to turn away as the grass clippings flew. We dodged past the Washington Monument—it always looked to me like the helicopter's standard route would someday clip the edifice—and swung down the Potomac before turning toward the Maryland home of Air Force One. There the great Boeing 707, Number 26000, was positioned like a dog on point, ready for its chief passenger to walk the short distance from helicopter to ramp. We always clambered aboard in haste, gave our hellos to the stewards and buckled in quickly. As soon as the President was seated, Colonel Paul Thornhill gave the airplane a shove, and we were shortly airborne.

One of Johnson's regular habits was to begin a conversation with someone in his cabin just as the jet engines were at their most thunderous on takeoff. This time it was with speech writer Harry Middleton, who strained to hear comments and instructions above the roar. Larry Temple and I, sitting three feet away, could not understand a word. Once aloft, the Presidential cabin in the rear of the plane was almost as noiseless as an automobile. Special padding over the windows insured this, and it was possible to sit around the President's table and work and talk as comfortably as in a conference room.

Free of his seatbelt, Lyn Nugent began punching the buttons on the President's telephone and listening to the receiver. This was also one of his favorite tricks in the White House, and Presidential assistants with direct lines from Johnson were accustomed to answering the phone with anxiety or expectation, only to experience dead silence or a few mumbles on the other end, followed by Johnson's voice in the background telling the baby to try another button.

The President was concerned, however, about toying with the phones on Air Force One, until one of the stewards, Jim Brown, told him he had warned the operator up front to ignore the buzzer unless informed otherwise.

Johnson ate a bowl of chili with crackers and a glass of milk, then worked for a time with Middleton and Bob Hardesty on remarks he would make in signing the two proclamations at President Truman's home.

After a stroll through the front cabin to greet the telephone operators, Secret Service agents, communications experts, and other support personnel who always traveled with him, the President settled down in his chair and went through the memoranda on the farm bill. As he finished reading something, he would pass it to me without looking up, and I would pass it on to Hardesty and Middleton. "Read all this stuff and tell me what you would do if you were President," he said. Included in the material were a signing statement and a veto message, both of which he directed us to edit, and "pro and con" memos from the experts on his staff. McPherson and Pierson had recommended he sign the bill, H.R. 17126, extending the Food and Agriculture Act of 1965 for one year.

"Well, what would you do?" Johnson finally asked.

"Sign," we said, repeating the reasoning of McPherson and Pierson.

"It's a sorry bill," he retorted. "Why should I put my name on it? If I veto it, Congress can still extend the Act when they come back in January."

We gave him a limited argument, based mostly on political considerations. We knew that he knew the importance of these considerations but merely wanted us to voice them. That was his way of stirring things up while he rolled a decision around. Finally, he told us we were putting politics above principle, and he would not act until he was ready to leave Kansas City. I could imagine Orville Freeman calling Hubert Humphrey and urging him to phone the President. Humphrey would not need much prompting to do that.

But the first calls came from Carl Albert and Gerald Ford, who informed the President that the House of Representatives had completed its business and they were happy to report the close of the Congressional session, save for the usual last-minute paperwork which would run into next week. The connection was not very good and Johnson had to shout his thanks to the two House leaders.

V · Independence

Just before seven o'clock, local time, Air Force One landed in Kansas City. Mayor Ilus Davis was at the foot of the ramp to greet the President and Luci. It was a twenty-five minute drive to

Independence and Johnson was already late, so the formalities were brief.

It was almost dark when we pulled up to the old, two-story home of Harry and Bess Truman. Like older houses in many cities, it is surrounded now by commercial buildings as well as residences, but the street is still relatively peaceful, comfortably Midwestern and tree-lined—completely in character with its most famous family. A crowd had gathered, kept by police and security men to the sidewalk across the street. Many of the people were neighbors; they had watched Johnson make this pilgrimage before. Tonight there were a number of teenagers. They cheered and applauded and got a wave from the President and Luci as they got out of the car.

The press pool car and bus pulled up behind the President, and the occupants hurried forward to watch Johnson enter the gate and head up the sidewalk. The Trumans and their daughter, Margaret Daniel, were on the porch. Local cameramen were already hard at work before the White House "reels" and "stills" could move into position, but the proceedings were quite similar to several other visits to Independence and the excitement was muted.

Bess Truman was particular about her home, and her orders were plain—and respected—on the number of people she would welcome into her parlor. We usually limited entry to one or two Presidential assistants, and if we were lucky a White House photographer also, though Mrs. Truman frowned on that. This time I shoved Tom Johnson to the front so he could squeeze inside and take notes.

At the top of the steps the smiling President shook hands with Harry Truman and said, "Sorry I'm late."

To which the elder statesman rather surprisingly replied, "You ought to be. It's your own damn fault."

The front part of the Truman home is composed of a dining room, a small library crammed with books in shelves and stacked on the floor, and a sitting room to the right of the door where the visitors were ushered.

Magaret Daniel, standing with Luci as the parents settled into the parlor, presented a striking contrast to the raven-haired young daughter of the incumbent President. Both were dressed in similar shades of red, Margaret in a knee-length skirt, Luci in a mini-skirt. Margaret's appearance was one of basic serenity, even impassiveness. Luci, standing with her weight braced on one leg to support the bulk of a king-sized baby on her hip, looked weary and worried. The clamor of White House events was obviously far behind the Trumans' daughter. The process of beginning a normal existence, even with a husband in Vietnam, would not occur for Luci for three more months.

After a brief exchange of pleasantries in the parlor and a report on the progress of grandchildren, a small table was readied and the President signed Proclamation 3878, designating October 24 as United Nations Day, and Proclamation 3879, pointing out that President Truman helped create the UN and "never flinched in the exercise of United States responsibility in and through the United Nations."

But in his spoken remarks Johnson's emphasis was on domestic affairs. With a press pool admitted for a few minutes, the President gave Truman a copy of a scroll, "Landmark Laws of the Lyndon B. Johnson Administration," which had been presented by the Cabinet on Johnson's sixtieth birthday. The President said the Truman Administration deserved to share the credit, because "as I look over the nearly two hundred measures on this list, I see so many that began with you." What better way to focus on the achievements of the Democratic Party at such a crucial time of year—and to emphasize the continuity of Democratic Administrations?

The former President, no longer strong enough for much formality, had few words in reply. But as always, he desired to be clear in his unwavering support for Johnson's policies; if he had ever deviated an inch, it went unrecorded. Tonight he said, "You always do right, Mr. President."

They moved to the front porch and waited during the rush of reporters and photographers who were admitted through the gate amidst yells from security men not to trample the shrubbery. Some of the radio men fought for position with their hand mikes, but got little except goodbyes. The Trumans and their visitors posed again for the cameras, standing under the bare globe of a porch light around which numerous autumn insects were orbiting. Then the Secret Service agents and press aides moved the newsmen back toward the fence. The President shook hands with the Trumans and Margaret and walked to the gate with Luci and Lyn as the television cameramen stumbled backward to capture the scene. On the porch, which was the farthest point Mr. Truman was allowed to go because of fear he might fall down the steps with such a ruckus in the front yard, the elderly couple and their daughter gave one last wave.

Thus Johnson made his final pilgrimage to Independence during the time of his Presidency. Each visit was symbolic as well as sentimental, a means of drawing attention, if only for a fraction of time, to the man whose Presidential program was a model for Johnson's. "You had the courage and the vision to propose laws when they were unpopular—because you knew that they were in America's interest," Johnson told him. Privately, Johnson always gave Truman credit for Medicare, Federal aid to education, and many of the housing and health measures of the 1960s. Tonight he told Truman: "They are our laws, but they were your dreams."

Johnson had a small town boy's propensity to engage in hero worship: Franklin Roosevelt, Sam Rayburn, a Texas lawyer named Alvin Wirtz. He recalled them with deep devotion frequently and openly. They had helped mold his early career and they were "the wisest men I ever knew." His affection for Harry Truman and Dwight Eisenhower was of a different kind. He had reached a status of power himself when they served as President; he had dealt with them on different terms, perhaps not clearly understanding their every move at the time, but now he was quite tolerant of all they had done and stood for in the national interest. In the Congress he had criticized both on occasion, but nevermore. They had been President; they did the best they could, and no fair man should fault them.

"Every President wants to do right," he said so many times. A favorite recital for visitors to his office was to show them a montage of inscribed photographs of the Presidents he had known, beginning with Herbert Hoover.

"They accused Mr. Hoover of wanting to starve little babies," Johnson would say. "He did the best he could to end the Depression, and he was treated as unjustly as any President we ever had."

Then he would tell of the criticisms leveled against Roosevelt, Truman and Kennedy—"most of them pure imagination."

About Eisenhower: "They say he didn't know what was going on. That's not true. He stayed right on top of everything. I know; I had to deal with him all the time. And right now I would rather have his advice than anybody's I can name."

Almost in self-defense, Johnson became a student of the worst trials of his predecessors in the White House, the arrows of their enemies, and their periodic disfavor with the people. It seemed to give him at least limited satisfaction to remember that other Presidents—all of them—had their bitter detractors, some far more venomous than his.

One was Harry Truman, now standing unsteadily on his front porch in Independence, Missouri, braced by a cane and the loving attention of a protective wife and daughter, well past his bedtime, watching that other commoner, Lyndon Johnson, climb into a black limousine and return to the world of the present.

In the cabin of Air Force One the President removed his coat, loosened his tie, and pinched a thoroughly wet shirt from the sensitive parts of his skin in hopes it would dry quickly. He drank a tall glass of ice water in one tilt, then picked up the material on the farm bill he had been studying earlier. The plane would wait on the ground until he made his decision. A Jetstar was nearby, ready to return the bill—dead or alive—to the capital. The flight would have little importance if he signed the bill, but a veto message would have to be officially registered.

Tom Johnson came aboard to await a press release. "What's he going to do?" he asked me.

"I think he'll sign it, but he's sure upset about it," I replied.

Three calls had come to the airplane during the President's absence and they were now placed again on the land line. DeVier Pierson reported on conversations he and Harry McPherson had had with key officials. Speaker McCormack called to express his hope the President would sign. Then Johnson talked to Hubert Humphrey, who made his feelings known plainly and urgently. "Thank you," the President told him.

Johnson looked at the veto message again, then the signing statement. With a fountain pen he began writing additional language into the signing statement, adapting it from the veto message. At 8:25 p.m. he said morosely, "Well, I guess I'll sign it. I hate to." With a stroke of the pen the deed was done. He entered the time on the bill and handed it to Jim Jones.

"Let's go home," he said.

I handed Tom Johnson the amended statement, and he departed hastily as the jet engines geared up for takeoff.

"Despite the short-term relief this extension gives," said the press statement, "I regret that the Congress did not act favorably on the recommendations in my special message of February 27, 1968. To be plain about it, the farmer has already suffered from this inactivity, and from those who have played politics with these farm problems this election year."

Then Johnson ticked off the specific complaints:

—Not a permanent Act—but a mere one-year extension.

—He had recommended creation of a National Food Bank— "but the Congress failed to act on this request."

—He had urged more bargaining power for the farmer—"but the Congress failed to pass this legislation."

—Nothing done about the fact that "some government payments are so large—while many small farmers find it difficult to survive even with government assistance."

Many of the farmer's problems, the President said, "have simply been swept under the rug this year."

Johnson rested until Air Force One touched down at Bergstrom Air Force Base, Austin, at 9:55 p.m., Central Daylight Time.

The night was warm as he stepped off the plane, shook hands with the base commander, and went to the waiting Jetstar for the brief hop to the LBJ Ranch. At eleven o'clock he was in the swimming pool with Luci, Lyn, and his secretary, Marie Fehmer. At midnight his head was on his pillow, and the light was out.

VI · Winding Down

Lyndon Johnson began the last lap of his Administration—his last hundred days—with the mixture of disappointment, struggle, and satisfaction that was becoming the way of life of his waning Presidency. The Congress was little pleasure any more. The appointment of a Chief Justice had been denied him. Ratification of the nuclear nonproliferation treaty had been denied. Possible discussions on arms limitations with the Russians were fading with each passing day. Congress had ignored almost everything he wanted in farm legislation. The gun control law had been watered down to cover only mail-order sales; registration of guns and licensing of gun owners were both rejected.

But Apollo 7 was safely in orbit, and the new stirrings in Paris posed an enticing question.

In a hundred days Johnson would end his stewardship as thirty-seventh President of the United States. Twilight was settling over his Administration. This was the time to begin winding down, but not surprisingly, others in the Administration were winding down a lot faster than he was. Many were looking for new jobs; several Cabinet members had departed or would depart soon; many other officials at various levels were simply waiting for the election, three and a half weeks hence.

A suburban realtor told me that the housing market in the Washington area would be creeping along slowly until November 5 ended the uncertainty. It happened every four years, he said, despite the fact that very few government employees were actually affected that much by elections.

For many weeks after the March 31 announcement that Johnson would not run again, there was little perceptible change in White House activity. There was that small matter of a successor, and although he adhered rather strictly to his pledge not to embroil himself in partisan politics, Johnson made no bones about his choice for the Democratic nomination. Hubert Humphrey inherited the Johnson apparatus, which was still a formidable nucleus for a campaign despite the onslaughts of Eugene McCarthy and Robert F. Kennedy. Johnson's heavy contributors became Humphrey contributors. The abortive organization called Citizens for Johnson-Humphrey, which was just getting off the ground in March, became Citizens for Humphrey—and Whoever.

But still during those months between April and August—with their political murders, riots and bitter dissension—Johnson and Johnson alone was the national leader, the man with the power of the nation at his command, a little tarnished but quite adequate. The Republican Convention did little to change this picture. Then came Chicago.

When does an outgoing President become a lame duck? In some ways, never. The country cannot afford one any more. When Congressional sessions lasted only a few months, and the British Navy ruled the seas, and the Federal establishment was only something to hold the union of states together, a lame duck now and then caused few problems. Americans could wait for their new leader, and during the interim they either endured the incumbent if they were out of sorts with him, or revered him like a cherished relic if he were still in favor.

But in the last third of the twentieth century, the Congress is in session most of the time and has grown more dependent than ever on Presidential leadership. Few programs are initiated by the Congress any more. It has become the President's program, to be expedited or delayed, voted up or voted down. Lyndon Johnson, history's most prolific legislating President, established this practice even more firmly. Of course, the voice of the President of the United States in international affairs must remain strong, although Johnson's final weeks showed how it can be muffled at crucial moments when a foreign country knows it will soon be dealing with another President.

So while it can be argued that the lame-duck Presidency is an anachronism with little modern relevance, there was a time in 1968 when Johnson psychologically became less a President than he was before. That time was, of course, during the Democratic Convention in Chicago. This was his party, split apart at the seams. This was, in words Johnson himself once used to describe national disunity, like a tree with part of its bark knocked off, the wound exposed to every irritating breeze. It was the national bile rising in the national throat. It was hawk versus dove, establishment versus revolutionary, age versus youth—all on color television.

Remarkably, it was all of this despite the fact that it was a cut-and-dried convention. Humphrey had the votes. McCarthy and McGovern never had a chance. The Ted Kennedy bid was wishful thinking on the part of a few delegates, egged on by certain television commentators; a candidacy was created where none existed. Yet the Democratic Party showed its backside to the American people and asked to be kicked. Outside the hall, youthful demonstrators sought a confrontation with police and were accommodated. President Johnson suffered in silence at the ranch, having decided that Chicago was the last place on earth he wanted to be in August.

When the ordeal was finally over, and a Humphrey-Muskie ticket was put together as the odor of the stench bombs and tear gas wafted away, many in the Johnson Administration were asking: "What will Hubert do with this mess?" Humphrey himself was enduring a psychological letdown. He was acting like the loser, not the winner, of the convention. Then the political adrenalin took hold, and the man from Minnesota began the uphill climb—pretty much as his own boss. Now, Humphrey was the head Democrat, the rallying point for the party regulars. He had moved from the shadow of his President and was on his own.

From that point, Lyndon Johnson walked a narrow line until

election day. He had sworn to be President first, politician second. He would try to stand above the partisanship of the three-way Presidential race. He would work for peace while others politicked. He would help Humphrey where he could but wanted no part of directing the campaign. These were his feelings, and they varied little from August to November.

He also became increasingly aware of the subtle changes in his life as President. The pressures began to ease somewhat, especially from the news media. Their prime attention had shifted to Richard Nixon, Hubert Humphrey, and George Wallace. More and more of the front-line White House correspondents were drifting off on the campaign trail. The news was being made elsewhere. Leaders of other nations were carrying on business as usual with Johnson, but with one curious eye cocked on the Presidential race. The Congress was sharpening its partisan arrows. The cooling of the humid summer air in Washington heralded the changing of the leaves—and the guard.

But in large part a Presidency is shaped by world events, even in its twilight months. There could have been a cosmetic Presidency after March, or after August—a whirlwind of activity, speeches, travel, and controversy, all designed to keep Johnson in the public eye. As a matter of fact, nothing like this was necessary to keep Johnson moving, busy, frequently quite newsworthy—and controversial. He was far from ready to permit his Administration to die peacefully in bed.

TWO

I · *The Bombs of October*

The President, in khaki and wearing a golf tam, had just picked up the Reverend Norman Truesdell at his home and was driving back onto the LBJ Ranch when Jim Jones radioed from the ranch house that a message from Walt Rostow was being delivered to the car by the Secret Service.

In the Texas hill country, mid-October is late, late summer. It had been warm enough the previous evening for the President to take a midnight swim. Autumn was only a whisper in the early dawn and at dusk. The live oaks were a dusty green all year round, but at this time of year all of the foliage and grasses were still holding out gamely against the brittle, brown colors of the Texas fall.

With Johnson were Bob Hardesty and Harry Middleton, the two veteran writers who worked on the President's speeches and statements and were being recruited for post-Presidential duties after January 20. The Reverend Truesdell, a burly young man from Ohio who was a relatively new pastor at Trinity Lutheran Church in Stonewall, had become a favorite companion of the President's along with Father Wunebald Schneider, a priest at St. Francis Xavier's Catholic Church. Trinity Lutheran is the elderly gray church that juts into the LBJ Ranch not far from the family cemetery. Johnson took a proprietary interest in Trinity's welfare, and the earnest social conscience of Truesdell and his wife had attracted Johnson to the young couple.

When the President was in residence at the ranch, the Truesdells and Father Schneider were frequent guests at meals and at after-dinner movies in the airplane hangar. Johnson was thoroughly at ease in their company; the three were adopted citizens of the neighborhood who were due hospitality and help, which the President offered whenever he could. They were also fresh sparks in a tiny community which hadn't budged much, one way or the other, for many years. If Lyndon Johnson were anything, he was a man who liked to budge things. As it turned out, the Truesdells were somewhat less than permanent residents; within a few months they had moved on.

The Saturday morning message from Walt Rostow was the reply from Ambassador Ellsworth Bunker and General Creighton Abrams to the urgent message sent by Dean Rusk on Friday. Their interpretation of Hanoi's overture was the same as that voiced in Paris and Washington. It appeared to the Saigon team that Hanoi was ready to move from the battlefield to the conference table.

Johnson and his guests resumed their drive, then at noon the President telephoned Rostow on the "secure" line to discuss the recent developments. Clark Clifford and General Earle Wheeler would return from Europe Sunday night. A meeting should be scheduled Monday morning to bring everyone up to date. The President wanted Maxwell Taylor to join the "regulars"—Rusk, Clifford, Wheeler, Rostow, Dick Helms of the CIA, Christian, and Tom Johnson.

Saturday evening the President hosted Father Schneider and

the Truesdells at a movie, a Dean Martin-Robert Mitchum shoot-'em-up called *Five Card Stud*. Johnson was appalled at certain gory aspects of the film; *Five Card Stud* became a topic of conversation whenever the new morality of the motion picture industry was discussed around the President.

On Sunday he attended the nine o'clock service at St. Francis Xavier, where he encountered NBC correspondent Carl Stern and his wife. Since this was Mrs. Stern's first visit to Texas, the President invited them for coffee on the ranch house lawn, then took the two of them to Trinity Lutheran for the 10:30 service. Johnson, a member of the Disciples of Christ, and the Sterns, who are Jewish, all seemed to enjoy their ecumenical Sunday.

That evening the President flew back to Washington, still only half hopeful that something was really in the wind. He had become cautious long ago on North Vietnamese peace feelers. He wanted substantial evidence, not guesses, and for the next seventeen days the question would be hashed over so many times that frequently the participants would have to stand back and ask themselves, "Are we really getting anywhere?"

Perhaps the arrival in Washington was an omen of the difficult days ahead, when very little would be crystal clear.

Andrews Air Force Base in Maryland, the home of Air Force One, was so badly fogged in at midnight that a safe landing was impossible. The nearest "open" airport was at Richmond, Virginia. Then the word came from the Air Force weathermen that an instrument landing at Washington National Airport would be within the safety limits.

So Air Force One boomed through the thick mist for a landing at National, scaring some of those on board, but apparently it was done with reasonable ease. After the President had left by automobile for the White House, the chartered press plane also came down at National, bounced along the runway, and finally freed three dozen news people who were shaken up thoroughly by their pilot's intercom descriptions of the heavy fog and airport problems. I greeted them at the ramp.

"Was it safe for the President to land in weather like this?" Fran Lewine of the Associated Press demanded of me.

"Nothing to it," I said.

"Why did we come back tonight instead of Monday?" another reporter asked.

"I never said we were coming back on Monday."

"We always come back on Monday."

"Not always."

Because we rarely did return from Texas on Sunday and had no announced schedule for Monday, suspicions were already growing among the newsmen that something had brought the President back to the capital prematurely. They were usually as suspicious as we were devious, and during the next few days their anxieties would rise steadily.

The action began early Monday with the news stories on a speech at DePauw University, in Indiana, by McGeorge Bundy, the President's former Special Assistant for National Security. Bundy, one of Johnson's original counsellors for a troop buildup in Vietnam and bombing attacks against the North, and brother of William Bundy, top State Department official for the Far East, had come out for an unconditional bombing halt and gradual U.S. troop withdrawal. Bundy defended the decisions of 1964 and 1965, but said American policy must "not go on as we are going."

The President and his foreign policy team were well aware of Bundy's disenchantment with the progress of the war. He had expressed himself clearly in a meeting of Johnson's "outside advisers" on foreign policy the previous spring—before the President called a partial halt to the bombing on March 31 coupled with his announcement that he would not seek another term. But the timing of Bundy's speech shook everyone who was aware of Hanoi's move at Paris. A tentative feeler for substantive talks might be withdrawn if the North Vietnamese thought they could get a bombing halt for nothing—and it was known from intelligence reports that Hanoi paid close attention to any statements indicating disagreement among the President's inner circle and causing pressure on Johnson himself. If Hanoi were truly on the hook, it might be off again before Washington and Saigon could agree on a countermove.

Bundy's public proposal would have been of less concern had not Vice President Humphrey, in his famous Salt Lake City speech in September, indicated strongly that an unconditional bombing pause was an acceptable risk to get meaningful talks started at Paris. The Humphrey and Bundy statements, taken in tandem, appeared to be two big chinks in the Johnson armor.

But the series of Vietnam meetings which began at the White House on Monday, October 14, showed virtual unanimity among Presidential advisers from the very start. Hanoi's offer was interpreted as a reasonable opening, and should be pressed as rapidly as possible.

General Wheeler, briefed on the situation only hours before, did not hesitate to accept a package that entailed admission of Saigon to the talks, respect for the demilitarized zone, and no shelling of the cities. Because of bad weather in the panhandle of North Vietnam, he said, air strikes were becoming more difficult anyway, and this was a good time to test Hanoi's good faith by calling off the bombers. He and Clark Clifford agreed that the bombing could be renewed if Hanoi violated the terms of the agreement. The President warned them this would not be as simple as they made it out to be, because of world opinion against the bombing.

Dean Rusk was solidly behind the proposed agreement. But he cautioned that America should not invest twenty-eight thousand dead and seventy-five billion dollars in war and then toss everything away with a dishonorable peace. His admonishment: Move ahead, but make certain you are on sound ground.

From the outset, Johnson raised the spectre of a President playing election politics with the war. "Some people will call it a cheap political trick," he said. But it was argued that Nixon had been honorable on the war issue and had said he wanted the peace talks moved along as far as possible by the incumbent President.

Clifford argued that the date of the election should be of no concern in the decision. On the first of several occasions during the month, the courtly, deliberate-speaking Secretary of Defense said: "There comes a time in the tide of men's affairs that is a time to move."

We had met many times on Vietnam—so often that it sometimes was comparable to discussing the price of wheat, or the status of our trade with Venezuela. That first group meeting after the feeler from Hanoi was also pure business: calm discussion, cold deliberation, no evidence of anxiety. There were a few laughs at Presidential wisecracks, and even a reasoned discussion by Clifford and Wheeler of their European trip and the pulse of our NATO allies.

The smokers—Rusk, Wheeler, Rostow, and Helms—puffed along as usual, Rusk making points as always with an ever-present Lark vibrating between his right index and middle fingers. Maxwell Taylor, oldest man in the room but straightest in posture, spoke only when the President asked him questions and listened alertly with his mouth set in a half-smile. Clifford put his head in his hands occasionally, tired from the long trip home, but he listened intently to every word. As usual, Rostow and Christian doodled incessantly on White House pads and secret documents. Tom Johnson, Presidentially appointed "Keeper of the Notes," scribbled constantly to keep up with the flow of conversation.

Lyndon Johnson, now straight in his chair with elbows on the table, now waving a yellow pencil, now slumped back and reading a report over his spectacles, now glowering, now illustrating a point with a Johnsonian fable, now turning right or left in his chair to listen quietly to Rusk or Clifford . . . ; Johnson presided, debated, argued, sucked out opinions from his advisers as if with a syringe. He wanted to know everything there was to know up to that point. Only Lyndon Johnson could make the decision. Behind him was a bust of Abraham Lincoln, who had his share of hard decisions. And in the corner was another bust of John Kennedy; in this room he had deliberated the Cuban missile decision, a success, and the Bay of Pigs decision, a fiasco.

Rusk was awaiting word from the Soviet Union on its understanding of the North Vietnamese offer. Le Duc Tho, high-ranking adviser to Hanoi's delegation in Paris, was on his way home, via Moscow. Ngo Minh Loan, North Vietnam's ambassador to Communist China, had flown from Peking to Hanoi. In Paris, Averell Harriman and Cyrus Vance—the Harvan team—awaited further instructions from Washington.

Send the Bunker-Abrams cable to Harriman and Vance, the President ordered. Then be available for further meetings on short notice and keep everything close to our vests. Rusk reported that only four people in the State Department knew of the development. The President ordered me to avoid all press inquiries on the subject. The story was bound to leak when Saigon and the Allied countries knew of it—as soon they must—but anything the U.S. government did to lend credence could tilt Moscow and Hanoi the wrong way. The President wanted a "clean" decision—no premature speculations by government officials, no pressures, no bad faith with the other side, and above all, no politics.

At that time all of us thought the decision was only hours away.

I told the press at my morning briefing that Clifford and Wheeler had reported to the President on their European trip. The reporters accepted that with little question, but then they bombarded me on McGeorge Bundy's speech. Ironically, the reporter who asked me the first question referred to him as "George McBundy," which evoked smiles from his colleagues, but he had the tone of the speech correct.

I declined to comment on the substance of Bundy's remarks, or to confirm that the President had even read about them. I did not recall the last time Bundy had discussed Vietnam with the President, but thought it had been some time ago. I was sure it had been several months since Bundy participated in a group meeting on Vietnam policies.

It was obvious that some of the newsmen thought Bundy's speech might be a straw in the wind on a change in policy. That was precisely our fear of Hanoi's reaction. At any rate, the Bundy speech—completely unrelated to the events in Paris—began the wheels of speculation turning, especially when combined with the travel plans of Lyndon Johnson from Texas to Washington and

Le Duc Tho from Paris to Moscow to Hanoi. Of course, Bundy was not aware of the turn of events in Paris and would not have timed his speech deliberately to cause problems. He and his brother were among the country's more astute professionals in foreign policy; they gave 100 per cent effort to two Presidents. Bill Bundy was intimately involved in the conduct of the war and the peace talks. Mac Bundy had remained fairly close to Johnson after leaving the White House in 1966 and was still a consultant to the President despite his change of mind on Vietnam.

In the early afternoon the President called another meeting of the regulars, plus the military chiefs and Senator Richard Russell of Georgia. He felt that Russell's judgment as chairman of the Armed Services Committee was essential; the solemn old Southerner had a nose for bad deals and a delicate political touch. He also knew how to keep a confidence.

Rusk, Clifford, and Rostow gave the military leaders a complete summary of the developments at Paris, with no sugar coating. There was also word from Ambassador Bunker that President Thieu had concurred in the instructions to Harriman and Vance. "This is not the end of anything," Rusk cautioned. "It's the beginning of a new chapter which will be very difficult."

One after another, the nation's highest military officers gave their views.

General J. P. McConnell of the Air Force said: "If we're going to stop bombing, this is the time. The weather is bad over the North and we can put our air power where it's needed more. We must preserve reconnaissance over the North." Finally, after reasoning out the question, he added: "I recommend it."

Admiral Thomas Moorer of the Navy and General Leonard Chapman of the Marine Corps agreed. General Bruce Palmer, Vice Chief of the Army, commented: "Time is running against the enemy. I would go along."

Palmer's superior, General William Westmoreland, arrived late. But he added his support. "He [the enemy] doesn't have the capability for full attacks on the cities. If we do this I believe we can preserve GVN [Saigon] morale and our troop safety."

It was nearly five o'clock before the President went to the Family Dining Room for a hamburger with Senator Russell, Tom Johnson, and me. Russell was cautious, apparently because of the possible political repercussions of a bombing halt. "They'll accuse you of everything in the book," he said. Johnson agreed this was a factor that disturbed him.

The relationship between Johnson and Russell, two old friends, was somewhat cool at the moment. Russell thought Johnson had tried to pressure him to vote for Abe Fortas' confirmation by holding up a Georgia judicial appointment which the Senator had recommended. Actually, it was the Justice Department, not the President, which had opposed the appointment; Johnson from the beginning had backed Russell's man. But the matter had been handled clumsily and Russell blamed the President.

The subject was not discussed at lunch. For both men, there were more important matters at hand.

That evening Johnson again raised the political question in another group meeting of the "regulars." Clifford, contending that a bombing halt would not affect the campaign, quoted Mark Twain: "When in doubt, do right." To which Johnson retorted, "That's right, but let's not be pulled in."

In Saigon, Ambassador Bunker had briefed President Thieu. Bunker cabled that Thieu was for the plan without reservation and also concurred in the plan for Harriman and Vance to meet with the North Vietnamese and tie up the loose ends.

Harriman and Vance wanted an announcement of the agreement made by midnight the next day, October 15. They were confident Hanoi would accept the American proposal.

Now it was time to consult the troop-contributing countries. There was little doubt that these allies—the "TCC's" in State Department parlance—would approve the move.

The President asked Rusk and Clifford, "Do you know this is what we ought to do?" Rusk replied, "Yes, sir." Clifford answered, "I have absolutely no doubt that this is right."

"All right," the President said, "go ahead and execute. I do not

want one man to die tomorrow who could have been saved because of this plan."

Then he added, rather prophetically, "I do not think it will
happen, but there is a chance. We'll try it."

The next day the President held his regular "Tuesday luncheon," the appointed time each week to discuss foreign affairs with
his senior advisers. The regulars—Rusk, Clifford, General Wheeler,
Dick Helms, Rostow, Christian, and Tom Johnson—usually gathered in the West Hall of the White House living quarters for
sherry and preliminary palaver while the President was completing
his morning office schedule.

This was a time for swapping stories, going over reports, and
generally relaxing in the comforts of the First Family's parlor
while waiting for the President to arrive. Sometimes Mrs. Johnson
or one of the girls would drop by for a visit. In these latter days,
Lynda Bird Johnson Robb was nearing childbirth and was plainly
uncomfortable. She was also deeply distressed about her husband
in Vietnam, who seemed to have a professional Marine's passion
for running toward the sound of gunfire. Several of us had serious
doubts he would survive.

When the President arrived he sometimes joined us for a glass
of sherry. If he were late for the one o'clock luncheon, he would
go directly into the dining room, and we would trail behind him.
We took our places at the table in the same order nearly every
time—Rusk at the President's right, Clifford at his left (Bob
McNamara's old spot), Helms next to Rusk, then Tom Johnson
with his notepad, Wheeler next to Clifford, then Christian, and
Rostow at the opposite end of the table from the President. If
someone else joined the circle—Maxwell Taylor occasionally, the
Vice President rarely—the seating arrangement varied only
slightly.

The Mansion's Family Dining Room is the most warlike room
in the White House. Down the hall is the Treaty Room, done in
1880s style and replete with framed originals of peace treaties with
Indians and foreign countries. It is a stuffy, dim, peaceful room.
But in the Family Dining Room one eats his lunch surrounded by

colorful wallpaper depicting great events of the Revolutionary War, with Redcoats and Colonials falling before deadly musket fire.

Luncheon was usually calorie conscious in deference to the President's constant battle with his appetite. Lamb chops, baked fish, calves liver, spinach, baked eggplant were among the fare. Desserts were prepared with artificial sweeteners. Coffee was invariably the beverage, although Clark Clifford frequently had a glass of milk. Sometimes we were treated with special meat casseroles—a Presidential favorite—or with chicken and rice or seafood and rice. The President had a special fondness for rice, steamed so carefully that every grain was separate and delicious. The kitchen knew his attitude toward gummy rice.

At the luncheon on October 15, Rusk brought word that President Thieu had asked for twenty-four more hours to work out his problems before announcement of a bombing cessation. This was not deemed fatal. The bombing could be stopped at midnight Wednesday, which was noon Thursday in Saigon.

We marvelled that details of the discussions in Paris and Saigon had not yet leaked to the press. However, Hedrick Smith in the *New York Times* and Marvin Kalb on CBS had voiced tentative speculation that something was afoot, and I told the luncheon group that I doubted the story would hold through the day.

Midway in the meeting, Secretary Rusk went to the White House Situation Room to call Ambassador Bunker in Saigon and give Thieu his twenty-four hours. When the luncheon ended, Dick Helms shook hands with the President and said, "Good luck." Johnson smiled faintly but did not reply.

II · *Delay*

Later that day the fabric began to unravel.

Harriman and Vance reported from Paris that the Hanoi delegation had balked at one of their demands: that the broadened peace talks begin one day after the bombing stopped. At this point, the President and his advisers felt a quick move to the conference table by both new parties—the Saigon government and the NLF—was essential. Otherwise, it was feared that political opposition in Saigon might undermine President Thieu's assent to the arrangement.

Now, Ben Read, Secretary Rusk's top aide, told the President that Hanoi had said in Paris that it was not authorized to speak for the NLF. Hanoi could not get the Viet Cong representatives to Paris a day after the bombing stopped.

Harriman and Vance recommended that the plans proceed regardless of this. The announcement, they said, could state that the expanded talks would begin as soon as the Saigon and NLF representatives could get to Paris. The President disagreed. "I will not stop the bombing if I do not know that serious talks will start with the government of Vietnam at the table," he said. His suspicions were clearly aroused; he could visualize a bombing cessation, then prolonged delay while Hanoi sought excuses for avoiding the talks and the Saigon government hung on for its life against its political enemies. Thieu could well be toppled by the "hawks" in his own camp, who would then refuse to talk with Hanoi while the NLF was at the table. In the meantime, the panhandle of North Vietnam would be free of bombardment, enemy forces could assemble as they wished for further assaults, and the U.S. would have a nearly impossible task of renewing the bombing in the face of world opinion and the opposition of the domestic "doves."

Both Rusk and Clifford shared his concern. The Secretary of State said the troop-contributing countries should be flashed that the U.S. would not move until it had a definite day when talks would begin. Clifford added that it should be made clear the U.S. had no intention of stopping the bombing until it knew the date of a meeting at which the government of Vietnam would attend.

Thus began two weeks of frustration as first Hanoi, then Saigon raised problems which delayed a Presidential decision. On the fifteenth, however, we still thought the delay would be only a matter of hours. With unanimity of opinion in the American councils, with Bunker confident of Thieu's statesmanlike assent, and with the Communists having made a major concession, it seemed impossible that a hitch in the plans would develop.

So the next day we were not overly concerned when rumors of a peace movement began to appear in print and on the air. Saigon was the chief source. Ambassador Bunker had been spotted by the press in three visits to President Thieu, and all this activity gave credence to the rumors. Press calls to the White House began at seven o'clock in the morning.

When I went to the President's bedroom he was devoting his attention to other matters, particularly a call from Governor Buford Ellington of Tennessee urging him to come to that state in the interest of the Humphrey campaign. Tonight the President had also been invited to speak at the annual dinner of the Alfred E. Smith Memorial Foundation in New York City. Both Nixon and Humphrey would be there. Johnson wanted an especially good speech, and half a dozen writers were involved in polishing one that would meet his requirements. After receiving a suggested speech, the President would often send it out to a number of people for comment and editing. When I received a copy for this purpose I usually had no idea who else might be working on it. The final assembly job would be performed by Charles Maguire, an artistic, Irish-born intellectual with fiery hair and a temper to match. Feuds among the President's writers were commonplace.

The President agreed with the consensus that a White House statement should be issued on Vietnam. I told him we needed something—anything—rather than face a constant bombardment from the correspondents all day. It was decided we should try to "cool" the speculation until we had better evidence that a real breakthrough would occur. Rusk and Rostow prepared a brief comment which I distributed about ten o'clock.

The position of the United States with respect to Vietnam remains as set forth by the President and the Secretary of State.

There has been no basic change in the situation: no breakthrough.

As you have always been advised, when there is anything to report, you will, of course, be informed promptly.

The correspondents interpreted this as we wanted them to: Something was indeed afoot, but the bombing was still underway. Be ready for further developments.

As I opened my briefing shortly after eleven o'clock, Bill Gill of ABC asked: "Can you tell us whether we are hurtling toward peace?"

"I stand on the statement we put out," I replied.

Then I turned back a series of questions on possible meetings of the National Security Council and reports of a lull in the fighting in Vietnam. The government had been telling the press for several weeks that the low level of combat was indicative only of North Vietnamese efforts to regroup from military setbacks. Most qualified military experts thought this was still the case, regardless of developments at the conference table. But there was a great temptation for writers in Saigon and Washington to interpret the lull as a possible prelude to a cease-fire. This view was actively encouraged by some officials in both capitals who did not agree with military estimates of the situation.

Shortly after my briefing I went to the Oval Office to join the President, Rusk, and Rostow. Johnson was on a conference call with Hubert Humphrey in St. Louis, Richard Nixon in Kansas City, and George Wallace in Los Angeles. He had put the call on the speaker box so that the others in the room could hear.

The President told them that the government was anxious to stop the bombing and would be willing to do this if Hanoi would sit down with us, with the government of Vietnam present, and have productive discussions. He said that we had told Hanoi we did not think we could have productive discussions if they were shelling the cities or abusing the DMZ.

Johnson then read them the statement issued earlier in the morning and told them he would let them know if there were any developments to report.

Humphrey thanked the President for the information but made

no specific comment. Later, one of his assistants told me the Vice President felt hurt that he was informed of the developments along with the other two and felt that he should have had the matter discussed with him privately.

Nixon told Johnson that the actions taken were consistent with the position he had taken all along. "I'll make no statements that will undercut the negotiations and we'll just stay right on that, and hope that this thing works out," he said. Wallace agreed, adding that "we shouldn't play politics and foul up the negotiations."

After the call the President was due to go to the East Room to sign two educational bills. He said he would make mention of his conversation with the three candidates when he made his speech. Consequently, when a reporter asked me if the President was going to say anything "hot" in his remarks, I told him he might be interested in an announcement Johnson might make. This was a mistake. The rumor spread quickly through the newsmen that Johnson had an important announcement on Vietnam. When the President made no mention of the telephone call in his speech, confusion reigned. So I quickly returned to the press office, with the reporters trailing behind, and told them there that Johnson had talked with the candidates "in light of the uncertainty created by the various reports." I did not report the substance of the conversation.

Further fuel for speculation was added when the President was seen leading Democratic Vice Presidential nominee Edmund Muskie to a private meeting after another bill signing that afternoon. The press was grabbing for every possible item to add to a mounting storehouse of leaked information from Saigon, Bunker's frequent trips to Thieu's Independence Palace, tantalizing comments by North Vietnamese delegates in Paris, some hints in Bangkok, and above all, a blunt report by Prime Minister John Gorton of Australia. Gorton said he was in close contact with Washington, that discussions about ending the bombing were underway in Paris, that only one point remained to be ironed out, and that "with a bit of luck President Johnson could be expected to make a statement soon."

This was coupled with an Associated Press account of the

American briefing in Paris by our spokesman, William Jorden, in which Jorden was quoted in the lead as saying there was "movement" in the peace talks. The President wanted an explanation of the story, so Rostow talked to Jorden and got word that the briefing had gone like this:

> *Associated Press:* Could you tell us what happened during today's tea break, please?
>
> *Jorden:* No, I couldn't.
>
> *Associated Press:* I want to ask a question that has been asked many times before but has to be asked from time to time. Has there been any progress to date at all?
>
> *Jorden:* It's terribly difficult to judge progress until one arrives at a destination. One doesn't know if one has been moving forward or in circles. I would say there has been movement. I cannot characterize it as progress. I would hope that at some point in the future we can characterize it, and I hope that characterization will be positive. I cannot do so now.
>
> *Associated Press:* Would you characterize the movement?
>
> *Jorden:* No.

As it turned out, Jorden, a brilliant former *New York Times* foreign correspondent who was our White House expert on the Far East before being assigned to the Paris talks, had faced this same question several times before and had handled it in generally the same way previously. But in the context of the day's events, the word "movement" became a news lead. When Jorden discussed the matter with the Associated Press, the correspondent agreed his lead had been too strong and said he would damp it down in subsequent stories.

The politicians were also beginning to get into the act. Senator Everett Dirksen said in Chicago: "If there is a bombing pause the public may regard it as something of a gimmick." Senator George Murphy of California, chairman of the Republican Senatorial Campaign Committee, declared in Indianapolis that a peace move at this point would be suspect. Key Republicans had been voicing suspicions for weeks that Johnson had something up his sleeve on

Vietnam as a last-ditch effort to help Humphrey. With the rumors now prevalent that a peace move was underway, they were beginning to lay a backfire to head off any sudden Democratic surge from a favorable event in the war.

Some Republicans were telling reporters that the Johnson plan called for a halt to the bombing and the reduction of one hundred thousand American troops in South Vietnam, in the hope that this would lead to North Vietnamese de-escalation. The press "bit" on this one only temporarily; a unilateral step of this kind, without any assurances from Hanoi, was so uncharacteristic of Johnson that most diplomatic and military writers dismissed it as uninformed speculation.

Nixon himself was extra cautious after the telephone call from Johnson. His only comment in Kansas City was that "we hope the war in Vietnam may be over before this election."

Hubert Humphrey was equally reticent. Answering questions at Christian Brothers College in St. Louis, he remarked:

> If I say anything, I shudder because there are theologians on Vietnam who will write a whole new story. We have got more self-appointed Presidents and Secretaries of State and ambassadors than any ten countries in the world. If you want to know what the government's position is, listen to what the President has to say.

Johnson would see both of them at the Al Smith Dinner in New York that evening, but would have no opportunity to tell them more about the developments. Shortly before seven o'clock the President put Vietnam behind him and left by plane for New York. The only thing he could do now was wait for new reports from Harriman and Vance.

But there was plenty of action ten thousand miles away in Saigon. Ambassador Bunker had brought President Thieu a joint statement announcing the understanding with Hanoi and a halt to the bombing. Thieu was being urged to have a delegation ready to go to Paris within twenty-four hours. But now the South Vietnamese President—about whose fate Johnson had worried if there was a long delay between the bombing halt and the arrival of the Saigon delegation at the conference table—was telling Bunker that there was not that much hurry.

Furthermore, Thieu's National Security Council—which included the thoroughly independent leaders of the South Vietnamese Congress—got its first official briefing on the situation and decided the conditions agreed to by the Americans were unacceptable. Thieu and his advisers now felt the Allies were admitting defeat by halting the bombing with only silent concessions, rather than clear conditions, from the Communists. A proposed joint announcement with the Americans was turned down. Thieu wanted stronger language.

Bunker and his deputy, Samuel Berger, began the time-consuming task of trying to reason with each of the men who were making the decisions in Saigon. At every turn there was opposition. Berger was told by Vice President Nguyen Cao Ky, Thieu's longtime political rival, that he was 100 per cent behind Thieu. Ironically, American officials had been pressing Ky for months to remain unified with Thieu. Now he was, and the situation was becoming stickier in Saigon as Bunker and Berger worked to put an agreement back together.

Strange events were beginning to take shape in this war-torn and politically volatile country. Nguyen Van Thieu, elected by a minority of the votes and only half accepted as the President, was suddenly growing in stature as a national leader around whom divergent forces would be rallying as the news spread. He was no puppet; he had stood up to the Americans and reminded them that despite their five hundred fifty thousand troops and their bombers over the North, this was his country, and he had to decide what was best. By early November he was ten feet tall.

The developments in Paris and Saigon shifted the activity firmly to those two cities. Washington was calling the shots, but the diplomats had to carry through. Some on the American side—notably Clark Clifford and Averell Harriman—were growing impatient. The President became philosophical about the delays; he would act when he was certain it was right—not before. Hanoi wanted a communique announcing that the American bombing halt was "unconditional." Johnson would have none of that. The United States was willing to concede that no DMZ violations and no shelling of the cities would be "understandings," rather than "conditions," but Johnson wanted that much made clear to Hanoi.

From the standpoint of public anxiety over the recent reports, relief for the American government was at hand. At the height of the peace speculation, the announcement was made that Mrs. Jacqueline Kennedy would soon wed Aristotle Onassis. The national shock wave submerged the news about bombs and peace conferences.

"What a break!" I told Bob McCloskey, the State Department's hard-pressed spokesman. Agreement around the White House, State Department, and Pentagon was widespread. It was as if someone had suddenly relieved the pressure on a swelling balloon, just short of rupture. The newspapers and broadcast media became far more interested in Greece than in Vietnam. The country had a much-needed diversion from war and campaign politics.

Thursday and Friday became routine days. A unit citation for the Fifth Marines: "I never think of a Marine but what I think of a man who wants to do more, not less, a man you have to hold back and not shove." A signing ceremony for the hazardous radiation bill, the last of twenty consumer measures enacted during the Johnson years. A visit to the White House mail office to thank the employees, the first of several sentimental meetings with the rank and file: "I started my government career handling mail."

A presentation by Speaker McCormack was the beginning of a Presidential joke of several days' running. It seemed that Sam Rayburn when he was Speaker had been given a sculpture by Western artist Frederic Remington, depicting a mounted Indian with a lance bearing the scalp of an enemy. Appropriately named "The Scalp," the valuable statue had reposed in neglected and unappreciated splendor in some closet for several years. McCormack, knowing Johnson liked Western artwork and especially Remington, brought it to the White House one day and gave it to him. The President displayed it on a side table in the Family Dining Room, and since no one around him knew the circumstances of its sudden appearance or the fact it was a Remington, he promptly invented a story about it.

By his account, two of his Texas friends had discovered several of these statues in a Fredericksburg curio shop, where they were being sold as doorstops. They had bought one for a hundred dollars and sent it to the Johnsons as a gift. Mrs. Johnson, obviously unimpressed by the aesthetic tastes of the two "friends" her husband named, was victimized immediately. She declared the doorstop to be a dud and urged that it be removed from her dining room. This pleased Lyndon Johnson immensely; if he could fool Lady Bird, everyone else would be easy marks. So he repeated the act to other vulnerable souls, professing elaborate appreciation for the generosity of his two Texas friends for sending him such a fine doorstop. One staffer thought to be an expert in the fine arts (he shall remain nameless here) commented that the statue was "not too bad, but obviously not a Remington." Johnson showed him Remington's signature on the base and howled.

The President went to Camp David Saturday evening with the Walt Rostows. The Catoctin Mountains were bathed in the full glory of autumn, and the President spent a good part of the weekend walking and bicycling. Sunday was Elspeth Rostow's birthday; the President gave her an engraved julep cup and told her it would keep her company in the evenings while waiting for Walt to drag home.

Johnson used the Camp David retreat sparingly. It was strictly for short visits—a good place for companionship, relaxed meals, a little bowling, and outdoor recreation. After a day or two, his tendency was to become restless. Like the White House, Camp David was a place of confinement. Marines guarded the gates and there was a reinforced double fence all the way around. When the President was in residence, the Marines patrolled the fences against the possibility of intrusion. The woods were too thick for much hiking, although some of the family tried strolls among the trees occasionally. The paved roads could be toured by bicycle or golf cart, but the sightseeing was limited and the appearance was one of a military encampment. Its main attraction to Johnson was the opportunity to relax, take long naps, and enjoy conversation with friends and aides. A man as energetic as the President would thirst for more action after a short time.

Late Sunday afternoon in Aspen Lodge the President watched Hubert Humphrey on a special broadcast of the CBS program, *Face the Nation*. The interviewers tried hard to draw the Vice President into criticism of President Thieu's position that North Vietnam should reciprocate for any plan to curb the American bombing. Humphrey said the attitudes of the Saigon government obviously were important in securing an agreement at Paris; then he added:

> But this is an American mission. I believe there is very little bombing if any done by the South Vietnamese. This matter must be something over which the government of Vietnam— South Vietnam—cannot exercise a veto.

Although Johnson always cringed at public statements such as this, Humphrey was voicing the prevailing sentiment at the State Department and Pentagon. All of the machinery of the foreign affairs establishment was gearing itself toward cessation of the bombing and a new phase in the peace talks. All-out "hawks" were virtually nonexistent. The ponderous turn around toward de-escalation which began after the Tet offensive in February was now almost complete—yet was being frustrated at the eleventh hour by what many thought was a question of "face." Clark Clifford's view was the more probable fact: Saigon simply had a different objective in the war than Washington. Whereas Washington was ready to seek a political settlement after halting the North Vietnamese aggression, Saigon was for holding out as long as possible so its own military and political base would grow stronger and it could survive the so-called peace.

On Monday there was more routine for President Johnson. He presented the Employer of the Year awards in the Cabinet Room and then walked to the South Grounds to accept the new Presidential limousine from the Ford Motor Company. This Secret Service vehicle had been the subject of press comment due to its alleged high cost and formidable construction; to some reporters it symbolized the unhappy necessity of enclosing a President in a steel cocoon to protect him from his own people.

The President seized the occasion to praise the Secret Service and also took pains to point out that the vehicle would serve principally the next President, not himself. He was openly self-conscious about his personal protection since the rise of the war demonstrators and black militants.

On Tuesday morning Jim Webb of NASA called to report Apollo 7 was down safely in the Pacific. The President dressed early and went to the Cabinet Room to talk on the radio telephone with the astronauts. For some reason, a natural conversation between the Commander-in-Chief and three happy astronauts was not to be the case. The President used notes supplied by NASA, containing this prose:

> As the eyes of the earth have been open upon you, so have the hopes of the world lifted to you. And in this universal gladness, there is the making of a human partnership where space technology and science will serve as instruments of man's peace in the world. . . .
>
> And today, despite our triumphs, we have only our fingertips on the latch that could unlock a world of miracles that are practical and profound. And from the blessings that we already hold in our hands we know that neither complacency nor conceit can stay our hand from reaching higher. . . .

We could watch the astronauts on the television monitor as they listened to his words over the radio phone. I kicked myself for not urging the President to throw away his cards and say something more human. The reporters, appalled at the stiffness of the conversation, made not the slightest mention in their stories of their personal impressions. As so frequently happens, the historic significance of the event, and not the artificiality of the telephone call, overcame all else.

Later in the morning Johnson signed the shattered gun bill, squeezing as much favorable comment as he could from the remains of his original proposal to the Congress. He called it the most comprehensive gun control law ever signed, but he added:

> We just could not get Congress to carry out the requests we made of them. I asked for the national registration of all guns and the licensing of those who carry those guns. For the fact of life is that there are over one hundred and sixty million guns in this country—more firearms than families. If guns are to be kept out of the hands of the criminal, out of the hands of the insane, and out of the hands of the irresponsible, then we just must have licensing. If the criminal with a gun is to be tracked down quickly, then we must have registration in this country.
>
> The voices that blocked these safeguards were not the voices of an aroused nation. They were the voices of a powerful gun lobby that has prevailed for the moment in an election year. . . . We have come a long way. We have made much progress— but not nearly enough.

The guns of Vietnam were still active, also, and Bob McCloskey and I were bombarded daily by the press, which by now had nearly all of the story except official acknowledgment by the United States government. This is a sample of the line of questioning at the White House briefings:

> Q. George, over Hanoi radio it is reported that they are quoting the National Liberation Front as giving what is generally considered a rejection of whatever offer the President made last week or the week before concerning the Paris talks. Can you illuminate for us any on that?
>
> A. I am still not commenting at all on the Paris talks.
>
> Q. Should we assume from that that you do not consider this a rejection?

A. I am just not commenting at all on it.

Q. Why aren't you commenting?

A. Do you want to have me give you a lecture as to why?

Q. Yes.

A. My answer to your question is no comment.

A press secretary receives few compliments, so I was delighted when Dean Rusk asked the President, "Are Christian and Mc-Closkey still saying nothing well?"

During this week, President Arias was deposed in Panama and our State Department arranged for an Air Force plane to fly him from the Canal Zone to Washington. Arias promptly holed up in the Panamanian Embassy and said he was going to press his case before the Organization of American States, until he was finally persuaded to accept the coup as a fact of life. Secretary Rusk commented wryly to President Johnson that Panama was the sixty-second coup he had lived with since becoming Secretary of State.

Now some of the pieces were being put back together on a date for the bombing halt. Hanoi wanted a three-day lapse between the cessation of the bombing and the time for the first meeting in Paris with the Saigon and NLF representatives. Johnson, who earlier had wanted only a one-day lag, was content with three after being assured there was no added complication in Saigon. Clark Clifford urged that Harriman and Vance get an air-tight agreement with the North Vietnamese negotiators that the bombing would end at a time certain and a meeting would be held at a time certain. So a new target was set: a joint announcement by Johnson and Thieu Friday night, October 25, and the expanded talks to begin Monday.

Johnson wanted more detailed information from Ambassador Bunker and General Abrams in Saigon. How would this deal affect troop morale? What political repercussions would there be in South Vietnam? Could Thieu endure? Johnson was itching to talk to Bunker and Abrams face to face, but there was no feasible way at the moment. Bunker needed to stay on top of Thieu. The President was considering calling Abrams to Washington, but knew this would be difficult to do in secrecy. So he settled for another cable to Saigon requesting the information he wanted. The President found a temporary substitute for Abrams. General William W. Momyer had commanded the Air Force bomber strikes from Thailand and had been visited by Johnson in late 1967. Now Momyer was stationed at Langley Air Force Base, Virginia, fresh from the war. The President called him in for a secret meeting, laid out the situation, and asked his opinion. Momyer's reaction: If you can get the deal, stop the bombing. One more doubt was removed from Johnson's mind.

In the meantime, one of the most painful episodes in Johnson's Presidency occurred. He and Willard Wirtz, the brainy and sensitive Secretary of Labor, became involved in a bitter dispute over a reorganization order Wirtz issued against the President's wishes. Johnson, already harassed by Vietnam troubles, and Wirtz, who was sour on the war and increasingly out of step with the President, exchanged bitter words in a Wednesday meeting that left Wirtz on the verge of resignation. This will be treated later in my account. Suffice it to say that the argument with his Cabinet officer rubbed Presidential nerves which were already raw.

That night, after another meeting with the Vietnam "regulars," the President sat in his "Little Office" with Joe Califano, Larry Temple, and me, morosely discussing the Wirtz incident. Suddenly Lyn Nugent, newly arrived with his mother from Austin, rushed into the room, clad in an orange and yellow raincoat over pajamas, and assaulted his grandfather with a hug and a kiss. Luci followed with some soothing words about home, letters from Pat in Vietnam, and assorted items. All was set right again. The President invited us to late dinner, and when we joined Mrs. Johnson in the Family Dining Room there was not a hint of trouble, foreign or domestic. He joked, teased, laughed, told stories until time for bed and the pile of night reading on the folded-back sheet.

The next day the President agreed to a news conference, his first since the October peace move began. My briefings had been well populated with State Department reporters, along with the

White House press crew, since the peace talk stories had mounted from Saigon, Paris, Canberra, and other capitals. So at shortly after one o'clock a sizeable crowd was herded into the Cabinet Room by Tom Johnson and Loyd Hackler. The President sat in his regular chair, facing the newsmen across the table. He smiled a rather tolerant smile, knowing that the press anticipated more than he would tell them.

Douglas Cornell of the Associated Press opened:

Mr. President, has there been any change since George issued his statement of October 16 on the Vietnamese situation? There has been no basic change in the situation, no breakthrough?

The President replied:

The statement Mr. Christian issued was accurate at that time, and is accurate now.

We want peace very much. We have been doing all we could for several months to try to bring about some kind of an understanding that would result in substantive discussions and ultimate settlement of the Southeast Asian problem.

We do not want to make news until there is news. We realize that many times diplomacy can be more effective in private than to have all your discussions, recommendations, and prophecies carried in the press. But I would say, Mr. Cornell, on the statement Mr. Christian made on October 16, there has been no basic change, no breakthrough. Our position remains as set forth by the President and the Secretary of State. When there is anything to report, you will be informed.

He snuffed out two other questions on the subject and spent much of the news conference relating his Administration's efforts to fight crime and maintain law and order. This was a low-keyed answer to Richard Nixon's accusations that Johnson's Attorney General, Ramsey Clark, had been "soft" on the issue.

Afterward, Johnson read the news bulletins on his office tickers, rather noncommittally and bemused, then took me to a Mansion luncheon to help referee a debate among three staff members on whether he should sign or veto a bill affecting the tariff on wool fabrics. Harry McPherson, DeVier Pierson, and Ed Fried were the experts on this latest attempt by Congress to be protectionist. Johnson listened to the pros and cons for an hour, thoroughly enjoying the difference of opinions, before signing the bill.

That night Lynda Johnson Robb began her labor pains. Her father was still in his office when he received word. He walked to the Mansion and saw her off to the hospital. Tom Johnson, who had relieved Jim Jones for late duty on the appointments desk, sat with him the remainder of the evening while he worked, talked, and worried. The President ordered a message sent to Captain Chuck Robb in DaNang that he was about to become a father. Mrs. Johnson suggested by telephone that the President not come to Bethesda Naval Hospital until Lynda went into the delivery room. In another call to Liz Carpenter, the President appointed Liz, Helen Thomas of UPI, and Fran Lewine of AP as the "official midwives." At midnight Johnson drove to the hospital. Taken to the wrong elevator by mistake, he had difficulty locating Lynda's room. But his exasperation faded when Mrs. Johnson told him: "It's a little girl."

III · *The Secret Minute*

Lucinda Robb was born on the day the bombing halt was programmed for announcement: Friday, October 25. It was not to happen. Hanoi came forth with a new wrinkle. It would go along with the latest proposal, but only if the United States signed a secret statement, referred to as a "minute," that the bombing was being halted "without conditions." This was the face-saver. Worse, it put the American decision squarely in the context of North Vietnam's longstanding demand that the bombing be stopped unconditionally, with no reciprocity of any kind.

"That old dog won't hunt," the President asserted.

Rusk, Clifford, and the others agreed. So Harriman and Vance were instructed to try the American terms again.

Hanoi had already begun to step up its propaganda attacks on the U.S. negotiating position. Its radio declared there could be no discussions on substantial matters at Paris until the Americans stopped the bombing unconditionally. Hanoi claimed the Western press was fabricating news about a breakthrough in the negotiations. As for reports that the North Vietnamese had accepted U.S. conditions for a bombing cessation, these were "deceitful arguments of a psychological warfare nature aimed at sowing confusion."

Propaganda of a sort was also flying in the United States. General Curtis LeMay, George Wallace's running mate, said publicly that President Johnson was cooking up a "false peace." LeMay said he smelled a "political brew."

Far more important were remarks by Richard Nixon, whose restraint on Vietnam up to that point had been remarkable. But today Nixon said:

> In the last thirty-six hours I have been advised of a flurry of meetings in the White House and elsewhere on Vietnam. I am told that top officials in the Administration have been driving very hard for an agreement on a bombing halt accompanied possibly by a cease-fire in the immediate future. I have since learned these reports are true.
>
> I am also told that this spurt of activity is a cynical last-minute attempt by President Johnson to salvage the candidacy of Mr. Humphrey. This I do not believe.
>
> This latest suggestion of Presidential politicking on the Vietnam war is but one of many similar rumors and press speculations in recent weeks.

Thus the Republican candidate made certain the implication of brazen politics was well advertised, even as he denied personal belief in the reports.* He went on to say that Johnson had been

---

* Newspapers unfriendly to Nixon had a field day with his statement. The *Washington Post* ran a biting editorial entitled "Vintage Nixon," in which it pointed up "the shocking charge, from the anonymous source, followed by the pious but only partial disclaimer of belief which left the President vindicated, but a nameless assortment of advisers still guilty of

"impartial and candid" in his dealings with the Presidential candidates about Vietnam and that the President had assured him he would not play politics with the war. Nixon said he believed every Presidential candidate should "mind his tongue" to avoid weakening our diplomatic hand and said he would continue to back Johnson in his pursuit of an agreement.

Concurrently with the Nixon statement, an unnamed Nixon aide (reporters later told us it was Melvin Laird) listed four men as the culprits who were working for a bombing halt to assist Hubert Humphrey. The four were Clark Clifford, George Ball, Cyrus Vance, and Joe Califano.

Clifford most certainly was a party to the negotiations, as was Cy Vance, of course. The President had not discussed the matter with George Ball, whose disdain for Nixon had caused him to resign as United States Ambassador to the United Nations in order to help Humphrey. However, Ball publicly favored an early peace settlement. Joe Califano, the President's special assistant for domestic affairs, had had no part whatever in the deliberations on Vietnam. "Why are they doing that to me?" Califano complained. I told him not to worry about it; the only thing he had been really accused of was being an advocate of peace. "Don't look a gift horse in the mouth," I advised him. "This will put you in good with your dove friends." But Califano could see little humor in it. The President was distressed at Nixon's remarks and at the same time was amused at the report of the conspiracy, especially as it pertained to Califano.

Our efforts to maintain the secrecy of numerous White House conferences on Vietnam also brought some much-needed chuckles when we needed them.

Heading for the White House on Friday, Secretary Clifford and

seeking to press upon him a 'fake peace'." The Post went on to say "there are several things to be said about this shabby business, none of them very nice." Herblock's editorial cartoon was even more bitter. It depicted an unshaven Nixon, in kid gloves but with a bucket of paint over his arm, holding a sign saying, "Administration peace efforts are all politics!" The cartoon line read: "Mind you, I don't believe this sign which someone or other put into my hands."

General Wheeler followed the Presidential edict to come as unobtrusively as possible. Let Marvin Kalb of CBS tell it from there, as he did on the air a few days later:

... Secretary Clifford and General Wheeler rolled their long black limousine into the basement garage of the State Department, joined Secretary Rusk who was waiting for them in a small tannish car with license plate number 1209, and drove to the White House for another secret talk about the Vietnam negotiations.

Obviously, the President did not want the press to find out there was another such meeting, so he had his top advisers bunch up uncomfortably in a small unpretentious car for the fast five-minute ride over to the White House. No one was supposed to know, but they were spotted and seemed embarrassed about the whole procedure.

The advisers also had orders to use the southeast gate to the White House grounds—the farthest from the region usually observed by the press.

Once Clifford and Wheeler entered this gate, parked, went into the south entrance of the White House, and ran smack into an army of tourists who began asking for their autographs. On another occasion Dean Rusk was caught by what he estimated to be "at least four hundred tourists." The delighted visitors, recognizing him instantly, began waving and calling to him excitedly.

The issue over the "secret minute" again raised strong doubts in the President's mind that the North Vietnamese were seriously interested in broadened talks. It was possible that they were just trying to achieve a bombing cessation by playing on American anxieties and unrest. The possibility that Hanoi was also playing American politics—with Russian help—was a very real factor. Nikita Khrushchev had once said he tried to influence the 1960 election in John Kennedy's favor; whether he actually had any impact or not was immaterial.* With the election only a few days

* Khrushchev, in a filmed interview televised by the National Broadcasting Company in mid-1967, referred to Nixon as an "S.O.B." and said he had

away, there was also concern on the part of some American officials, the President included, that the Saigon government was working to head off a bombing halt until the vote was in; the Vietnamese leaders made no secret of their unhappiness with the Humphrey campaign and its efforts to corral the doves.

When Nixon and other Republicans spoke of intrigues, they were not completely inaccurate. Efforts had been underway in the U.S. government for many months to achieve a political settlement of the war, but their origin had nothing to do with the election. Long before the President's decision not to seek re-election, leading figures in the State Department and the Defense Department's civilian branch were working actively for policy changes that would scale down the fighting and lead to American disengagement. Several key Pentagon officials had lost faith in the bombing of North Vietnam by mid-1967. Most importantly, Secretary of Defense McNamara himself did not believe the bombing was as effective as claimed and thought it was only prolonging the war. When Bob McNamara went to the World Bank in early 1968, his successor, Clark Clifford, was exposed immediately to these sentiments among Pentagon civilian officialdom.

Clifford's hawkish reputation prior to becoming Secretary of Defense was not entirely earned, although he had opposed stopping the bombing on previous occasions. His attitude toward the war was close to the President's own: Keep up the pressure on the North, avoid rash actions that might widen the war, and seek peace talks on favorable terms. To be sure, this position was shared by Dean Rusk and Walt Rostow, and in earlier times by Bob McNamara. Differences among the American foreign policy decision-makers began to appear on the degree of risk the U.S. was

---

once told Kennedy: "The fact that you became President is due to us. We made you President. . . . You collected two hundred thousand more votes than Nixon. Nixon asked for Powers, the U-2 pilot, to be released . . . and if we had done it, he would have received half a million votes just for that— because that would have shown that Nixon could have established better contacts with the Soviet Union. But we guessed his plans. We decided not to give him any answer, and just to give it to you when you moved into the White House." Khrushchev claimed Kennedy agreed with his contention. (Quotations as printed in the *New York Times*, July 16, 1967.)

prepared to take in securing peace talks; on the value of the bombing itself; on the magnitude of the U.S. military commitment to Vietnam; and on the policies of the Saigon regime.

Clifford was outspoken in his criticism of South Vietnam's motives after a visit to Asia in the summer of 1968. He felt the governmental apparatus there would never put its political and military house in order so long as the United States was an invincible shield and generous provider. In his view, the situation was roughly this: As long as the U.S. troops were there, North Vietnam and the Viet Cong could not possibly win the war, and at the same time the U.S. was pouring countless dollars into the economic life of South Vietnam, building roads and bridges, docks, schools, hospitals, and other vital needs of an underdeveloped country, which would not come in such volume in normal times.

Clifford expressed it this way on one occasion: "Suppose you are a provincial chief. You see an American bulldozer up there on the mountain, building a road which your town has needed for a hundred years. Tomorrow the war will end. What will happen to the bulldozer and the road? The bulldozer will depart, and the road will never be finished."

The Defense Secretary believed simply that South Vietnamese leaders would have little incentive to succeed on their own unless the war was de-Americanized and little incentive to seek a political settlement until it became evident the American commitment had limitations. He had the backing of a number of officials, including his deputy, Paul Nitze, another trusted aide, Paul Warnke, and the Under Secretary of State, Nicholas Katzenbach. Later these men were referred to in press accounts as "secret doves." Actually, their views were anything but secret within the Administration, and they were "doves" only in the sense that they could see no way out of the war except by compromise and de-escalation. When George Ball, the original dissenter when he was Under Secretary of State, became Hubert Humphrey's chief foreign affairs adviser in the Presidential campaign, it was obvious Humphrey's leanings would be in the direction of those who were losing patience with the war.

The October peace initiative was not a struggle between Clifford on the one hand and Rusk and Rostow on the other, between soft line and hard line. Rusk, patient and tough-minded, remained in charge of the proceedings throughout. He wanted the bombing stopped and was willing to take reasonable risks, but to throw away military and political success in Vietnam because of war weariness was to him unthinkable. Rusk visualized not only a just settlement in Vietnam, but also a restoration of peace in all of Southeast Asia. That meant resolving the issue of North Vietnamese troops in Laos and Cambodia, and heading off the threat to Thailand. To Rusk, the essential first step was substantive talks in Paris involving Saigon and Hanoi. He was the architect of the Johnson policies that were now turned that way. Rostow's thinking was similar, and he sensed that Allied military success was largely responsible for this latest turn in the war.

It had now been two weeks since the Harvan message that an agreement was in the offing. The world knew the essentials of the story, but still there was no Presidential order halting the bombing. Humphrey's people were keeping their fingers crossed. Whether the President would play politics in their behalf or not, they thought a bombing halt might be all their candidate needed to edge past Nixon. In the meantime, the Nixon camp was waiting for the other shoe to drop.

On Sunday the Republican Presidential candidate devoted an entire radio talk to the question of Vietnam. He was protecting his flanks—preparing for what he thought was inevitable. It was a masterful political approach to a difficult situation.

Richard Nixon contended that delicate peace negotiations should not be upset by political talk. He hoped Lyndon Johnson could "honorably end" the war—and quickly. He wanted everyone to know that our negotiators in Paris spoke with a united American voice. Only the President could determine whether Hanoi's guarantees in return for a bombing halt were credible and adequate. An end to the bombing, however, "should not be wasted, or lightly played."

Nixon listed three *if*'s as conditions for his support of a Presidential order to stop the bombing:

—If it would speed an honorable peace;

—If it would save American lives rather than cost more lives; and

—If the President determined that the conditions have been met by North Vietnam.

Then Nixon fired volleys at both Johnson and Humphrey. He called the history of America's involvement in Vietnam "a sad chronicle of misjudgments." He accused the Administration of "a lack of candor at home and a lack of leadership abroad." He criticized a "misguided policy of gradualism" which he said had wasted America's military power. He said we had been fighting the wrong kind of war and had neglected the training and equipping of the South Vietnamese army. "The Administration has not been out-fought by a far weaker enemy," he said. "But it has been out-thought."

For Humphrey, Nixon reserved a complaint that "he has talked too much and too loosely about Vietnam." Nixon went on:

He has been for a bombing halt, and against it. He has called for pre-halt conditions, and then no conditions. He has demanded reciprocity, and then said he didn't mean it. He has held out hope that American troops could be brought home this year, and then backed away from it. He was against the minority plank on Vietnam at the Democratic Convention, then for it, and then against it again—and now he seems bewildered and straddling.

The GOP candidate spelled out his philosophy on Vietnam, and it sounded like an echo of Lyndon Johnson's:

—Not punishment for North Vietnam, but an end to its aggression;

—Not privileges for the U.S., but the basic right of the South Vietnamese to self-determination;

—No imposition of a coalition government, which would be a "thinly disguised surrender"; and

—Participation in the political processes of South Vietnam by everyone who renounces use of force and accepts the verdict of elections.

Nixon said Americans would have to decide whether they thought the war "can better be ended by an Administration hobbled by a legacy of past failure, or by a new Administration neither defending the old mistakes nor bound by the old record."

Johnson spent the weekend campaigning for Hubert Humphrey. On Saturday it was a speaking schedule in West Virginia and Kentucky. On Sunday it was a luncheon meeting of the All American Council of the Democratic National Committee in New York. This was an organization of ethnic groups whose votes were vital to a Democratic victory. On Vietnam, the President told them:

I wish I could give you some better news, and I wish I could tell you more than I have. I know how each of you feels. I am curious myself a great deal of the time. . . .

There are a lot of speculations. There are a good many reports. The press sometimes refer to these things as "political observers believe." That is what the fellow means that is writing it. That is him. But when we say something, you remember it a long, long time. There is one thing when we are dealing with the lives of human beings we must not do. We must not be careless, and we must not be soft, and we must not play it loose.

As eager as I am—and I work on it every day and every night, and I have for many, many months—I just cannot make news until there is news. As soon as there is news, you will be the first to know it—you, the American people and the people of the world.

Until there is, try to satisfy your curiosity with a cup of Sanka or a Coca-Cola or something. I am thinking now of the words I uttered when I got off the plane the day President Kennedy was taken from us when I began to try to assume the terrifying responsibilities of the Presidency. I said, "Give me your prayers."

What I need now is not your curiosity. I need your prayers.

At the time he spoke, Johnson already knew of another vital development in Paris. Walt Rostow had called him as the Jetstar sped toward New York. Rostow told him the talks between Harvan and the North Vietnamese negotiators had just been concluded. Hanoi had folded on the secret minute. A deal was ready to close.

When he landed at La Guardia, the President called Rostow on the land line. "Our friend Abe should be asked to come to Washington, alone," Johnson said. This was his summons of General Creighton Abrams from the field. It was time to look Abe in the eye and make certain this was a square deal that would not kill more Americans—and to have the field commander so firmly "on board" that criticism by the hawks might be muffled.

As the day wore on, the President brooded over the decision that was closing in on him. A reception at the apartment of Arthur and Mathilde Krim delayed his return to Washington. By the time he got to the White House, he was quite agitated. The delays had shoved the bombing halt to the virtual eve of the election; he was convinced that the people would say "old wheeler dealer Johnson" had pulled another one. He was also worried that his soft line on conditions would encourage Hanoi to take a cavalier attitude toward the American position. Rostow had warned earlier that Hanoi would test U.S. will by causing DMZ violations and tossing some shells into population centers. What concerned Johnson, however, was flagrant violation of the American understandings—with higher Allied casualties—and himself impotent to resume the bombing because of worldwide reaction.

Once the bombing of the North had ceased, he believed, it would be lost forever as a military tactic. The woods ahead were too dark for his satisfaction. He was not yet convinced he was right.

Rusk, Clifford, Maxwell Taylor, Earle Wheeler, and Walt Rostow were ready to act. That Sunday night, as we all sat around the table having a late dinner in a tense and nervous atmosphere, I realized how truly anguished Lyndon Johnson was in shaping this final decision. A new timetable was put before him: Approve the package tonight; Bunker would inform Thieu and Harvan would inform Hanoi's negotiators within an hour; orders to halt the bombing would be issued Monday night; the troop-contributing countries, the Presidential candidates, and the Congressional leadership would be informed Tuesday; the bombing would end at 7 p.m. Tuesday, October 29, and public announcement would be made at that hour.

Not until he had seen Abrams, the President ruled. And not until Harriman had gone back to the North Vietnamese one more time to make certain they understood about the DMZ and the shelling of the cities. And not before Rusk had gone back to the Russians again to make certain they understood, too.

Looking back now, it is easy to pinpoint these hours as the most discouraging in the whole exercise. After all of the haggling with Hanoi and Saigon—the jockeying for position, delays, and suspicions—the most formidable barrier of any was the doubt in Lyndon Johnson's mind that he should end the bombing. All of his men who had squirmed through the thicket with him were convinced. It appeared that he was not. The President was the last holdout. And perhaps all of us somehow sensed that he would be.

Also looking back, I suggest that Johnson had a peculiarity in making decisions that often fooled even those who worked with him the closest. On many occasions, a major decision was preceded by the severest form of soul-searching. Instinctively, the President would recoil from the decision, drawing up from every recess of the imagination the reasons he was wrong. A course of action he spoke of with assurance and delight on one day would become an act of stupidity the next. Confidence would turn to doubt, conviction to suspicion. This was no time for men whose feelings bruised easily to be around him. It was a punishing process, but especially for the President himself. In times like these the person to whom he turned was Lady Bird Johnson. She was the last sounding board, the last reasoner, the voice of calm, logic, and remarkable understanding. I am confident they had many private conversations during this period.

IV · *Abe*

In Vietnam General Creighton W. Abrams, in civilian clothes, slipped aboard a C-141 StarLifter for the grueling flight to Washington. Johnson had wanted to bring Ambassador Ellsworth Bunker home, too, but Rusk deemed it more important for Bunker to remain in close contact with President Thieu. Prime Minister Keith Holyoake of New Zealand was in Saigon, giving Thieu the opportunity to declare again in a joint communique that he would not accept the Viet Cong as a separate entity in the Paris talks. But Bunker was reasonably satisfied that Thieu's hard-lining, necessary to maintain stability in his own government, would not prevent his full acceptance of the terms for expanded talks at the proper time.

By coincidence, the third man in the top American team in Vietnam was in the news Monday. Robert W. Komer, pacification chief under Abrams, was named by President Johnson to be Ambassador to Turkey. His had been the thankless task of "building confidence in the countryside," a program set back sharply by the Communist offensive at Tet, but still a measurable success. Johnson wanted to give Komer and his family a break before he left office; he hoped that the incoming President, whoever he was, would leave the new Ambassador in Ankara long enough for Komer to enjoy some of the privileges of a peaceful post. Komer had been particularly ravaged by a tropical intestinal disease resistant to treatment.

All day Monday, I sweated the possibility that Abrams' trip home would be discovered. I did not see how a four-star general could leave his battlefield command, fly to Alaska for refueling and on to Washington—an elapsed time of nearly a full day—and not be seen by someone or be missed by the press in Saigon. Abrams told me later it was because he did not have much to do with the press; they had gotten so they did not pay much attention to his movements.

We had word that Abrams would land at Andrews Air Force

Base not long after midnight. His scheduled arrival was changed a time or two because of prevailing winds, but we were alerted to begin meeting with him at whatever hour he could get to the White House. I had been staying with the Larry Temples ever since my family had returned to Texas, and we watched the Green Bay Packers defeat the Dallas Cowboys on television while waiting for the StarLifter from Vietnam. It was 2 a.m. when the White House car picked me up. "This is one way to beat the traffic," I told the driver, who had been in the business long enough not to ask why various staff members were reconvening at the White House at such an unhappy hour.

When I arrived, I went to Walt Rostow's office in the basement. Clark Clifford was there, talking with Rostow. I staked Clifford to a carton of milk from the vending machine, and together we went to the Cabinet Room. The President arrived at two-thirty, his dark brown suit and pale yellow shirt highlighting his unusual paleness. He was plainly tired and had the beginnings of a cold. But he was in good spirits as the Cabinet Room began to fill: Rusk, Wheeler, Dick Helms, Maxwell Taylor, Clifford, Rostow, Christian, Tom Johnson, and a relative newcomer to the bombing halt proceedings, Harry McPherson. The President liked to call Harry his "philosopher." McPherson, a slender Texan who had worked for Johnson on and off for a dozen years, was an outspoken liberal intellectual who was never reluctant to give his views to the President in highly literate, lengthy memoranda noted for their subliminal technique. Harry also knew how to roll with the punch and keep his silence on relatively minor matters. Some of the staff pushed Lyndon Johnson rather hard; Harry liked to pick and choose his thrusts at forming Presidential opinion.

At 2:38 a.m. Creighton Abrams, looking like a grizzled Spencer Tracy in a snap-brim hat never intended for a general, came in through the outside French doors and accepted the President's warm handshake. He had been picked up by Brigadier General Bob Ginsburgh, Rostow's aide, at Andrews Air Force Base and driven straight to the White House. At the east gate a guard was reluctant for a moment to admit the stranger. No one came in the

White House grounds without identification. Ginsburgh pulled rank to solve that problem, while Abrams remained mute with his civilian hat helping to hide his identity.

The President sat with Rusk on his right and Abrams on his left. The rest of us arrayed ourselves on the other side of the table, the better to hear the general express his views. Johnson, with few preliminaries, read swiftly a background paper to bring Abrams up to date on everything—beginning with indications from the Russians in the summer of 1968 that they had grounds to believe prompt results would emanate from a decision to halt the bombing of Vietnam.

Abrams was informed of the more recent contact with the Soviet Union: The message was that he, the field commander, would respond to violations of the DMZ and attacks against the cities, and that useful talks could not proceed if the North Vietnamese committed either of these acts.

"It will be on-again, off-again Flanagan if they do anything," Johnson remarked bluntly.

Abrams was also informed of a report from Harvan that the North Vietnamese in Paris "understand clearly" the American position on the DMZ and the cities.

At three o'clock Jim Jones brought a tray of orange juice from the White House kitchen, and Abrams, at the President's bidding, began explaining his views on the military situation in detail. I recalled the first time Abrams had been at the White House, the preceding spring, when Johnson was considering his appointment to succeed General William Westmoreland. He gave the impression then of a tough, inarticulate, nuts-and-bolts military pro with none of the polish of "Westy." One official remarked then, "He would be cut to pieces at a Congressional hearing." That judgment was premature. Abrams was not smooth, true. But he said nothing he had not rolled around in his mind, he seemed to know the position of every battalion of Allied soldiers in Vietnam, and he could pinpoint the strengths and weaknesses of every unit of the South Vietnamese Army. In his brassy New England idiom, he told a story this morning that pumped reassurance back into Lyndon Johnson.

Assaults across the DMZ were no problem. The enemy in recent months had reduced his own capability to do this by withdrawing forces into other areas. The threat now was not in I Corps, but in III Corps, where the enemy had sanctuary in Cambodia and still was capable of hitting Saigon. Even at that, a major assault on Saigon could not succeed. If the bombing were stopped and the North Vietnamese then precipitated some emergency, the situation could be handled easily by the military until the political decisions were made to resume the bombing.

Johnson asked him the point-blank question: Had we reached the point where bombing North Vietnamese territory could be ended without causing additional Allied casualties?

Abrams answered without hesitation, "Yes, sir."

The President leaned back in his chair, looked at Rusk, and then at the faces across the table. I made a mental note to remember that moment as the high-water mark of his fear about stopping the bombing. From then on, the tide would recede.

The general went on with his review of the military situation, including a detailed report on improvements in the ARVN (Army of South Vietnam). As he talked, I scribbled a note to General Earle Wheeler on my left: "If this was some other war, we would be convinced now we had won it." Wheeler nodded and wrote under my note: "We have—we won it in Feb, March, Apr & May. We didn't know it until mid-May."

In this account of the October peace move, I have used direct quotations sparingly, and only where necessary to give the flavor of specific discussions. Since Abrams' views on the bombing halt were reported fully in the days following the decision of October 31, I feel the following exchange should be in the words of the principals as several of us jotted them down:

President Johnson: General, I think you have all the information I have. In light of what you know, do you have any reluctance to recommend we stop the bombing?

General Abrams: No, sir. I have absolutely no reservations about doing this. I know it's stepping into a cesspool of comment and interpretation. It will be a difficult time for everyone. But I think it is the right thing to do.

To get everyone on the record again, the President polled the room. He got nothing but assent. Dean Rusk commented wryly that he had no reluctance at all "as long as we recognize this isn't moving us into paradise." As he frequently did, he reminded us that we undoubtedly faced many more months of frustration and heartache at Paris, as well as more trouble in Saigon and more dead on the battlefield.

Walt Rostow had put together a new schedule which called for the bombing to cease at 7 p.m. Washington time, which was 8 a.m. Saigon time, today. The President was now ready to issue the orders, contingent upon another report from Ambassador Bunker on the situation with Thieu. He was satisfied that the cessation would not cause additional casualties or impair troop morale. He had been assured it would not cause a coup in Saigon, because South Vietnamese politicians knew that would be the beginning of the end of any relationship with the United States.

At five o'clock Johnson told Abrams to go to the Mansion and get some sleep. The group would meet again in the Cabinet Room at noon. In the meantime, Rusk would have a later report from Bunker on the timing of a joint announcement, and the Presidential order to the military could be handled by telephone. Abrams went to bed and the President, too edgy and exhilarated for sleep, sat in the West Hall with McPherson, Jim Jones, Tom Johnson, and Christian, awaiting Rusk's report. The President was pleased with the unanimity of the decision he would make. And he obviously felt it was proper that he, the Commander-in-Chief, should be the last man to agree it was the right move. Otherwise, the military and other advocates of the bombing might undercut him, and there was still that matter of election politics. The negotiations had been tricky, and they hung on very slender threads.

As Abrams had said, there might be a cesspool of comment and interpretation, but the President alone did not select the date of the bombing halt; it had been worked out at the conference table with the enemy, and a prompt decision was backed by every senior military adviser, including the field commander.

Several times during our discussions I had dwelled upon one theme: To wait until after the election to call the bombing halt would be blatant politics. Once an agreement was reached with Hanoi and Saigon, to then permit the November 5 election to delay the announcement would subject the President to well-deserved condemnation. I could picture what those in the President's own party would say if Humphrey were defeated. To many of them, the blame would be on Lyndon Johnson for failure to make a turn toward peace when he had the opportunity.

To Harry McPherson would fall the task of framing the President's radio and television report to the people, which we hoped would come that evening. McPherson said he needed some sleep first so Johnson gave him a pair of his own pajamas and told him to go to the third floor for a nap.

Around six o'clock Rusk called with an unhappy report on Thieu. The South Vietnamese President thought three days between the bombing halt and the widened talks in Paris was not long enough. He could not get his delegation there by then. Furthermore, it would be nine o'clock this evening, Washington time, before he could discuss the matter with Vice President Ky, whom he wanted to go to Paris as an adviser. That would eliminate any possibility of stopping the bombing today. I thought President Johnson showed admirable restraint in receiving the report. But he had no sooner hung up the telephone than a memorandum came in advising him that someone at a meeting of top Republican leaders had said the word was being passed to South Vietnam to try to hold up the bombing halt. The evidence was too flimsy to vouch for, but it was still ominous.

The President headed back to the Cabinet Room to meet Rusk and Rostow for a more thorough discussion of the revised situation.

We enjoyed a beautiful dawn as we walked through the colonnade to the West Wing, then plunged into another meeting with much less optimism than had prevailed an hour or so earlier.

Was Thieu conniving with the Republicans? If so, should he be saved from himself? Public opinion in this country would turn on him like a tiger. Should he be told everything had gone too far to turn back now, that he had originally blessed the entire package and should not change his mind, that we had everything we wanted in the deal? Finally, caution ruled the day. The President ordered patience, along with a full explanation to Thieu on the gravity of the situation. He would go that last mile with the South Vietnamese leader, however difficult it might be. Scrambled eggs and bacon were brought to the Cabinet Room by the Filipino waiters from the White House Mess. At least we would suffer our anxieties on full stomachs.

The third floor of the White House living quarters contains the laundry, a solarium used mostly by the Johnson girls for entertaining guests, the First Lady's secretarial office, and a number of guest bedrooms. The wide hallway is lined with bookcases, and many of the volumes date back to Franklin Roosevelt and earlier. It is of small historical note that many of the books are like those which reside year in and year out on public library shelves without ever being checked out—outdated and rather dull reading. The guest rooms are comfortably furnished with antiques, including four-poster beds in some of them, and cooled by erratic window units rather than central air conditioning. This is where Presidential guests get their thrills from spending a night under the White House roof. The President also graciously offered rooms to staff members who were uprooted temporarily for one reason or another, and during the Washington riot of 1968 he ordered two of my secretaries in the press office to share a room there rather than go home to their apartments near the riot area.

This is where the President bunked Creighton Abrams, weary from his long flight from Tan Son Nhut airport, in a single bed under a print of two doves touching their beaks in a gesture of affection. Abrams napped only briefly and had breakfast from a tray before the President walked to the Mansion after his Cabinet Room meeting and rode up the elevator to the general's room. They sat and talked privately for nearly an hour, Johnson filling him in on the latest tangle. Then Johnson went to his own bedroom in hopes of getting some rest. But there is no evidence that he did anything other than work on accumulated papers and talk on the telephone.

We reassembled on the second floor for lunch and learned that Thieu's National Security Council had been in session four hours on the talks proposal. They were apparently having quite a row. In Paris, Cyrus Vance was using his best bedside manner on the Hanoi delegation, advising them that the U.S. had a number of countries to consult before the final word could be given.

Dean Rusk reiterated his greatest fear—that our own impatience would flush everything down the drain after thousands of lives had been sacrificed to give South Vietnam a chance to survive as a nation. The President, despite his exasperation over the developments, was resigned to the fact that it would be a day or two longer before he could move. On Sunday he was reluctant to face the decision; on Tuesday he was eager to get it over with. He was not feeling very well; he thought he had picked up a cold on his trip to Kentucky the previous Saturday, and his voice was becoming a little hoarse. "If you all don't settle this pretty soon I might not be in shape to announce it," he groused.

Abrams was eager to return to Vietnam immediately. Just before he departed the White House, the President took him aside and gave him a Distinguished Service Medal. It was not the time for ceremony, so the presentation was brief and private. The general's absence from the field had still not been discovered. I secured an agreement from the President that I would announce he had come to Washington for consultation if I had a single press inquiry about it. I thought that any attempt to cover it up if it began to leak would create a credibility problem of mammoth proportions. I was also certain that Abrams would eventually be missed and someone would put two and two together.

At my four o'clock briefing no one raised a question. I produced

Walter Humann and Doris Kearns, officers of the White House Fellows Association, to brief the press on a report the Association would give the President later in the day. The afternoon was so ordinary that I thought for a moment Abrams might have pulled the cleverest stunt since Grover Cleveland's secret operation for cancer.

But this was short lived. Just before six o'clock, Dan Rather of CBS called and asked: "George, has General Abrams been in Washington today?" Rather's sources were always remarkable. Without delay, I answered that he had. I think my candor startled Rather, who expected an evasive answer.

I promptly called the President and told him CBS had the fact Abrams had been there. He felt there was a security leak somewhere and wanted me to find out where. I later was told that an Air Force reserve trainee with some sort of CBS connection thought he had seen Abrams at Andrews Air Force Base. I could never verify the story and don't know to this day whether Rather really had information or was just playing a hunch.

I called in all of the press from the lobby and told them:

> I have had some inquiries that prompted me to bring you in here so you would all have an even break on the matter. As most of you know, the President, for several weeks, has desired to see General Creighton Abrams. You are all familiar with the reports from time to time about possibilities of meeting with him somewhere. The President determined this weekend that it would be best for General Abrams to come here to Washington, which he did.
>
> The President reviewed the military situation in Vietnam with him today. He also conferred with appropriate Pentagon officials. The President asked him to attend the regular Tuesday luncheon meeting today. General Abrams has now returned to Vietnam; he is en route.

The newsmen probed for details, without a great deal of luck.

Q. I think you realize that this is going to be fairly widely interpreted in the light of what is going on.

A. You interpret it any way you want to.

Q. Do I have your permission to do that in the light of what has been going on?

A. I can't stop you from doing anything you want to do. I don't want to add to any speculation. We have told you time and time again what the situation is. It is still the situation. I don't have anything new to report to you. There was a military review, as I said. I don't think it is to be expected that I would get into the deep particulars of that review.

The White House reporters, and news analysts all over town, did not need much more than that to conclude that a bombing halt was indeed only hours away. For the first time, the White House had given them hard news about the Presidential decision the world was discussing. They had no inkling yet of other developments which might have had a bearing on the South Vietnamese foot-dragging which was currently upsetting American desires.

V · *The Lady*

In addition to the rumors of contacts between the South Vietnamese and Republican campaign officials, we now had hard evidence of such a move. Mrs. Anna Chennault, lovely widow of Flying Tiger hero General Claire Chennault, had had consultations with officials of the South Vietnamese Embassy in Washington. Here was intrigue right out of a Cold War movie. Mrs. Chennault, Chinese-born but now an American citizen, happened to be a vice chairman of the Republican National Finance Committee. She also served as co-chairman, with Mrs. Dwight D. Eisenhower, of the Nixon-Agnew National Advisory Committee. The information we received left no doubt as to Mrs. Chennault's mission. The question was whether Richard Nixon had any knowledge of it.

Mrs. Chennault became known to us as "the lady," and her movements in South Vietnamese circles were followed closely before and after the bombing halt decision. President Johnson asserted that he did not want her activities revealed by any of his people, as this would only further complicate our dealings with Saigon.

However, Johnson made certain that Nixon was told of the implications of Mrs. Chennault's movements. When Hubert Humphrey learned of her activity, he faced the hard decision of whether to use the information for his benefit in the last days of the campaign. Humphrey decided that it would not be proper to do so. He had no proof that Nixon had anything to do with Saigon's reluctance to enter the peace talks, and to accuse the Republican candidate of prolonging the war would be a quite serious matter. To his credit, the Vice President ignored the incident rather than risk damaging the American political system any more than the events of 1968 had already done.

Later, reports of contacts between Republican campaigners and Saigon officials prior to the November 5 election appeared in the press, but it was not until January that Tom Ottenad of the *St. Louis Post-Dispatch* uncovered the full story of Mrs. Chennault. Rather than precipitate a controversy then, government spokesmen were instructed to neither confirm nor deny the story. But Nixon aides confirmed it, while denying that the GOP candidate had anything to do with Mrs. Chennault's activities or with overtures certain South Vietnamese made to the Nixon camp. Ottenad quoted one Republican official as saying, "She wasn't our baby." The *Post-Dispatch* headlined its story, "Was Saigon's peace talk delay due to Republican promises?"

The real significance to Johnson was not so much the fact that Mrs. Chennault did what she did, but the knowledge that Saigon probably believed it could get a better deal out of the Republicans than he had arranged. As one adviser put it, "they're beginning to make their choice between two months of Johnson and four years of Nixon."

The immediate task was to overcome this obstacle without destroying the alliance with South Vietnam. The differences between Washington and Hanoi had been ironed out. Hanoi—and

Moscow—were awaiting Johnson's order to stop the bombing. Now it was a question of American credibility in negotiating for peace. Furthermore, the President doubted he could hold the country together in its commitment to South Vietnam if it became known Saigon was causing a complete breakdown in the Paris talks. This he communicated to President Thieu.

Johnson, who badly needed sleep, went to bed Tuesday night with his cold getting worse and his throat tight. He tossed about for a few hours, awake for much of the time, then got up early for telephone calls to Rusk, Clifford, and Rostow. All of them had been contributing passages to the Presidential speech coordinated by McPherson, which was now in its fourth or fifth draft. At ten o'clock we gathered in the Cabinet Room to go over the speech and get everyone up to date on the cable traffic from Saigon and Paris.

Ambassador Bunker was applying the hard squeeze to Thieu and his associates, but they were arguing back—both publicly and privately. The early edition of the *Washington Star* carried the banner headline: "Thieu agrees to bombing halt." If the situation had been that simple, much grief and antagonism would have been avoided. The true fact was that relations between Washington and Saigon were reaching their lowest ebb.

Thieu had rejected the first version of a joint communique. A revised version acceptable to Thieu went too far toward upsetting the delicate balance in Paris. Thieu wanted assurance from Hanoi that the National Liberation Front would not constitute a separate entity in the expanded talks. Giving such stature to outlaws, he felt, would undermine the legitimate government in Saigon. This was not to be a four-power conference, in his view. Thieu also wanted assurances that Hanoi would enter into direct talks with Saigon—a condition Ambassadors Harriman and Vance could have never sold.

Harriman, the seventy-six-year-old expert on Communist diplomacy who thoroughly enjoyed the code name "Crocodile" once assigned to him, confronted the South Vietnamese observer in Paris, Pham Dang Lam, with the impossibility of forcing Hanoi to agree to rigid conditions. Harriman, who rarely hid his distrust of "the Saigon generals," was apparently irritated enough with the South Vietnamese demands to use blunt language in rejecting them. In any event, Lam's report to Thieu on the conversation badly complicated Bunker's dealings with the Saigon government. Thieu reportedly believed his people were being told one thing in Paris and another in Saigon. Despite Bunker's best efforts to smooth over the new controversy, Thieu summoned Lam home from Paris to give him a face-to-face report on Harriman's rejection.

Thieu understood by now that President Johnson had made up his mind and was ready to act. He had been assured by Bunker that the United States would not recognize the NLF as anything more than part of the Hanoi delegation. But this was not enough for Thieu, Ky, Prime Minister Huong, and the others, who were united against the American position. It appeared to them that Ho Chi Minh was tricking Johnson in an effort to relieve the pressure on himself, while at the same time undermining Saigon by achieving equal status for the NLF. It was difficult to dispute some of this reasoning, but Johnson was convinced after all of his doubts that he could not get a better deal than he already had. He had no illusions that the decision was anything more than a gamble.

At one point the President showed a copy of his proposed speech to Mrs. Johnson. "Does this ring any bells with you?" he asked.

After she had read it, she replied, "It's a grand and glorious relief that something is happening."

"It hasn't yet," the President said glumly.

VI · *Belay All Bombs*

The tension began to creep up our necks that Wednesday afternoon, October 30, as we struggled to shape up an agreed version of the President's announcement. Drafts were torn apart and put back together on the basis of new thoughts, and changing moods. Johnson devoted his number one pencil to the rewrites, which were being typed by Marie Fehmer in his outer office as fast as we could get the pages to her.

We still did not know whether the President could go on the air that night or would have to wait until Thursday. A complicating factor was his voice. It was beginning to grow hoarse. His eyes were bothering him, his chest was sore, and his nose was running. As the anxieties mounted, so did the aches and pains.

Finally, it was decided that Bunker should have a little more time. Dusk in Washington was dawn in Saigon. Another working day for the weary Ambassador would not make that much difference in timing and might produce a better frame of mind in Thieu, Ky, and their colleagues. We were still hoping for a joint communique with Thieu.

But Johnson wanted to rehearse his speech that evening—and to film it for broadcast later if he liked it. He was concerned he would not be in condition to make a live broadcast Thursday evening. It might be noted that an announcement in prime television time was all that was ever considered. It was essential that the President reach as many people as possible with a reasoned explanation of his decision, for it was worth little without public understanding and support.

After our final speechwriting session, Johnson said he was near to being satisfied. He would rather not use prepared texts for his speeches, he told us, but had little choice when the subject was so critical. He felt he always did better when he just "got full of the speech and then let it all out." Warming to the subject of speechmaking, he told us a story about Jim Ferguson, a Texas governor who was impeached and couldn't run again, so he ran his wife in three elections in the twenties and thirties, winning two of them.

It seems that one of Mrs. Ferguson's opponents had botched a literary speech because he couldn't pronounce the words someone else had written for him. As Johnson related it, Jim Ferguson had commented: "I've known some people who could write a speech but couldn't say it, and I've known people who could say a speech but not write one. Now I see an ignoramus who can't read it, write it, or say it."

Late in the day Jim Jones turned the final draft of the speech over to the teleprompter operators, who were sworn to secrecy in regard to the contents.

Because of this need for secrecy, and to avoid premature disclosures while Bunker was still negotiating with Thieu, we could not use a network television crew for the filming. We had no facilities for video taping a Presidential speech, but would have to use ordinary color film with all of its attendant delays in processing. The equipment would be manned by Commander Tommy Atkins, the White House movie cameraman, and his small crew.

It was after eleven o'clock before Atkins and his men were ready in the theater. They had received short notice of the magnitude of their task, but the White House photographers had a good record for responding to any emergency. Once in Bonn, Germany, I smuggled Yoichi Okamoto, the President's "still" photographer, into a tightly guarded room where Johnson was to meet Charles de Gaulle. The German hosts had decreed no photos, but "Oke" and I bluffed our way through the guards, and he snapped several quick pictures of the austere handshake between the two leaders with a camera he had hidden under his raincoat. Later we gave the roll of film to the AP and UPI photographers who were travelling with us, and the world had pictures of historic significance at the time. Between them, Atkins and Okamoto saw to it that the Johnson Presidency was recorded on film better than any other. While this drew some press criticism late in the Administration, I have no doubt about the significance of the film library in the future. Their cameras were admitted to every type of meeting—most of which were barred to press photographers for security reasons—and someday their labors will be viewed as monumental.

Tonight Atkins was apprehensive. He had only one camera position, so he used a shoulder camera for different angles of the President as he talked. This was a makeshift procedure, but it worked reasonably well. It was the middle of the night, Johnson was tired, and his temper was short. But he plowed through the speech, sore throat and all. The film processors would work through the remainder of the night to have a print ready for him to view in the late morning. If it was not of sufficient quality, he would have another chance at it. But he said, "I'll tell you right now that I don't think I can go through that whole speech again tomorrow."

The President went to bed at midnight but slept little. Two or three times the Navy corpsman on duty in the White House dispensary was summoned to administer medicines in an effort to clear his chest and nasal passages. Before 5 a.m. Rostow was on the phone to the bedroom to report on Bunker's efforts to win Thieu over to a joint announcement. Bunker would go into session with the South Vietnamese leader again on the evening of October 31, Saigon time, which was morning of the same day in Washington.

Now occurred one of the oddest mix-ups of the period. I had announced that the President was going to make a political broadcast for the Democratic ticket, which would be taped in advance. My briefings had been crowded with foreign correspondents of late, including several Japanese reporters with only a limited grasp of English. I am sure my own drawl made it even more difficult for them to comprehend what I said. After my announcement, Helen Thomas of UPI overheard a spirited discussion among the Japanese outside my door, in which she detected that some believed the President had begun to tape a broadcast on Vietnam, confusing my announcement on the political speech.

Within hours, the Kyodo News Service quoted "government sources" in Tokyo as saying they expected a suspension of the bombing to be announced within several hours. In a classic example of building something out of nothing, the report said that the U.S. government "was believed to have informally intimated to the Japanese government that the U.S. bombardment of North Vietnam would be stopped."

The belief of the informal intimation was backed up by the report that "the sources . . . had heard President Johnson was having his statement on the bombing halt prerecorded."

This caused a flurry in the White House press room, of course, but as it turned out, the fact caught up with the error. Johnson did prerecord part of his speech, so by accident and misunderstanding the Japanese reporter who started it all managed to scoop the world.

At noon McPherson and Rostow brought Johnson two additional pages for the speech. The President had been dissatisfied with the ending of the original statement and had directed that a new close be tacked on. He okayed their handiwork as "real good" and ordered the theater prepared for further filming. I spent some time with Ken Gaddis, Johnson's valet, looking for the shirt Johnson had worn the night before so he would be wearing the same clothing in the second segment of the film.

It was all the President could do to complete the job in the theater. His voice had worsened from the night before, and the change in tone was noticeable, but he struggled through it with grim determination. Atkins rushed to process the film and splice it onto the earlier segment, trusting to luck that he would be able to complete it in time. We were shooting for an eight o'clock broadcast, provided we had any decent word at all from Bunker, and that meant getting the film to one of the network studios a half-hour before that.

Lynda Robb was bringing baby Lucinda home from the hospital that afternoon. The Johnsons went to the South Portico to welcome them. The reporters and photographers had congregated nearby, under the tutelage of Liz Carpenter and Loyd Hackler, and they watched as President and Mrs. Johnson strolled in the Rose Garden. It was a sunny, still day. Johnson did his best to appear healthy and happy with the press watching, when in fact he ached from the chest up and was waiting anxiously for some word from Bunker. When Lynda and the baby arrived, accompanied by Luci Nugent, the President got close enough to Lucinda only to satisfy the cameramen. Then it was back to his labors.

In Saigon, Bunker and Thieu were deadlocked at the Presidential palace. In the dark of the night, Viet Cong rockets fell in the city. One of them crashed into a Catholic Church, killing nineteen people who were worshipping there. Thieu was furious. The U.S. was preparing to give up bombing North Vietnam's military targets, while the Viet Cong were shelling churches in Saigon and killing civilians. The rocket attack also angered Lyndon Johnson, but Walt Rostow pointed out that we were also still bombing the North and there was no agreement as yet.

Johnson repeated an earlier order that General Creighton Abrams' rules of engagement be perfectly clear when and if the bombing came to an end. There must be appropriate retaliation if the enemy shelled the cities or violated the DMZ. Rostow had predicted early in the negotiations that we would be tested periodically by Hanoi—that we could expect some attacks and even some activity in the DMZ. Rusk and Clifford agreed that violations of the "understanding" must be dealt with. Clifford was especially determined that reconnaissance flights over North Vietnamese territory be continued and that the enemy learn to live with them. The U.S. was careful to agree to nothing that would bar such flights and was prepared to attack antiaircraft positions which fired on the reconnaissance planes.

The meeting between Bunker and the South Vietnamese leaders broke up at dawn. Bunker, a taciturn, seventy-four-year-old New Englander who had handled some tough assignments for his country, never cracked this one. It has been put to Thieu on instructions from Washington that Johnson had made a firm and hard decision to stop the bombing in return for expanded talks. Nearly three weeks before Thieu had concurred in the negotiating formula. The questioning came later, after Ky and other Vietnamese officials—including Thieu's National Security Council—had debated the issue. But it was too late to turn back. The bombing would stop at Johnson's order on November 1, and on November 6 a meeting would be held in Paris at which the government of South Vietnam would be "free to attend." We still believed Thieu's delegation would show up on schedule, despite his refusal to join in the announcement.

Now Johnson moved ahead quickly to clear away the last preparatory items on the agenda before the speech went on the air. The candidates for President would have to be notified, and the Congressional leaders. There should be a meeting of the

National Security Council and the military chiefs and service secretaries from the Defense Department. Few of these men had ever been officially advised of the negotiations in progress since early October. But unless they were blind and deaf, nothing Johnson told them would come as a surprise. The grapevine had been at work steadily since the President's first order to maintain tight secrecy on these developments.

At 5:45 p.m. I called the press into my office and told them:

> The President has called a meeting for six thirty tonight in the White House of the National Security Council, the service secretaries, the Under Secretaries of Defense and State, and other appropriate civilian and military officials.
>
> The meeting will be in the Cabinet Room. It will relate to Vietnam and will be a follow-up to the President's consultations with General Abrams on Tuesday and numerous consultations by cable with Ambassador Bunker.
>
> I will shortly advise the networks that the President's present plans are to go on the air any time after 8 p.m. tonight for a statement.
>
> That is all I have.

The reporters barged out so quickly that several bounced off the door jam in the crush.

At six o'clock the President, in his Oval Office, placed a conference call to Hubert Humphrey, Richard Nixon, and George Wallace. Humphrey was in Elizabeth, New Jersey, Nixon at his apartment in New York, Wallace at the Golden Triangle Motor Hotel in Norfolk, Virginia. Stenotypist Jeri Rudolph took down the conversation, and the President's "Tuesday luncheon group" listened on the box. Johnson leaned forward in his rocking chair to talk into the speaker. Rusk, Clifford, Wheeler, Dick Helms, Rostow, Tom Johnson, and I grouped around on the two sofas and a couple of chairs, beneath the portrait of Franklin D. Roosevelt which Johnson had hung over the mantel a couple of years before.

This was a depiction of the latter-day Roosevelt. His black cape was around his shoulders and his face was haggard. It was not the Roosevelt of the first hundred days, admonishing depression-struck America that it had nothing to fear but fear itself. This was the Roosevelt who had been through twelve years of the Presidency and more than three years of war. In his hand he held the Atlantic Charter, and in the background was the sea itself.

In the mind's eye of those around Johnson, he could have been substituted in this portrait, holding a symbolic Pacific charter in his hand, and the sea in the background would be the Pacific.

Johnson's times dictated that he should be the Pacific President. Because of events but also because of attitude, his eyes were nearly always turned westward. When we travelled from Washington we usually raced the sun, east to west, seizing every ray of light, stretching the day as far as it would go. Campaign trips were planned to take advantage of the time zones. And only once during his Administration did Johnson fly east, to Europe. It was always to the west—to Honolulu, to Guam, to Australia and New Zealand, to the Philippines, Malaysia, Thailand, Korea, and Vietnam. I doubt that any other President will ever receive a noisy Polynesian welcome from the residents of Pago Pago, American Samoa, twice within fourteen months.

"I'm interested in Asia because that's where the people are," he said time and again.

And he also believed firmly that this was where the danger lay —that an American presence in Asia and the western Pacific was essential to national survival. When in his enthusiasm he sometimes said we might be pushed all the way back to Hawaii if we ever showed weakness in meeting our commitments to the free countries of Asia, some called this World War II rhetoric with no bearing on the late 1960s. But Johnson was not comparing the present with Japanese aggression in Asia and the Pacific. He was merely explaining that an absence of U.S. power in the perimeter around Red China would open the entire region to Communist attack or subversion, and ultimately the surviving countries would have to reach an accommodation with the Chinese, thereby making Hawaii the westernmost outpost of American influence save possibly for Australia and New Zealand. In his view, anyone naive enough to believe otherwise was blind to Chinese imperialism, or simply didn't care what happened to hundreds of millions of Asians who might have the opportunity to develop their own future in freedom if they had a shield to work behind.

"Hubert . . . Dick . . . George?"

The man to whom Johnson would turn over this problem was on the other end of the line, along with two others who wanted the responsibility.

Briefly, the President reviewed his October 16 call to the three candidates. Since then, he said, he had been informed by the U.S. negotiators in Paris that Hanoi would permit the Saigon government to attend the talks, and Hanoi understood fully what would happen if we stopped the bombing and they shelled the cities or abused the DMZ. He said he had told the Russians that he had doubts Hanoi would live by the understanding and had been told in return that his doubts were unjustified. Then the President related problems that had developed:

Speeches that we ought to withdraw troops, or that we would stop the bombing without anything in return (a slap on the wrist for you, Hubert); and

Implications by "some of our folks, even including some of the old China lobbyists" that a better deal might be made by another President (the same for you, Dick).

Johnson said he was prepared to issue an order stopping the bombing, based upon the understandings in Paris and the recommendations of the Joint Chiefs, Abrams, and Bunker. He pointed out that he had stepped aside as a candidate in an effort to achieve peace, and now that Hanoi had moved in that direction he wasn't inclined to put it off because he might be concerned with an election. The President said the plan had nothing to do with the election and hoped all three candidates would give him their support, as they did on October 16. "Let one man speak with a single voice to the Communist world and to the rest of the world," he appealed. "Over and out. I'll be glad to have your comments."

Nixon wanted to know if military activities would continue in

South Vietnam. Apparently he could smell a cease-fire, or a Korean-like situation wherein Allied forces were shackled while the talks proceeded. Johnson assured him this was not the case, that the enemy would be given no advantage in the South.

When Johnson told them he would soon go on the air, George Wallace said: "Mr. President, I just pray that everything you do works out fine, and I am praying for you."

Nixon said: "We'll back you up. Thank you."

Humphrey said: "We'll back you, Mr. President."

And Wallace came back on: "We'll back you, Mr. President."

Johnson thanked them and hung up. He grinned at those in the room (he had told the candidates others were listening to the conversation) and clasped his hands together as he was wont to do when something turned out well.

Then Johnson talked on a conference call to the Senate and House leaders: Senators Mansfield, Dirksen, Tommy Kuchel, Speaker McCormack, Hale Boggs, and Leslie Arends. House GOP leader Gerald Ford was on the line at one point but hung up when he couldn't determine who was calling him. White House staffer Barefoot Sanders later passed the word to Ford and Democratic leader Carl Albert, who could not be reached when Johnson wanted him.

The President walked into a crowded Cabinet Room to break the news to the military and foreign service leaders. His voice was hoarse from the previous conversations, but he was assured and businesslike as he went over the background of the peace negotiations and told them of his decision. There was general pleasure— perhaps too much optimism—in the room when he finished. The press photographers were admitted for pictures, then there were handshakes and congratulations as the State and Defense Department officials filed out.

Hubert Humphrey called back, requesting advice on how to handle his response when the story broke. He agreed he should keep partisanship at arm's length.

In the meantime, my office had its hands full trying to get the President's speech on the air. The assistant press secretary, Loyd

Hackler, escorted the film to the studios of the National Broadcasting Company and stood by as it was fed over the lines for broadcast at eight o'clock. When the "feed" began, Channel 13 in New York City—the educational station—put it on the air immediately, breaking the eight o'clock embargo. As soon as he saw what had happened, Hackler pulled the plug. Hackler, an Oklahoma farmer's son with a psychology degree and a distinguished career in journalism, was never one to dillydally when a decision was needed. A controversy over Channel 13's action, and the subsequent network protests, boiled for several days thereafter.

Simultaneous press "backgrounders" were held at the White House, Pentagon, and State Department to explain the President's decision to the three sets of correspondents. Then at eight o'clock the President's somber face appeared on the nation's television screens and the bombing of North Vietnam, begun on February 7, 1965, came to a close, after unloading more explosives than the Americans dropped on Germany in World War II, and after the loss of more than nine hundred U.S. planes.

The President explained carefully the series of events since his March 31 decision to halt bombing except in the southern part of North Vietnam. He related the recommendations from his advisers, including General Abrams, then:

"As a result of all these developments, I have now ordered that all air, naval, and artillery bombardment of North Vietnam cease as of 8 a.m., Washington time, Friday morning."

He said a meeting in Paris would be held on November 6, at which the representatives of South Vietnam would be free to participate. He said Hanoi had advised that representatives of the NLF would also be present, but emphasized that "their attendance in no way involves recognition of the National Liberation Front in any form." That was as far as he could go with President Thieu's complaint.

The President warned that such arrangements are never "foolproof" and that we could be "misled." If so, "we are prepared for such a contingency." Johnson took great pains to avoid public expectations that the war might be about to end, adapting Rusk's words that some "very hard fighting" and "very hard negotiating" loomed ahead.

"What is required of us is a courage and a steadfastness, and a perseverance here at home, that will match that of our men who fight for us tonight in Vietnam," the President said. "So, I ask you not only for your prayers but for the courageous and understanding support that Americans always give their President and their leader in an hour of trial. With that understanding, and with that support, we shall not fail."

Then came the addendum recorded earlier in the day, aimed at allaying suspicion that it was all a political trick to help Hubert Humphrey.

Johnson said he had devoted every resource of his office to the search for peace, and had kept all of the Presidential candidates briefed, without special favor to any. The cooperation had been good. There had been a united voice. Hopefully, it would continue until January 20, "because in this critical hour, we just simply cannot afford more than one voice speaking for our nation in the search for peace."

The President concluded:

I do not know who will be inaugurated as the thirty-seventh President of the United States next January. But I do know that I shall do all that I can in the next few months to try to lighten his burdens as the contributions of the Presidents who preceded me have greatly lightened mine. I shall do everything in my power to move us toward the peace that the new President—as well as this President and, I believe, every other American—so deeply and urgently desires.

Johnson watched the television speech in the Oval Office, with Mrs. Johnson and some of the staff. Not long before airtime, Luci brought in young Lyn Nugent, decked out in a costume and mask. Emblazoned across his small chest was the title, "Super President." It was the first time most of us remembered it was Halloween.

THREE

I · *Fallout*

"As you are probably aware, tonight the President announced another bombing halt in Vietnam," Richard Nixon told a Republican rally in Madison Square Garden. His audience booed.

Hubert Humphrey sat in his car at Newark Airport and listened to President Johnson's speech on the radio. His comment afterwards: "Let us hope and pray that the negotiations in Paris will be able to move forward now toward an honorable and lasting settlement." He had had no part in the President's decision, he told reporters, and had stayed away deliberately from tonight's National Security Council meeting in order to avoid "political implications."

But the smoke of the last bomb on North Vietnamese territory was still settling when Republican and Democratic leaders began open speculation in the press on the possible political effect of the decision. The new Harris Poll, taken before October 31, showed Humphrey had closed the gap to only three percentage points behind Nixon.

In Washington, Mrs. Anna Chennault was active again in South Vietnamese circles.

And in Saigon, President Thieu said "no" to South Vietnamese participation in the scheduled session November 6 in Paris.

Thieu laid down his terms for his entry into the peace negotiations. In brief, they were these:

—North Vietnam must guarantee it was ready to hold direct and serious talks with the Saigon government;

—These talks must be a new phase in the negotiations and were not to be considered a continuation of the exploratory talks between Washington and Hanoi; and

—Hanoi must abandon any pretense that the National Liberation Front was a separate party in the Paris talks, since this would be a North Vietnamese maneuver toward a coalition government.

For nearly a week, Thieu and Ambassador Bunker did not meet. Saigon officials made frequent comments to the press that Johnson had betrayed them. South Vietnamese newspapers condemned the U.S. President for yielding to Hanoi. Keyes Beech, highly regarded correspondent for the *Chicago Daily News*, wrote from Saigon that the Vietnamese had turned on Johnson "with all the fury of a poor recalcitrant nephew who had been rudely ignored by a rich uncle." Beech declared, "No Vietnamese stopped to recall how many times they had let Mr. Johnson down during the last four years."

Johnson went home to Texas for the weekend, where he planned a ranch reception for the Apollo 7 astronauts. The weather was good, and he retreated to the farthest ranch roads to see the deer, which he pampered outrageously. The hunting season would open in a couple of weeks, but there was no hunting on the LBJ Ranch proper any more and very little elsewhere as far as Johnson was concerned. He preferred to drive around and watch the herds of deer race across the pastures, their white tails flashing in the early evening light.

On the Sunday before the election, Richard Nixon said he would go to Saigon if the Johnson Administration thought it would promote the cause of peace. "I think that if the United States right then could present a united front with President Johnson . . . if he could knock down the idea that Hanoi is going to gain by political division in the United States what they cannot gain on the battlefield . . . this might get these talks off dead center."

Nixon telephoned Johnson to volunteer to help resolve the problem if he could. He denied any knowledge of Mrs. Chennault's contacts with the South Vietnamese, or any other activities on his part which might be contributing to the delays. On election eve, there was press speculation from Saigon that Nixon was responsible for Thieu's attitude. Johnson ordered Rostow and me to refuse comment on the story.

The next day Nixon was elected President.

Thieu dispatched a cable of congratulations, in which he said: "The Vietnamese government, the Vietnamese people, and our soldiers fighting in the front lines against Communist aggression will be most happy to receive on Vietnamese soil a staunch defender of freedom, which you have been for many long years." He asked Nixon to make an "on-the-spot assessment of the war and the situation" in Vietnam.

It appeared to us that the stage was fast being set for a repeat of Eisenhower's I-will-go-to-Korea notion in 1952. Thieu had picked up Nixon's gambit of Sunday. Nixon headquarters in Key Biscayne put out the word, however, that the President-elect would not go to Saigon or any other foreign capital before his inauguration unless President Johnson wanted him to. That took care of that, for Dean Rusk set the Administration policy in short order: Nixon should not go to Saigon but should take himself entirely out of the situation by telling Thieu he sided with Johnson on the need for the South Vietnamese to get their delegation to Paris.

American strategy at Paris was also set, based upon the recommendations of both Rusk and Clifford. The U.S. should proceed in its talks with Hanoi without Saigon participation. Saigon would soon get the message. The talks could center on such questions as restoring the demilitarized zone and getting North Vietnamese troops out of Laos.

The hang-up was especially galling to those around Johnson because we knew of the lengths he had gone to protect the Thieu government, and the fact that he would be the last one to negotiate a peace settlement ruinous to that government. Johnson had already demonstrated his patience and perseverance—too much so, in the eyes of some—but we all sensed that the new President would be more determined to get out of the war on the best terms he could. We reasoned that neither Humphrey nor Nixon would allow the Vietnamese conflict to drag him down in the same manner it did Johnson. We felt President Thieu should be made to understand this.

While Saigon balked, the Viet Cong took full propaganda advantage by putting on display a full-fledged Paris delegation, headed not by a general but by a woman. But the absence of South Vietnam brought an indefinite postponement of the November 6 session. Hanoi's delegates also raised the first quarrel over the conference table arrangement when and if Saigon finally sent a team. Hanoi was going to push for the NLF as a full partner, in accordance with the line it had taken before Johnson stopped the bombing. Part of the "understanding" had been that Hanoi would tell the story its way and Washington would do likewise; as Walt Rostow put it, each side would have its own mythology. Admittedly, this would lead to problems, but at least the two sides would be there to thrash them out in conversation that might lead somewhere.

As the argument over representation bloomed, the Administration stuck by its guns. Our original proposal to Hanoi was that there be two sides: ours would be the U.S. and the government of Vietnam, their side the North Vietnamese and whomever they wished. Both sides would organize themselves as they chose. We had not agreed to a four-sided conference which in effect would recognize the NLF.

North Vietnam also challenged our right to fly reconnaissance aircraft over its territory. Clark Clifford and the military had insisted from the start that such flights were essential to the whole plan, since we had to know whether North Vietnam was going to take advantage of the bombing halt by building up men and supplies in the neighborhood of the DMZ. There had already been some artillery and rocket fire across the DMZ since the President's order against bombardment, but the abuses were sporadic and no one considered them dangerous at the moment. In Clifford's words, there was no "pattern" to the violations of the DMZ. We had agreed to stop "acts involving the use of force" against North Vietnamese territory, carefully avoiding any term that would preclude reconnaissance.

In addition to isolated violations of the DMZ, the enemy had also shelled a number of smaller cities. Some of this undoubtedly involved the type of "testing" Walt Rostow had warned would occur, to see what our reaction would be. Also, General Abrams had been ordered to keep up the military pressure on the enemy. It was logical to assume that the enemy would continue to do some fighting of his own and would toss shells into provincial capitals just to remind us that he was still alive and kicking.

The American people—many of them lulled into thinking peace was just around the corner despite all of President Johnson's caution in his speech—were being reminded in early November that the war was still nasty and people were still dying. While Johnson had won praise from most of the nation's press for trying to move toward a peace settlement—and Thieu had been criticized—much of the mail the White House received during this period indicated a sizable segment of the public was as hawkish as ever, or at least highly suspicious of Johnson's motives. Immediately after the speech on October 31, we were hit with numerous messages of dismay and anger. Some thoughtful editors were also beginning to write that Thieu indeed had a severe problem, and we ought to be patient with him. After all, he was the ally and not the enemy.

Clark Clifford and Averell Harriman were the two American

leaders whose patience was most thin, just as it was in October when Bunker was getting nowhere with Thieu.

Clifford chose a news conference on November 12 to show his exasperation publicly. Pointing out that Thieu had been consulted every step of the way and understood everything we were discussing in Paris, he insisted that Washington had bent over backwards to accommodate Saigon's position. Then recalling the visit of General Abrams to Washington on October 29, the Defense Secretary said:

> We broke up that morning meeting on Tuesday with the sure knowledge—I did—that finally we had arrived at the end of this journey that had taken some five and a half months, and we were all to go to bed and get some rest, and then the President was going on the air that night, Tuesday night, the twenty-ninth of October and make his speech and announce that he was stopping the bombing that night, because that was the date, and that he was going to meet with the other side and with the GVN in Paris on Saturday, the second of November. [His use of the pronoun *he* in reference to the November 2 meeting did not mean a personal conference by Johnson himself.]

Growing more nettled as he talked, Clifford accused Thieu of stopping that deal "because he said he didn't have time to get his delegation to Paris by Saturday," and then stopping us again on October 30 with new reasons for not agreeing.

"So here came a whole new set of concerns and objections, every one of which would consume a substantial amount of time," Clifford told the newsmen. But we had reached the point, he went on, where the President was committed and could not turn back, so it was necessary to go on the air without the firm assurance that Saigon would have a man in Paris on November 6, the new date for the expanded talks.

"Now here is the position the President was in on Thursday. . . ." He worked through five and a half months to reach an agreement that he thought could be a major step toward peace, and then in the last out of the ninth inning, why suddenly they say, 'No, we can't go along.'" The President, Clifford said, "was absolutely right in not giving Saigon a veto on the plan."

A reporter asked: "How do you characterize Saigon's operations, then, during these dealings? As sabotaging or as a doublecross, or what?"

Said Clifford, "Take your pick."

The news media thus had a confirmed story of worsening relations between Saigon and Washington and of a Saigon "doublecross." The immediate reaction of some analysts was that Johnson encouraged Clifford to take this public stance as further pressure on Thieu.

The fact was that Johnson was quite unhappy over the news conference and its repercussions. He knew that the story of a doublecross would make it more difficult for Bunker to bring Thieu around. So on his instructions the State Department issued a statement the next day, blasting Hanoi on the issues of reconnaissance planes and NLF presentation at Paris. The aim was to soften the impact of Clifford's words and to reiterate to Thieu that we stood by his demand that the NLF not be recognized in any form other than as the stooge of Hanoi. This went a long way toward salving our allies in Saigon.

Clifford's role in the deliberations on peace had been one of constant pressure, sometimes subtle and often not. His suspicion that the Thieu government did not favor an early peace was heightened by recent events. He pressed this view on Johnson, but he obviously did not desire an open break with Dean Rusk, whose patience with Saigon had worn a little thin but who still felt we were in dangerous shoals when we talked of cease-fires, troop withdrawals, and de-Americanization of the war. Rusk's prime objective was what it had always been: somehow bringing to Asia a "durable peace" which would not be threatened in Laos, Cambodia, Thailand, or somewhere else if we wrote off Vietnam. To him, any weakening of our commitment to Saigon had far greater implications than retaliation against an ally with whom we were temporarily out of sorts.

Clifford began to speak of American troop withdrawals as soon as the understanding was reached with Hanoi on expanded talks. He saw this as the logical next step, and from November to January he held out hope that Johnson might lay down a schedule for partial withdrawal before he left office. The present troop level in Vietnam had come about with Clifford's approval and recommendation shortly after he became Secretary of Defense, but that was in a time of uncertainty after the Tet offensive. For months now he had devoted his energies to those matters which would hasten the day the war could be turned over to the Vietnamese. An example was his insistence that the South Vietnamese army be supplied promptly with M-16 rifles, a slow process under Robert McNamara.

Clifford's open criticism of Thieu, and his advocacy of troop reductions, found little favor with the President. But their personal relationship had always been strong and Clifford was willing to gamble their friendship in the interest of having his views prevail. So he was never dispassionate nor retiring about the matter, even when rebuffed by others in the Administration including the President himself. Johnson sometimes gave the impression that he was tuning him out, but as a practical matter Clifford lost little of his influence and continued to present his views forcefully to the end. He was Secretary of Defense, not of State, but he ignored the dividing line and pushed on.

This fuzzing of responsibilities for American foreign policy could have brought a bitter feud with Rusk. It did not. Both men worked manfully to differ without being difficult; they respected each other, argued when they had to, and worked together in reasonable harmony. The *Washington Post* called it, aptly, "a civilized collision." This was made easier by the fact that Johnson's faith in Rusk never wavered. He listened to Clifford, McNamara, George Ball, and others who sometimes differed with Rusk on specifics, and he might blend these views into a decision; but mainly it was Rusk's judgment he wanted in the end, and Rusk's judgment he followed.

Three days before he left office, the President went to the State

Department to join Dean Rusk's colleagues in honoring the man who served as Secretary of State for eight years under two Presidents. He awarded the Presidential Medal of Freedom to Rusk and called him "this decade's man of the ages." The President went further: "History will rank him high above those who deserve to be called statesmen." And at the Lyndon B. Johnson School of Public Affairs, to be a part of the University of Texas, there would be a two-hundred-thousand-dollar endowment in the names of Dean and Virginia Rusk to provide scholarships to young people interested in public service. It was the first time I ever saw any betrayal of emotion by the wispy haired diplomat from Cherokee County, Georgia, whom one writer called "Buddha" but who preferred another's description: "the neighborhood bartender." Bob McNamara sobbed in public when the President praised him upon retirement. Dean Rusk may have shed a tear or two; at least his eyes became misty.

II · *The Military*

General Earle G. Wheeler was a scholarly military professional who understood diplomacy and politics far better than he would usually concede. The President called him "patient, forthright, steady as a rock—a soldier for every season."

Once at a Tuesday luncheon when Johnson was chiding Rusk and Clifford over their alleged efforts to win the Nobel Peace Prize, Wheeler turned to me and whispered. "If they will leave me alone, I'll win 'em their Nobel Prize."

Facetious though that remark may have been, Wheeler and the establishment he headed were never timid about their advocacy of more military pressure on North Vietnam, and unwavering in their belief that the war could be won on the battlefield. After the bloodbath at Tet, the almost universal military opinion— beginning with that of General William C. Westmoreland in the field—was that the Viet Cong and North Vietnamese suffered a staggering defeat. There is no question that they did, in terms of terrible losses, inability to capture the cities, and failure to topple the South Vietnamese government. But the blow to the American public was also staggering. The credibility of our military assessments suffered irreparable damage, there was universal shock that the enemy could still mount that type of offensive, and though the Allies had intelligence reports that an attack was coming, its ferocity and scope stunned Washington.

The Tet offensive changed the complexion of the war for Lyndon Johnson. The strategy of "wearing down" the enemy, advocated by most American war planners from 1965 on, was discarded. It was also too late to worry that the companion strategy of "gradualism"—about which the hawks complained—might have been a mistake. It may have prevented a wider war by keeping the Chinese from being backed into a hole. But it also gave the enemy time to respond to Allied activity, and in the case of the bombing, it helped him prepare tougher and deadlier defenses. "Maybe we went too slow," Johnson mused to a reporter one day late in his Administration. "But I still have to think that we did what we had to do, and if we stick with it we will accomplish our objective."

The military reaction to the Tet offensive was to request some two-hundred-thousand additional American troops, spread over a period of several months because of training and logistical problems. Johnson balked. More troops would be sent on an emergency basis, but two-hundred-thousand was out of the question. Thus, although troop levels were escalated slightly, the policy from that day forward was de-escalation. The U.S. would again attempt to obtain a political settlement, based upon the unilateral cessation of the bombing of three-quarters of North Vietnam which Johnson announced on March 31. His statement that he would not seek another term, but would devote all of his energies to the quest for peace, was the dramatic footnote that very likely brought Hanoi to the table.

Doves in the Congress and war protestors in the streets were willing to sheath their swords only temporarily after March 31. Bombs were still raining down hard on the panhandle of North Vietnam, a long argument developed over a suitable site for the talks, and after the discussions began there was no visible progress at all. Hanoi still demanded an unconditional halt to the bombing as the prelude to any substantive conversation. Senators Eugene McCarthy, Robert F. Kennedy, and George McGovern all campaigned for President on peace platforms, and Hubert Humphrey edged closer and closer to the same position. Outspoken hawks were few and far between, though the President spoke in harsh terms about those who would "cut and run" from our commitments.

In August, as the Democrats were preparing to meet in Chicago to name their candidate, General Abrams and his superiors in Washington built a strong case against halting the rest of the bombing of the North without guarantees from the enemy that the DMZ would be restored. American outposts along the border had been in jeopardy for months; thousands of North Vietnamese regulars were enjoying sanctuary across the DMZ; an all-out enemy attack, made possible if the bombing ceased, could not be dealt with in the I Corps Area without a high cost in American lives. Simply put, the military told the President that a complete bombing halt would result in increased casualties.

Between August and October there was a dramatic change. North Vietnamese troops were withdrawn deeper into their own country and Laos. There was a lull in the fighting in I Corps, so much so that Abrams withdrew some forces to other areas. When he was in Washington on October 29, Abrams was grilled by Johnson on the diminished danger. He gave the same answers Wheeler and the Joint Chiefs had given earlier: The threat of mass attack was no longer there, and the monsoon rains prevented much bombing of the North anyway.

This was a factual assessment. Yet there was more to the military judgments than that. The military was responding to a change in political strategy, in effect conceding that a battlefield victory was no longer in the cards and a political settlement was the alternative. Wheeler, Westmoreland, Abrams, and the other military leaders were willing to take greater risks because that was the course the diplomats had set. There could be little doubt in their minds that once the bombing ceased, it would never again be instigated, short of a highly unlikely mass invasion of North Vietnamese divisions across the DMZ. The effort to destroy Ho Chi Minh's capacity to support the war was abandoned. The military had failed repeatedly to widen the range of targets, and every step they took had been rigidly controlled by civilians in Washington.

The memoirs of many military leaders of this period will reflect disappointment at the manner in which this curious war was fought. Pilots who flew the missile-and-shell-filled skies of the North from bases in Thailand and aircraft carriers in the Tonkin Gulf will speak bitterly in their middle age of the times they fought with their hands tied. The President got a taste of that when he sat in the officers' club at Korat, Thailand, late one night and listened to the combat fliers talk of targets they wished they could hit.

But the compelling fact of this era in history is that the civilian again ruled the military, and the military accepted their lot. When all of the rhetoric is brushed aside, the Vietnam War always had a limited objective: to turn back the aggression against South Vietnam. The United States went into a war with no deliberate aim to win it in the classical sense, and it took the military a while to adjust to this. Even in the Korean War there had been a freewheeling invasion of North Korea and unlimited bombing targets. In Vietnam these customary tactics were off-limits and never seriously considered.

Military planning always contemplated other, more drastic steps if the war dragged on. The civilian leadership was probed consistently to do something about the enemy sanctuaries in Cambodia and Laos, the docks of Haiphong, the concentration of enemy troops across the DMZ. But these probes were made in the knowledge they would be tempered by political judgment. When Dean Rusk said "no," the plans were folded up and tucked away without further discussion.

The atmosphere was usually clear in military-civilian dealings under Johnson primarily because Earle Wheeler was the type of military man he was (Wheeler in a pair of pearl-handle revolvers would have been ludicrous) and because Earle Wheeler's voice was heard, not muzzled. If he wanted to argue, he could argue with the Commander-in-Chief and knew he would always have a hearing. Furthermore, he knew he had his Commander's confidence and that he was part of a team which was trying to do the best it could with an unhappy war. Lyndon Johnson trusted his generals, without compromising his belief in civilian control. From all indications, the trust was returned.

General Westmoreland caught the brunt of the criticism for the Vietnam stalemate, mainly because of optimistic statements he had been prone to make. Westmoreland had also been in Vietnam four years, and when Johnson pulled him out in mid-1968 it was as much out of sympathy as the need for a change. He was given command in Vietnam because he was one of the three or four best generals in the United States. He was just as good a general when he left as he was when he arrived, but he suffered the same fate as some of his civilian superiors—including the President—who learned the hard way about quagmires.

Johnson resented criticism of Westmoreland within the Administration, and when someone told a reporter that Creighton Abrams was more aggressive and imaginative than his predecessor had been, the President was furious. "Westmoreland did everything he was expected to do, and more," Johnson said. "I will not have him made a scapegoat."

The greatest misjudgment in Washington was not in military tactics, and not in underestimating the enemy, but in overestimating the American people. "Persevere" was Johnson's admonition to America, and it worked for a time but began to fade in the latter part of 1966. Recalling Valley Forge, the President remarked that some footprints were getting bloody and folks were falling out. Walt Rostow and others dug up historical records of similar public impatience in previous wars, especially the terrible times Lincoln had in holding the North together when a speedy victory did not come about. But history was only temporary comfort. Battlefield successes in 1967 were forgotten after the enemy offensive of February 1968. The word we denied, *stalemate*, became the unspoken fact of life. Ho Chi Minh must have watched American public opinion change, listened to the criticism of American leadership, and congratulated himself on formulating the best possible strategy for the war: Hold out till the Americans get weary, start fighting among themselves, and take French leave.

Throughout the October deliberations, the President worried about the reaction of the hawks to a bombing cessation. When he finally stopped the bombing, the initial reaction in terms of telegrams and early mail was predominantly critical. But how many of these people were angry because they thought Johnson had pulled a political trick to hurt Nixon? By late 1968 the question was no longer hawk-dove, or military-civilian. The question was how to resolve a war that no longer had enough support, in the Congress or abroad in the land, to carry it to a conclusion through the established strategy. Military leaders like Wheeler understood this, and they adapted. Ho Chi Minh had won the battle of perseverance.

III · *Armistice Day*

November 11, 1968, was the fiftieth anniversary of the armistice which ended World War I. It was also the first day Richard Nixon came to the White House as President-elect, to be briefed on the knotty international problems facing the man he would soon succeed.

Washington had had its first snow of the season on Sunday the tenth. It had melted quickly, but the air was cloudy and chilly when the Nixon party arrived at the South Portico about 1:15 p.m. on Monday. The President and Mrs. Johnson were waiting for them, along with scores of reporters and photographers lined along the South Lawn facing the White House. When Nixon got out of his limousine, one member of his party stood against the door and the automobile could not move forward, so press pictures of the greeting had to be taken across the top of the car while the cameramen grumbled and fought for position. Finally, we got the errant aide out of the way, and the car moved. The two couples then posed for pictures rather self-consciously, with the photographers requesting different alignments. At one point, Mr. and Mrs. Nixon did a little shuffling dance-like maneuver to get into better position for the cameras.

The four of them went upstairs for a private luncheon. Then, while Mrs. Johnson showed Mrs. Nixon the house and "counted closets," the two men went to the Cabinet Room to meet Johnson's national security advisers.

Quickly and candidly, Dean Rusk laid out the Paris situation and detailed Thieu's problems on NLF representation. He said the U.S. could probably meet most of Thieu's demands. Nixon responded that he wanted to help and was willing to travel if the President and the Secretary of State thought it would be beneficial. Johnson pointed out that the basic decisions on the peace talks were made in Washington, and that Nixon could contribute more by helping present a united front. The President-elect readily agreed, asserting that both Saigon and Hanoi should be convinced that American policy would continue after January 20.

Rusk urged Nixon to designate someone in whom he had "absolute confidence" to occupy an office next to his at the State Department so that the two Administrations would have an immediate contact point. Nixon thought Henry Cabot Lodge might be this man, although he would have to consider the feelings of the Germans since Lodge was now the ambassador to Bonn. He said he was not ready to appoint his Secretary of State, so he would come up with an interim choice for liaison with the outgoing Administration.

Thus far the discussions had been amazingly successful. Now Johnson inserted a question somewhat more touchy for Nixon: the treaty to halt the spread of nuclear weapons. The President-elect was brought up to date on the Russian intervention in Czechoslovakia—his stated reason during the campaign for advocating delay of the treaty—and showed interest in the reports of Russian troop withdrawals. Johnson told him frankly that both

Mike Mansfield and Everett Dirksen opposed a special session to ratify the treaty but that other Senators were favorable and he was considering this move. He did not think there would be very many votes against the treaty.

Nixon was careful not to endorse the idea of a special session. He would support the treaty if the President "wanted to call" the Congress into session. Johnson said an alternative would be to bring up the treaty soon after Congress returned on January 4, as proposed by Dirksen. To the President's obvious eagerness for ratification prior to inauguration day, Nixon remained rather noncommital. Apparently feeling this was not the occasion to inject a sour note in the proceedings, he waited for a few days before putting out the word that he did not think it wise to rush ratification of the treaty. Even after that, Johnson held out hope he might be persuaded to change his mind. For without Nixon, ratification during the Johnson Administration would be a herculean task. The same coalition of Republicans and conservative Democrats could find adequate reasons for further delay.

A briefing on the Middle East and a request for concurrence in an invitation to the NATO countries to hold a meeting in Washington in 1969 ended the session on a warm note. Later in the Oval Office, Nixon aides Herb Klein and Ron Ziegler joined me in asking the two principals to give the newsmen and cameras a rundown on the meeting.

"We could go out together, as far as I'm concerned," the President said.

"That would be the way," Nixon said.

I asked for a minute to notify the press. "We will give you five," Johnson grinned.

Johnson and Nixon walked through the press lobby to the door, where I had cleared a wide walkway through the newsmen so they could go outdoors to the cameras side by side in a show of unity.

Johnson squinted into the television lights and reported that he and his advisers had briefed the President-elect on international issues. "Both he and I," Johnson said, "are going to do everything that we possibly can to see that the wheels of government operate at maximum efficiency, not only from now until January the twentieth, but for all time to come."

When it was Nixon's turn, he spoke of the candor of his briefings on Vietnam, the Middle East, and U.S.-Soviet relations. Then he said:

> I gave assurance in each instance to the Secretary of State, and, of course, to the President, that they could speak not just for this Administration but for the nation, and that meant for the next Administration as well.
>
> For that reason I think these discussions were not only very helpful from my standpoint, but I think, Mr. President, you would agree that they were helpful, too, from the standpoint of seeing to it that in these next sixty days—this very critical period—rather than having the lapse of a lame duck Presidency in effect, we might have some very significant action and progress toward peace.

They departed for the Oval Office without taking questions, but none were needed from the press' standpoint. Nixon had given Johnson carte blanche to speak for him in conducting foreign policy, and in a rather astonishing way. Johnson said later he had no idea Nixon would go that far. Not only would it help in Saigon, but it might encourage the beginning of talks with the Russians on arms control.

"Nixon says LBJ speaks for both in foreign policy," headlined the *Washington Post* . . . "Nixon move welcomed as prod to Thieu." In the *Washington Star*, Garnett Horner wrote that "for the first time in modern American history, an outgoing President and a President-elect of different parties are sharing responsibility before the public for key foreign policy decisions and actions."

We should have known the whole thing was too good to last. Within hours, other Republicans began questioning Nixon's rather broad statements. To Senators Clifford Case of New Jersey and Mark Hatfield of Oregon, both opponents of the Vietnam War, it looked too much like a blank check. Senator Dirksen defended Nixon's stand, but there was plenty of grumbling elsewhere in the GOP.

On the morning of November 14, three days after his visit to the White House, Nixon called Johnson from New York to advise him that Robert D. Murphy, former Under Secretary of State, had agreed to serve as his liaison to the Administration in the foreign policy field. He thought it would be better to leave Henry Cabot Lodge in Germany. Johnson, an unabashed admirer of Bob Murphy, told Nixon that the veteran diplomat suited him fine.

But in making the announcement of Murphy's appointment in a news conference at the Hotel Pierre, Nixon said considerably more about Murphy's role—and the President-elect's power—in Johnson's policies. The first we learned of this was when Loyd Hackler brought me the UPI bulletin, which read: "President-elect Richard Nixon personally announced today that he had assurances from President Johnson and Secretary of State Dean Rusk that he will be consulted on any major foreign policy move involving Vietnam, the Middle East, or NATO and that no action in these fields would be taken without his agreement."

Amazed at this revelation, I took the ticker stories straight to the President and asked him, "Did you and Mr. Nixon agree to this?" He looked at the stories with puzzlement and answered: "Of course not. They're bound to be misquoting what he said. You were there when he called me this morning. Nobody said anything about this kind of announcement."

He ordered me to "no comment" the stories until we could find out what was said. Tom Johnson called Ron Ziegler, Nixon's press aide, to request a transcript of the news conference. It was several hours, however, before Ziegler's wire arrived.

In the meantime, I went down the news stories paragraph by paragraph with the President, pointing out such direct quotations as were available. While Nixon had insisted he did not have "veto power" over Johnson's decisions, the clear implication was that he had reached a formal arrangement with Johnson that would give him a major hand in foreign policy—particularly Vietnam, the Middle East, and U.S.-Soviet relations—in the two months before he became President. Johnson was incredulous, but I finally convinced him that both the AP and UPI could not be all wrong in their reporting of the news conference.

The President then telephoned Nixon, and after the barest of preliminaries told him we were getting press queries on the basis of his statements. Johnson reiterated that he intended to consult Nixon on major issues in the interim, but that he was free to make his own decisions. "You can't have two Presidents," Johnson declared. Nixon replied that he had tried to make it clear there was no veto power, but Johnson argued that the whole premise of a formal understanding was erroneous. The President told him he was instructing me to stay out of a fight, but to inform the press that nothing had been done between the two men which would weaken Presidential authority. Nixon concurred in this approach and indicated his press spokesmen would follow the same line.

By now my afternoon press briefing was forty-five minutes late, and I still had not received the transcript of Nixon's news conference. So when the sharp questions began at the briefing, I ducked them, saying I was reluctant to comment until seeing the transcript, while denying flatly that either Johnson or Nixon had done anything, or would want to do anything, that would dilute the power of the Presidency.

Ziegler's telegram came at seven o'clock, and I went through it quickly to find the key phrases.

> *Nixon:* As you ladies and gentlemen may remember, at the White House the other day I indicated that this nation could speak with only one voice and that I wanted to make it clear to all foreign nations that any decisions which were made by or any negotiations that were being undertaken by the present Administration would be honored by the next Administration. In order to make this a viable arrangement, it is, of course, necessary that there be a prior consultation on such policy decisions and that the President-elect not only be informed but that he be consulted and that he agree to the course of

action. . . . Ambassador Murphy will be my representative in conducting those discussions at the State Department level and at the Administration level.

Question: Do you have the President's assurance that you will be consulted on any foreign policy and decisions taken in the next sixty days?

Nixon: Not only his assurance but his and my insistence that that be done. When I made the statement that I did at the White House the other day, it was made with the knowledge that in the meeting with Secretary of State Rusk and President Johnson and Secretary Clifford, that we discussed not only Vietnam but a statement that was to be made by this government at the NATO conference and other matters that are not currently in the news.* Each of those statements was submitted to me prior to their being made and that is why it is so essential to have this kind of prior consultation before any major decisions are made so that if they do carry over that the prospect or the responsibility of implementation to the next Administration that it will be a decision that I have approved of and not one that I would have rejected.

Question: Would you clarify on a point . . . on the need for agreement on the course of action, are you saying that the President will not take a course of action unless you have approved of it?

Nixon: We did not discuss it that precisely. But, in the discussions we have had—and I presume your question relates primarily to Vietnam—in the discussions we have had there is no disagreement at this time on the broad general policies that this Administration will stand for in a negotiation once the

---

* The NATO statement to which Nixon referred, to be delivered by Secretary Rusk, was an invitation to the NATO foreign ministers to celebrate the twentieth anniversary of the founding of the organization in Washington during the spring of 1969. Rusk asked permission to tell them that Nixon joined in the invitation, since he would be President at the time of the celebration, and to also state that those who had read Nixon's statements on NATO or talked with Governor William Scranton on his recent European trip "will have no anxiety about Mr. Nixon's firm commitment to NATO and to the collective security of the NATO area."

South Vietnamese and North Vietnamese attend negotiations. And I think President Johnson is keenly aware of the fact that it would be very difficult for him to make any kind of an agreement on a major policy matter unless he could give assurance to the parties on the other side that it would be implemented by and respected by the next President.

The newsmen continued to press Nixon on the exact format of the understanding. The President-elect termed it "a form of commitment" but when a reporter asked if Johnson was giving him veto power, he replied:

No, it's nothing of that sort. No, this is one of those periods in which no Constitutions can be written and no position papers can be written which can cover the situation. What we're really trying to do is to work out as best we can a relationship which will see that the United States of America speaks with one voice in a vital period of sixty days where if the United States is unable to speak with one voice it cannot speak at all. . . . I have emphasized time and again I don't think this country can now afford—I don't think the cause of world peace can afford—a period of sixty days in which everybody is waiting for the next President . . . and I'm simply trying to set up a procedure whereby the parties on the other side cannot and will not have as an excuse that they must wait for the next President before dealing with matters on which progress could be made by the present President.

By the time I sent the transcript in to the President, he had already called Bryce Harlow, a Nixon aide, to object to the tone of the news accounts indicating that he (Johnson) was virtually sharing decision-making authority with the President-elect.

The next morning the headlines were disturbing to those in the Administration aware of the discussions on Monday. The *New York Times* headlined, "Nixon says Johnson gives him key role on foreign policies," and correspondent R. W. Apple, Jr., described the agreement as "apparently the most explicit transitional

arrangement in history." After quoting me as denying any dilu-
tion of Presidential authority, Apple reasoned: "Nevertheless, the
burden of much that Mr. Nixon said suggested he had been given
a veto in fact if not in name."

Conversations between Johnson and Harlow, between Harlow
and Nixon, and between Harlow and me left the question about
as confused as it was. The Nixon side kept coming back to the
NATO invitation for which Rusk had sought concurrence. But
to the Johnson side a statement of that minor import was a far
cry from an issue such as negotiations with the Russians on arms
reductions. Johnson wanted full consultation, and he welcomed
Murphy as an excellent agent to keep Nixon in touch with every
situation, but he also wanted freedom to maneuver for as long
as he was President.

"I wish I could turn it over to him right now," he remarked.
"But I can't, and I'm still President, and I can't shirk the responsibilities of the President."

Murphy had an appointment to see the President that Friday
morning. Rostow escorted the seventy-four-year-old diplomat into
the Oval Office, and a few minutes later I arrived on the scene
to urge both the President and Nixon's representative to see the
press and straighten out all of the confusion. Murphy said he
doubted Nixon wanted to leave the impression he would have
"prior approval" of Johnson decisions and said he was willing to
try to clarify the matter. Johnson nodded and told me to call in
the press. The reporters clustered around the President's rocking
chair, with Murphy sitting on a couch to his right, and heard
Johnson praise Nixon's selection of Murphy. The first question
was on the so-called consultation agreement.

Johnson, speaking deliberately and with a trace of acid, noted
that Nixon had replied to a question on an agreement of prior
approval with these words: "We did not discuss it that precisely."
The President went on to say that Rusk and Clifford had asked
that their successors be designated as early as possible in order
that the new President have the "background of knowledge and
information" upon which to make judgments. He said Nixon had

stated he had not made up his mind about the State and Defense appointments but would entertain the thought of an interim observer. "As Mr. Nixon said, on the question of the President taking a course of action unless it was approved, 'We did not discuss it that precisely'," Johnson repeated for emphasis, just in case the reporters missed his point.

The President said he welcomed Murphy and hoped for an orderly transition. Then he declared:

> Of course, the decisions that will be made between now and January 20th will be made by this President and by this Secretary of State and by this Secretary of Defense. Mr. Murphy, not being Secretary, not having been confirmed by the Senate, will be there as an observer and will be following these decisions very closely in order to keep the new Administration informed and prepare it for its obligations . . . beginning January 20th.

The President, in reply to a question, read the reporters the Rusk statement on the NATO anniversary. He added:

> The Secretary said two things [to Nixon]. First, designate a liaison man, and second, here is a matter I would like to include: quoting you inviting them here and saying that a change in administration does not mean a change in NATO policy. This was not only speaking for this President, but speaking for the next President beyond January 20th.

Johnson concluded with the pledge that he would submerge party differences for the rest of his term and that "after January 20th, I will try to do anything I can to make Mr. Nixon's burdens easier."

The Associated Press said in its lead: "President Johnson told the nation and the world emphatically today that he—not President-elect Richard Nixon—will make all decisions on U.S. foreign policy until Nixon is inaugurated."

Thus ended the flap over "prior approval." The question was never raised again by Nixon, and Johnson had re-established his authority as President, with no co-President.

Ron Ziegler and I discussed on the telephone the need for close consultation in dealing with the press. I said my line was that Nixon and Johnson had established a straightforward relationship and that any problems would be settled amicably and with understanding. Ziegler agreed we should go out of our way to preserve peace. The incident made both of us more conscious of the need to keep each other informed of developments.

I think it also made the entire Nixon camp more aware that Johnson was not ready to yield all of his marbles just yet. His shooting thumb might be sore, but he was still in the game.

IV · *The Round Table*

Ellsworth Bunker, United States Ambassador to Vietnam, was fifty-seven years old when President Truman appointed him ambassador to Argentina in 1951 after a lengthy career with the National Sugar Refining Company. He rarely saw his home in Putney, Vermont, after that. Following a stint in Italy, President Eisenhower assigned him to India. His first major mediation of international differences occurred in 1962 when he settled the Dutch-Indonesian dispute over West New Guinea, or Irian. As ambassador-at-large, the State Department's troubleshooter, he was sent by President Johnson to the Dominican Republic in 1966 to restore political order in the wake of civil war. He carried out his mission with distinction.

Now he was Henry Cabot Lodge's successor in Saigon, and in his thin hands rested U.S. prestige in the weird politics of Southeast Asia. A widower, he had wed Carol Laise, the American ambassador to Nepal. At least he and his wife were in the same part of the world and could visit on occasion. But this hardly lessened his burden in what undoubtedly was the most frustrating and dangerous foreign post in the diplomatic service.

With the patience of a man who has learned that time heals many a crisis, Bunker set out to secure South Vietnamese agreement to attend the Paris peace talks. For a week he and President

Thieu did not see each other after Johnson's October 31 speech. Impatience in Washington did not make Bunker's problem any easier, but finally on November 8 Thieu decided to crack open the door to renewed discussions. He proposed that "our side" in Paris be headed by his government, and "their side" by Hanoi. By now the issue between Washington and Saigon hinged upon two words, the definite article *the* and the indefinite article *a*. Saigon wanted to have *the* leading role in the Paris discussions; Washington wanted Saigon to have *a* leading role. The U.S. Constitution, of course, does not permit any other government to speak for this country in international affairs.

For the next several days Bunker met periodically with Thieu to work on an agreement clearing the way for the Saigon government to participate in the talks. After a half-dozen drafts, Thieu appeared closer to an understanding but still reluctant to be pushed. If anyone doubted his independence before, all such doubt was removed by now. Hanoi's frequent charge that he was Johnson's puppet had a hollow ring now in political circles all over the world. Thieu also was playing a canny political game at home. Conscious of his limited public support throughout his tenure as President—and with temporary allies like Ky always hovering nearby awaiting a false step—Thieu needed time to garner enough confidence among his people to enter the Paris discussions on sound footing. If it were thought he was joining in a sellout of South Vietnam—through recognition of the NLF or any other move pointed toward a coalition government—his chances of continued leadership were slim indeed. But by late November he was feeling the sting of world opinion, and this had to be balanced against his instinct for self-preservation in delaying a final decision.

Clark Clifford continued to press for substantive discussions with Hanoi and the NLF in Paris regardless of whether Saigon showed up. He thought a formal agreement might be approached on the sanctity of the DMZ, the lowering of the level of combat, and the withdrawal of foreign troops. The Secretary of Defense spoke regularly of U.S. troop withdrawals—the subject which had been virtually taboo in Administration circles.

When he appeared on ABC's *Issues and Answers* on November 24, Clifford called for gradual reduction of our forces and reciprocal action by Hanoi. "I think the time will come when under certain conditions there can be a cease-fire, and during this phase of it, I would hope also that Saigon and Hanoi would be able to be conducting a dialogue that would look toward the ultimate, final solution of the problem."

Clifford expressed the view that "Hanoi wants peace," but declined to say the same about Saigon. He commented only that "Saigon understands the basis on which an acceptable peace could be formulated today."

Rusk shared Clifford's view that talks on military questions should move ahead at Paris. He was concerned that the impasse would drag on until January when Congress reconvened and opponents of the war and the Thieu government would have a fresh new forum to conduct an assault.

Vice President Humphrey was just back from a post-election stay in the Virgin Islands: "You don't wear shoes and you get over being mad." He joined a meeting of the regulars long enough to say the present situation was unhealthy "and the people don't like it." Certainly, Humphrey had had more opportunity lately to feel the public pulse than anyone else around Johnson.

Hanoi continued to enjoy its propaganda advantage and to engage in a sort of hunt-and-peck violation of the DMZ. Like some mischievous little boy harassing the neighborhood cop, the North Vietnamese army fired volleys across the border and sent troops into the demilitarized area (some of which were snatched by American squads sent there for the express purpose of proving they were there). Hanoi also gloated over the downing of a U.S. reconnaissance plane in North Vietnam, and shells were still falling in population centers of South Vietnam, although the targets appeared to be mostly military.

American response to enemy activity was usually sudden and

spectacular. Clifford reported with mock gravity one day that the North Vietnamese had fired machine guns at an American unit on the Cambodian border, and in response we threw six hundred and eighty-two artillery shells. I thought this episode could pretty well describe the whole Vietnam war.

By November 25 there had been two hundred and thirty violations of the demilitarized zone since the bombing stopped. The enemy had attacked population centers sixty times, and we had lost three planes in reconnaissance flights over the North. Truck, rail, and water traffic in the lower part of North Vietnam was described in military reports as "very heavy."

But there was good news, too. Bunker reported that progress was being made with Thieu on sending a delegation to Paris. The ambassador credited Nixon's November 11 statement supporting Johnson as a major factor in Thieu's acceptance of U.S. assurances that Saigon's voice would not be secondary and a coalition government would not be forced upon South Vietnam. Subsequently, Nixon sent private word to Saigon about his feelings on the matter.

The seventh draft of a seven hundred and fifty word statement gave South Vietnam the main role in discussions on matters "which are of principal concern to South Vietnam," while reserving U.S. leadership on such matters as troop withdrawals and cease-fires. The NLF would not be recognized as anything other than part of the group sitting on Hanoi's side of the table. The U.S. would not recognize any government for South Vietnam that was not chosen through democratic and legal process by the people of the nation. And the talks would be "new" talks, not a continuation of the discussions between the U.S. and North Vietnam.

Again, President Johnson warned the world that the agreement did not mean peace was just around the corner: "We must expect both hard negotiations and hard fighting in the days ahead."

On December 8 Vice President Nguyen Cao Ky arrived at Orly airport in Paris in his role as supervisor of the Saigon delegation. He said:

I have come with all my good will to search for peace. We will not demand that those on the other side surrender. We only ask that justice and reason prevail. It is only just that aggression be terminated. It is only reasonable that the people's choice be sovereign. . . . This conference must not be regarded as a meeting resulting from Soviet Russian, Red Chinese, or American pressure. It must be considered as a meeting made possible by the determination of the Vietnamese—both in the North and the South—to put an end to this war and stop killing one another for the sake of alien ideologies.

But the good will was rather limited in the early days of the "new" talks. As we expected, the first and meanest debate involved the position of the NLF, with North Vietnam insisting that the South Vietnamese Communists have equal status with the legally elected government in Saigon. The argument focused on the type of conference table to be used. A four-sided table would signify four equal sides to the conference, which we could not accept. The hassle took on comic-opera aspects which exasperated the American press, but the overtones were deadly serious in the long-term chances of gaining an honorable peace.

Clark Clifford again was chomping at the bit. He was convinced that Saigon was still raising every obstacle it could in order to delay the talks. The Defense Secretary was watching the clock: only a little over a month was left in the Johnson Administration. And he wanted two things to occur before the final hour struck: real military de-escalation in Vietnam and the beginning of arms control talks with the Russians.

On December 15 he appeared on the CBS program *Face the Nation,* and in answer to a question from Peter Lisagor of the *Chicago Daily News* on the willingness of the American people to accept continued casualties, Clifford replied:

I would say to you I can tell you how I feel about it. I am becoming inordinately impatient with the continued deaths of American boys in Vietnam. I would like to get going at the Paris conference. I would like to get started on these plans to lower the level of combat. This isn't difficult to do. I would like to start getting our troops out of there. I would like to see a cease-fire. All of that can take place while these lengthy negotiations on a political settlement can also be handled by the parties. . . .

Steve Rowan of CBS: Is there anything wrong with just sitting down at a four-sided table, then, in Paris?

Clifford: Well, I have not heard that the Americans have raised any objection about any of the details . . . we are ready to agree to anything. Ambassador Harriman and Ambassador Vance—whom I might say have done a superb task—have said "we are ready to sit down at any kind of a table." It is Hanoi and Saigon that have raised the questions about these details, and it seems to me that there ought to be sufficient pressure of world opinion on them to get them going on the talks.

Questioned about the possibility of a winter offensive by the enemy and its effect on the Paris talks, Clifford denied that a new attack would wreck the negotiations because Johnson had warned there would be "hard bargaining and hard fighting ahead."

The repercussions of Clifford's comments were immediate.

In Paris, Ky protested bitterly: "He seems to have a gift for saying the wrong thing at the wrong time." Feelings at the U.S. State Department were ruffled. Unnamed "senior U.S. military and diplomatic officials" in Saigon—obviously the top team— criticized his statement about the winter offensive's impact on Paris. But Johnson did not censure Clifford. "He's giving me the image of a peacemaker, but he went too far," the President said.

I fielded press questions as best I could, contending that Johnson had neither approved nor disapproved Clifford's approach to the Paris problem. Chalmers Roberts in the *Washington Post* interpreted this to mean the President had given tacit approval, which was not the case. But there was considerable suspicion that Johnson was using Clifford as a hatchet man against Saigon in an effort to break the deadlock. The President's failure to repudiate the Defense Secretary's statements gave credence to this. My own view is that Johnson was trying to take as much advantage as he could of a situation over which he had little control. He did not muzzle Clifford, so Clifford kept talking. It was always possible that his public statements might prove to be beneficial in the long run, if disturbing at present.

Johnson was now pulling every bluff, every manipulation he could to retain his power in international politics. He was like a poker player with jacks for openers, but no help after that. He had to play the hand he had, with no opportunity for a new deal. He could not afford a blowup in his Cabinet, with his Defense Secretary opposing his Secretary of State, so he did his best to accommodate the views of both. Rumors erupted that there had been a bitter argument between Rusk and Clifford at a Tuesday luncheon, and many reporters doubted my vehement denials. The fact was that Clifford's controversial statements were not even mentioned at the meetings during this period; there were no angry arguments on any issue. Indeed, this in itself worried Clifford who wanted very much to have the President's ear on troop withdrawals and a cease-fire but could get nothing but noncommital answers and a minimum of debate.

Other pressing issues commanded Johnson's attention: a new financial crisis in Europe; the tragic war in Nigeria; continued trouble in the Middle East and a decision on whether or not to consummate a deal with the Israelis for Phantom jet fighters; concessions to Prince Sihanouk in Cambodia in order to obtain the release of American prisoners; a last-gasp effort to retrieve the crew of the Pueblo from North Korea; the ever-present desire to get the nuclear nonproliferation treaty ratified before January 20; and the on-again, off-again prospects of arms talks with the Russians, perhaps even a summit conference with Kosygin.

"So little time" was the Administration byword as the Christmas season approached.

It was not until four days before Richard Nixon became President that Hanoi and Saigon settled their first argument in Paris. The conference table would be round and unmarked, flanked at midpoint on either side by two rectangular tables to be used by secretarial personnel. There would be no flags nor nameplates. At the initial meeting, the U.S. side would speak first, and Washington and Saigon had agreed that the individual would be Nguyen Xuan Phong, number two man in the South Vietnamese delegation. Cyrus Vance would follow him. The North Vietnamese and NLF would decide between themselves who would lead off for their side.

The talks would still be on procedural matters. They would still be the kind of probing, antagonistic exchanges we believed would continue for some time, while men still died on the battlefield. There were few illusions in Washington that substantive discussions would begin anytime soon. But at least all four parties would sit down together; that in itself was an accomplishment of sizable proportions.

Again, some extra "clout" by Richard Nixon undoubtedly helped sway Thieu into accepting the formula for breaking the deadlock. Nixon sent the word directly through Ambassador Bunker that he favored the compromise backed by Johnson.

Walt Rostow called President Johnson at 5:45 a.m. on January 16 to advise him of the agreement on the round table. "In exactly fifteen minutes," said Rostow, "they are going to stand up in Paris and say, 'We've got a deal'."

V · *Remember the Pueblo*

The stepchild of American foreign policy for the year 1968 was the communications ship Pueblo and its hapless crew in a North Korean prison. "Remember the Pueblo" became a bumper sticker, a crusade by the skipper's wife, and the rallying cry of several patriotic endeavors. He would not permit the United States to be pushed around like that if he were President, Richard Nixon told his audiences during the campaign; there would be no more Pueblos, just as there would be no more Vietnams.

In the days following the seizure of the ship, a Presidential task force grappled with the problem to see if a decent solution could be found. I served for a time with this group, until other duties interfered. It was an exercise in frustration; there simply is no pat answer to acts of force or intimidation by a small antagonist against the United States. Should we bomb Wonsan? That would probably kill the crew, and could touch off another war. How about seizing one of their naval vessels? Good idea. Where are the beggars? All they have are a few gunboats, and they're hugging the coast; we would have to violate their territorial waters to bag one. Abandon that scheme. What about that big cannery ship built in the Netherlands which is their pride and joy? Good idea . . . only it's in port and shows no sign of moving onto the high seas.

One of the early proposals was that the United States Navy merely pick up one of those Russian trawlers used as spy ships. That would show the Communists two could play their game. Dean Rusk vetoed that one: "Two wrongs won't make a right. One act of piracy does not justify another."

It finally boiled down to a need for diplomacy, not force. So help was sought from the Soviet Union, and at Panmunjon talks were commenced between the United Nations (i.e., United States) representatives and the always angry North Koreans, now tasting even headier wine. One proposal after another was rejected. North Korea was not to be denied its self-satisfying opportunity to rub American noses in the ground.

Periodically, rumors circulated that North Korea had tired of its fun and would release the men. But every American overture was rebuffed.

The Pueblo capture helped spark one of the more bizarre incidents in personal diplomacy during Johnson's Administration. President Chung Hee Park of the Republic of Korea, justifiably aroused by attempts by North Korean commando squads to assassinate him, met with President Johnson in Honolulu in the spring, convinced that we were more disturbed about the Pueblo than we were the repeated violations of the demilitarized zone and enemy invasions of his country. Park, meeting with Johnson in the plush living room of the Kaiser mansion, demanded stronger commitments from him than he was prepared to give. Finally, the U.S. President asked to be excused, turned over the meeting to his aides, and retired to his bedroom for a nap. Park apparently got the message. When Johnson returned, an agreement was reached much more to American liking.

On December 10—nearly a year after the Pueblo was captured —Johnson made one last effort to secure an acceptable formula for release of the crew. Recalling the Russians' release of American prisoners under similar circumstances as a gesture to the then new President Kennedy, Johnson thought the Nixon Administration would have more luck with North Korea than he would. But he agreed to a procedure suggested by Rusk, whereby we would sign a North Korean paper admitting grievous crimes against that sovereign country, and then issue a statement of our own repudiating what we had signed. We would make it quite clear to the North Koreans that we would repudiate their paper, but it was hoped they would be satisfied.

Not one of the President's advisers thought this stunt would work, much less the President himself. It was a final shot in the dark and to everyone's surprise it hit its mark.

By Christmas the Pueblo crew was turned over to American authorities, ending one of the most painful episodes of the Johnson Administration. North Korea had milked all of the propaganda it could from the issue, old enemy Johnson had only a few more weeks in office, and the Americans had been made to swear to a lie. In the old days, gunboat diplomacy was the prerogative of the Western powers in keeping the brown and yellow men in line. North Korea had shown that gunboat diplomacy could also be used to tweak the nose of a super-power without much fear of retaliation.

The Christmas season was also release time for eleven Americans held captive by Prince Sihanouk since their boat had strayed into Cambodian waters, as well as a wounded helicopter pilot. This was the result of a visit to Cambodia by Presidential emissary Eugene Black and a conciliatory message from Johnson to Sihanouk delivered by the French chargé in Phnom Penh.

Sihanouk had treated his prisoners almost as well as royal guests. Unfortunately, in the treatment of the Pueblo crew the North Koreans reminded the world that barbarism is still extant in the late twentieth century.

VI · *Summit*

When President Johnson met Chairman Kosygin in Glassboro, New Jersey, in June of 1967, it was expected that the two leaders would resume their discussions at a later date—possibly in the Soviet Union, if events permitted a visit by the U.S. President. Glassboro contributed little to the settlement of tensions in the Middle East, although it was one important peg in the cribbage game that eventually led to the Paris talks on Vietnam.

It was also the scene of an impassioned plea for arms control, voiced at the luncheon table by Secretary of Defense Robert McNamara, egged on by Johnson. Kosygin made no firm commitment to enter into such talks, but constant diplomacy in the following months brought the two nations closer to consultations focused upon the nuclear arms race. Also, a state of belligerency still existed between the Arabs and the Israeli, and the United Nations had been incapable of extending the uneasy armistice to a settlement. After the Paris talks began on Vietnam and much of the bombing of North Vietnam was curtailed, an invitation to the American President to visit the Soviet Union had also become easier for the Russians.

Arms discussions could begin at a low level, looking toward a summit after months of preparation, or they could begin at the top, filtering down the decisions to be ironed out by the professional negotiators. Johnson favored the direct approach: leader to leader, meeting in private to talk things over and cut away the red tape. At Glassboro, Johnson found he liked Kosygin, even though the Soviet Premier was much less free to meet issues head-on than the American President. "He has to check with the committee," Johnson mused after that experience.

Now, in 1968, Johnson very much wanted a second meeting with the Soviet leadership. He had approached Khrushchev on the dangers of the arms race early in his Presidency, and he would like to end that Presidency with serious discussions well underway, or possibly an agreement. Johnson gave his full backing to the need for a defensive missile system—the latest twist to the arms race—but it was a reluctant, cost-conscious decision which could be reversed if some understanding could be reached with the other side.

Finally, in August, the stage was set. I was prepared to announce on the morning of August 21 that the leaders of the two nations would soon meet "within the Soviet Union." Only the city was undecided; Leningrad had been suggested, since Kosygin had stayed away from Washington deliberately in 1967. But Moscow itself was also in the picture and was preferred by the President.

On the evening of August 20 my wife Jo Anne and I were having dinner at the apartment of Peg and Bob Lucas. He was head of the Washington bureau of Gannett Newspapers. The White House called before I sat down to eat, and the President informed me sardonically that Soviet Ambassador Anatoly Dobrynin had just come to advise him that Russian troops had moved into Czechoslovakia. Johnson was calling a special meeting of the National Security Council.

When I got to the White House, the President related that Dobrynin had asked urgently to see him personally, at the direction of his government, and had read him a statement, written in long hand, on the invasion of Czechoslovakia. Dobrynin had very little else to offer about the situation, and Johnson did not press him. The ambassador then went to the basement office of Walt Rostow and dictated his prepared statement to a secretary, translating it from Russian to English.

The Soviet Union complained of a "conspiracy of the external and internal forces of aggression" against Czechoslovakia and said that the government of that country had approached the Warsaw Pact nations with a request for military assistance. It said the

threat to the socialist order in Czechoslovakia was also a threat
to the foundations of European peace and security. Accordingly,
Russian and other Communist bloc troops had entered the territory of Czechoslovakia "to satisfy the request of Czechoslovakia."
These stated reasons were so blatantly untrue that they could not
be "sold" even to other Communists, as events later showed, but
the distinguished Soviet ambassador was required to read them
to an incredulous President of the United States.

The statement contended the action did not involve U.S.
interests and "should not harm the Soviet-American relations to
the development of which the Soviet government as before at-
taches great importance."

Dean Rusk told the President at the National Security Council
meeting that no joint announcement of a summit meeting should
be made as planned and that he would advise Dobrynin.

The timing of the invasion and the summit announcement was
puzzling. We thought it inconceivable that the Soviets would
exercise diplomacy over a long period to arrange a summit, and
then within hours after the decision was made, launch a brazen
invasion of another country and plunge Europe to the brink of
disaster. But from the wording of the Soviet message to Johnson—
denying harm to Soviet-American relations—it appeared that the
Russian leaders did not relate the two issues. Because Czechoslovakia was one of "theirs," they were free to do as they wished
to resolve its internal situation. And because President Johnson
wanted a summit meeting, he would come to Russia regardless
of the invasion. And it need not be a topic on the agenda, since
Czechoslovakia was none of our business.

Ultimately, Johnson passed the word to Kosygin that there
could be no summit meeting while Soviet troops were victimizing
the Czechs. Our NATO allies stunned by the invasion and the
fact that Russian soldiers were now poised like a dagger at the
heart of Bavaria would not understand American willingness to
discuss disarmament with the Soviet Union in these circumstances.

There was some speculation, when reports of the abortive
summit conference leaked out, that the proposed timing of the

announcement—only a few days before the Democratic Convention—had deep political implications. A few suspicious souls suspected, as a matter of fact, that Johnson would use it as a lever to secure a "draft" for the Democratic nomination. If this were true, the President never confided it to those around him, or to Democratic officials. He wanted a summit, and wanted it as soon as possible, but only because there was a faint hope that arms control talks could blossom quickly and he could leave office with an agreement locked up, or nearly so.

During the fall and winter the Russians played a curious game of summitry. Through diplomatic leaks to friendly newsmen in Washington and London, they let it be known they were still much interested in talking with Johnson even though a new President soon would be on the scene. The continued presence of Eastern bloc troops in Czechoslovakia, however, made this impossible for Johnson.

On November 11—the same day Nixon was visiting Johnson at the White House—Robert McNamara, now president of the World Bank, was in Moscow on a brief stop en route to Afghanistan. Out of the blue, Kosygin sent word he would be "pleased" to see McNamara at the Kremlin, on a private basis. So the Soviet Premier and the former U.S. Defense Secretary renewed the discussion they had begun at Glassboro a year and a half before on the nuclear arms race. For nearly two hours, Kosygin talked with him about the need for serious negotiations on disarmament and the heavy expenditures for weapons in both countries. Kosygin contended that U.S. suspicions of Soviet intentions were unfounded. The meeting was interpreted in Washington as evidence the Russians wanted to get moving on talks before Johnson left office, possibly because of their uncertainty about Nixon.

Rusk, returning a few days later from his meeting with the NATO foreign ministers in Brussels, reported that the allies were still against a summit. Czechoslovakia had not cooled enough. Clark Clifford and Treasury Secretary Henry Fowler (he had been in Europe on the latest monetary crisis) had had a different view of the allied attitude, but Rusk dashed cold water on that. The

President was highly skeptical about reopening the summit issue. He thought the Russians were after one "to take some of the polecat off of them" after their aggressive actions against the Czechs.

Senator J. William Fulbright, who was usually reluctant to give Johnson the benefit of the doubt on anything, was an eager advocate on the subject of arms control. He urged the President not only to call a special session for December 1 so the nuclear nonproliferation treaty could be ratified, but also to meet with Kosygin immediately and open the broad subject of bilateral disarmament. Other Senate leaders, notably Richard Russell and John Stennis, were not nearly so eager.

Clifford, in speeches and news conferences, advocated the beginning of arms talks before Johnson left office. "I would rather see the talks start next week than four weeks from now or four months from now," he said. "I think the sooner they get started, the greater benefit there can be."

On a television program, Clifford was asked by Martin Agronsky of CBS to justify this in view of President-elect Nixon's statements that the United States should increase its production of strategic missiles and maintain a greater nuclear superiority over the Russians than we now had. "How could the Russians sit down at a table with us if this is the attitude of the President-elect?" Agronsky asked.

"It is my belief," said Clifford, "that Mr. Nixon is very likely to change his mind in that regard." He thought that Nixon and his new Secretary of Defense would come to realize we did not need additional superiority, since we already had forty-two hundred deliverable nuclear warheads against twelve hundred for the Soviet Union.

Johnson by now had begun to waver in his opposition to a summit. He reasoned that a meeting now with Kosygin might make it easier for Nixon to develop disarmament talks by taking him off the spot, since his campaign oratory had been against such talks. But Robert Murphy, Nixon's liaison with the State Department, plainly did not agree. Murphy thought a summit would be premature, and it had to be assumed that he was reflecting Nixon's view even though he did not say so.

Nixon's reluctance on both the summit and speedy ratification of the nuclear nonproliferation treaty became more evident to the President in the early days of December. At one point, it appeared that Nixon would approve of a meeting with Kosygin only if he accompanied Johnson, but later Nixon indicated he did not want to attend such a conference. It was clearly a slowdown by the Republicans on these two related issues in East-West diplomacy. Accordingly, a confrontation between Johnson and Nixon was entirely possible, despite the relative smoothness of the transition thus far. Johnson chose not to make an issue of it. The idea of a special session of the Congress was laid quietly to rest. And though the demand for arms talks was still strong in some quarters—the *New York Times*, for example, wanted Johnson to set a course that Nixon would have a difficult time abandoning— the chances of a summit also faded. Columnists and other newsmen familiar with the prevailing view in Nixon's camp discounted the worth of a lame-duck summit. Nixon himself avoided public discussion of the issue.

Finally, the Soviet Union's diplomatic leaks took a new turn. Newsmen were told that the Russians really did not see any point in meeting with Johnson. The full circle was closed.

One last hope for foreign travel remained in Johnson's mind as his Administration rushed toward its demise. It was his wish, forlorn though it might be, that he could pay a final call on "the boys" in Vietnam. He mused aloud how much he would like to spend Christmas with the troops. But the plans were never made, Christmas came and went, and his wish went unfulfilled. Except for the spectacular journey to the moon, the attention of his Administration in its last weeks turned to the thankless chore of taxes and budget. When all is said and done, these things too are vital to a Presidency and a nation.

FOUR

I · *The Successor*

Richard M. Nixon and Hubert H. Humphrey have at least one thing in common: They were the only American Vice Presidents since Martin Van Buren who ran for President while their chiefs were still in office.*

Nixon fought valiantly in 1960 to escape the shadow of a popular President whose public utterances did little to help his candidacy. In 1968 it was Humphrey's turn, and Nixon must have enjoyed watching his Democratic opponent bob and weave in an effort to run his own campaign without alienating his President, while trying to attract the anti-Johnson dissidents in the party.

Lyndon Johnson had a sympathetic attitude toward the office

---

* I exclude Vice President Breckenridge in 1860, a fractured political year for the Democrats, in which he was the candidate of the Southern states in the race to succeed Buchanan.

of Vice President. It had been no easy task for Senate Majority Leader Johnson, a man who made things move as no one else in government did, to endure the political limbo of being second man to John F. Kennedy for three years. While Kennedy went out of his way to keep his Vice President informed and to seek his judgment on important issues, some of the Kennedy staff were not so considerate. They called him "Colonel Cornpone" and ridiculed his loyalty to Kennedy.

Johnson felt great personal affection for both Hubert and Muriel Humphrey. In the Senate, Humphrey was far and away his favorite liberal, and it surprised few people when the Senior Senator from Minnesota was tapped by Johnson to be Vice President. Toward the end of the 1968 campaign when questions were being asked in print about whether Johnson truly wanted Humphrey to win or not, the President reacted strongly. One night he demanded of a reporter: "Who put him on the ticket over everybody else in '64? Who got out of the race and opened the way for him? Whose delegates put him over in Chicago?"

As Vice President, Humphrey stayed busy with the "make-work" assignments the second man has been given in recent history. In addition, he represented the President well in foreign travel and in a variety of pinch-hitting jobs at home. Johnson assigned him to work with the nation's mayors and sought his judgments on urban affairs. Humphrey also served as a sounding board; the reports on visits around the country were a window to happenings outside the insulated White House. He lent valuable assistance in Congressional activities, of course.

But on war policy Humphrey was left pretty much to his own devices. He sat on the National Security Council, but this body dealt mostly with broad policies other than Vietnam. The critical decisions on the war were made at the "Tuesday lunch" and supplemental meetings, especially in the last two years of the Johnson Administration. Humphrey was only rarely a participant in these sessions. Most of his insight into the President's deeper feelings about Vietnam came from private conversations with Johnson and from the routine flow of war information. As Vice President he participated in a few Vietnam decisions—such as the decision to bomb the North Vietnamese oil depots in 1966—but only a few.

In a way, this may have helped Humphrey in his campaign. If he wanted to take a slightly independent position on a specific matter involving the war or the peace talks, he could do so without the moral problem of having supported Johnson's position in some policy-making conference.*

Humphrey's position on Vietnam was Johnson's only real problem throughout the Presidential race. As early as the Democratic Convention platform hearings, the pro-Johnson regulars at Chicago worked to keep Humphrey from defecting toward a platform plank on the dovish side. They even used the implied threat of a "draft Johnson" movement to keep the Humphrey forces in line on Vietnam—a tactic the President let simmer as long as it was effective. Then those who held out hope to the bitter end that Johnson would get back in the race were knocked out of the saddle when Johnson said on August 24 in San Marcos, Texas, on the eve of the convention, "I am not a candidate for anything, except maybe a rocking chair."

Until then, many of the LBJ loyalists—including several Southern and Border governors—believed it was still possible that Johnson could be persuaded to move forward at the last minute and salvage the badly split party. Cool toward Humphrey and afraid he was a loser from the outset, some of these convention leaders made enough overtures to Johnson and enough comments around Chicago to cause momentary dismay in the Humphrey ranks. But if Johnson were tempted, it was only a fleeting twinge. One governor told me later that the rocking chair statement at San Marcos "took all of the wind out of our sails . . . it was impossible to convince delegates that Johnson might return to politics." When the showdown came, Johnson remained far, far

---

* Unfortunately, at one point late in the campaign his advisers gave background information to reporters that Humphrey had opposed a certain action Johnson had taken in the conduct of the bombing. As it turned out, the action had been debated on one of those infrequent occasions when the Vice President participated, and the record showed he had been four-square behind Johnson in the discussions.

away, and the momentary defectors returned to Humphrey to assure his lopsided victory.

Soon after Humphrey entered the race for the nomination following Johnson's withdrawal, I recall watching television with the President as the Vice President was delivering a rousing Democratic speech. Johnson hung intently on every word, commenting occasionally to Mrs. Johnson as Humphrey made an especially good point. At the end, the President—sitting in the dining room with his wife and one or two aides—applauded as vigorously as those in the live audience.

There was no applause September 30 when Humphrey delivered his Salt Lake City speech declaring that a bombing halt would be "an acceptable risk for peace" in a Humphrey Administration.

Some of Humphrey's advisers had been urging him for days to issue a declaration of independence from Johnson on Vietnam. But the candidate recognized a particular problem: It was one thing to say what he would do as President, but another to undercut his incumbent President on key negotiating points. So he tried to have it both ways, by giving the doves some delicious crumbs without yielding the entire cookie.

The impression one would likely receive from watching the speech on television was that the Vice President was for stopping the bombing. "As President," he began, "I would stop the bombing of North Vietnam as an acceptable risk for peace because I believe it could lead to success in the negotiations and thereby shorten the war. This would be the best protection of our troops."

But Humphrey dropped in this proviso: "In weighing that risk, and before taking action, I would place key importance on evidence—direct or indirect—by deed or word—of Communist willingness to restore the demilitarized zone between North and South Vietnam. Now if the government of North Vietnam were to show bad faith, I would reserve the right to resume the bombing."

Humphrey went on to say he would "take the risk" that the South Vietnamese would meet their responsibilities to defend themselves, so that the war could be de-Americanized. Then he added another crumb for the doves: He would call for an immediate cease-fire, with international supervision, followed by supervised withdrawal of all foreign forces from South Vietnam.

This turned out to be one of those curious human dramas involving politicians in the heat of a bitter campaign, when the greatest desire is to pull the pieces together and hold them together at all costs—even using a little flim-flam if necessary.

Johnson was unable to get his hands on a copy of the speech until I obtained one from the Democratic National Committee only minutes before the broadcast, although it had been billed as a major policy declaration and his anxiety was at a peak. Shortly before air time, Humphrey called Johnson to read him the pertinent parts—after the speech had been taped for television and released to the press.

Confused over Humphrey's meaning, the President asked for written interpretations from his foreign policy advisers. The consensus was that Humphrey, as President, would order a cessation of bombing if he believed the North Vietnamese would respect the DMZ and enter into serious negotiations. Humphrey himself stated this as his view in the telephone conversation with Johnson. He contended he was not making a radical departure from Johnson's position. But some of Humphrey's aides in background information to the press said that the key statement was the intention to stop the bombing. And Humphrey gave this impression in follow-up remarks on the campaign trail.

This speech was actually the third in a series of statements on Vietnam involving both Humphrey and Johnson, resulting in mass press interpretation of troubles between the two men. Humphrey fired the first round rather carelessly by saying in Philadelphia: "I would think that negotiations or no negotiations, we could start to remove some of the American forces in early 1969 or late 1968." This contradicted Johnson's contention, voiced previously, that troop withdrawals could not be predicted when there was no evidence of enemy de-escalation. The night after Humphrey's statement, Johnson said in a free-swinging speech to the American

Legion in New Orleans that he agreed with Truman, Eisenhower, and Kennedy "that a Communist military takeover in South Vietnam would lead to developments that could imperil the security of the American people for generations to come." After making it clear that the allies would keep on the pressure and not "surrender on the installment plan" until a way to peace could be found, the President declared: "We yearn for the day when the violence subsides. We yearn for the day when our men can come home. No man can predict when that day will come, because we are there to bring an honorable, stable peace to Southeast Asia, and no less will justify the sacrifices that our men have died for."

This was interpreted as a cruel slap at Humphrey, and the press made much of it. I contended that the President was only repeating a position he had taken many times before and voicing a yearning which he had certainly voiced before. The newsmen were somewhat less than convinced that this was the full story.

This set the stage for Humphrey's Salt Lake City speech, which in turn was interpreted as different from the position taken by Johnson. After sober reflection, however, a good many news analysts decided there was not that much difference after all— different in tone, perhaps, but similar in substance.

Some considered the speech to be a turning point in the Humphrey campaign, despite its ambiguities. It instilled doubt in the minds of the war protestors who had been baiting the Vice President at every turn. Reporters covering Humphrey said it seemed to make him feel better about his independence and gave him a psychological lift at a crucial time. In retrospect, the words of the speech indeed were not far from Johnson's position, not far from the Harriman-Vance instructions in the Paris peace talks, and not far from the actual course of events in Administration foreign policy during Johnson's last hundred days. But in early October, before Hanoi had moved an inch in Paris, the White House view of the moment was that Ho Chi Minh had been offered a better deal than Johnson's, if he only had the patience to wait a few months until Johnson was gone.

As the President once wisecracked: "If I were trying to sell my house for forty thousand dollars and had a man just about ready to buy it, and then Lady Bird took him out on the porch and told him, 'You can get it for thirty thousand dollars,' and then Lynda Bird took him out in the yard and said, 'He'll really sell for twenty-five thousand dollars,' that fellow will be a whole lot harder for me to deal with."

Johnson did not want Humphrey to rubber stamp every policy of the Administration. He asserted many times that he wished Humphrey would "be his own man" and "stake out his own positions." While the President naturally did not want Humphrey attacking him or his record, he was not so naive as to think the Vice President should campaign only as a cheerleader for Lyndon Johnson. Yet from the outset, Johnson feared that campaign oratory would confuse North Vietnam as to what U.S. policy was. Some of his advisers expressed the view that Hanoi was sophisticated enough to separate the wheat from the chaff, and that if it wasn't, Moscow certainly was. However, it could not be disputed that Hanoi might be less likely to buy Johnson's forty thousand dollar house if it thought it could get a better deal in January.

One of the President's principal concerns was that Humphrey's backers, in their eagerness to rebuild a sagging campaign, would encourage him to champion causes that would make the candidate a first-class hypocrite. This, Johnson reasoned, could destroy Humphrey. Moving to the left might pick up a few votes there but would cost him heavily with organized labor and more moderate Democrats.

Humphrey's campaign leaders ranged over the political spectrum, and they acted and reacted accordingly. There was a McCarthy wing which hated Johnson and the war, a wing that backed Johnson all the way, and a group which tried to walk the tightrope and unify as many Democrats as possible under the banner of a new leader.

Through it all, Johnson himself did a remarkable job of keeping hands off. I doubt if any reporter in Washington really believed the President when he announced at the outset—and repeated many times thereafter—that he intended to devote all of his efforts to peace and not to politics. "When Nixon starts attacking him, Johnson will be right in the thick of it," was the general comment. While of course Nixon campaigned against the Administration, his personal attacks upon Johnson were infrequent. He used the old Republican cliché of "cleaning house in the State Department," he baited Attorney General Ramsey Clark on the law-and-order issue, he criticized the President for ignoring Europe, and he sniped away cautiously on the Vietnam War. His most sweeping criticism was that the Democratic Administration had failed to resolve a single one of the major national crises and could not be entrusted with continued leadership. Still, there was little there to arouse the President's wrath. Johnson had been denounced more penetratingly than that by Gene McCarthy, Robert Kennedy, and others in his own party.

It was not always so. Johnson and Nixon had served together in government for nearly fifteen years before Nixon's involuntary retirement after 1960. There had never been much love lost between them. One of Sam Rayburn's most compelling reasons for urging Johnson to accept John Kennedy's offer of second place on the ticket was to "save the country from Nixon." Mr. Sam, Johnson's mentor, had never forgiven Nixon for trying to hang the "traitor" label on Democrats during the Truman Administration.

In 1966, a few days after the President had returned from a lengthy visit to Asia and a few days before the important Congressional elections, Johnson momentarily broke a self-imposed silence on comments made by private citizen Nixon. The United States and its Pacific allies had worked out a communique at Manila which established a policy of foreign troop withdrawals from Vietnam. Allied soldiers would be pulled out, said the agreement, "as the other side withdraws its forces to the North, ceases infiltration, and the level of violence thus subsides."

Nixon charged this would leave South Vietnam to the mercy of the Viet Cong. Needless to say, Johnson thought he had been hit below the belt.

"Could you comment on that?" a reporter asked the President at his next news conference.

"I would be glad to comment on the communique," Johnson plunged in eagerly. And he continued:

I do not want to get into a debate on a foreign policy meeting in Manila with a chronic campaigner like Mr. Nixon. It is his problem to find fault with his country and with his government during a period of October every two years. If you will look back over his record, you will find that to be true.

He never did really recognize and realize what was going on when he had an official position in the government. You remember what President Eisenhower said, that if you would give him a week or so he would figure out what he was doing.

Since then he has made a temporary stand in California, and you saw what action the people took out there. Then he crossed the country to New York. Then he went back to San Francisco, hoping that he would be in the wings, available if Goldwater stumbled. But Goldwater didn't stumble. Now he is out talking about a conference that obviously he is not well prepared on or informed about.

Johnson went on to explain the communique, then concluded: "Mr. Nixon doesn't serve his country well by trying to leave that kind of impression in the hope that he can pick up a precinct or two, or a ward or two."

The vehemence of his counterattack on Nixon surprised the press and made good partisan viewing for the millions who watched on television. But it kicked off a tempest and was labeled Presidential overreaction to criticism, especially in his reference to Eisenhower's statement about Nixon. Ironically, in late 1968 the President—before and after the election—chided reporters for "trapping" Eisenhower into saying something he didn't mean when he denigrated Nixon as a noncontributor to his Administration.

Johnson avoided public criticism of Nixon after the 1966 news conference and its aftermath of press comment. He retreated to his stance of remaining silent when criticized by a political leader, foreign or domestic. "When they sail a spitball by my head, I just duck and try to smile," said the former baseball coach at the Cotulla, Texas, Mexican school. He deviated from this cool position a few times, notably when Gerald Ford or some other Congressional Republican nicked him with a pitch, but there are only rare instances on record where Johnson retaliated in kind—publicly, at least.

His punches at Nixon during the 1968 campaign were not numerous; these will be noted later. So there was, for all practical purposes, a tentative truce between the two old enemies to "keep it clean."

Johnson did not look upon Spiro T. Agnew as an enemy at all. The Maryland governor had been helpful to the President, and Johnson appreciated it. He had affection for Agnew, and some genuine sympathy which might have been based upon his own experiences with criticism. He thought Agnew was abused unfairly during the campaign. "He told me he did not understand how a reasonably progressive and successful governor was suddenly the village boob when he became a Vice Presidential candidate," Johnson paraphrased an Agnew comment to him. "And I agree with him. He does not deserve it."

The President's relations with the Vice Presidential candidate of his own party, Ed Muskie, had not been close. Muskie was not in the "inner circle" of Johnson's Senate friends, although he had carried the ball on part of the Administration program. He had been one of the Senate liberals who had rebelled against Johnson's control over the Senate as Vice President. And he was not the President's choice for the nomination as Humphrey's running mate. Johnson leaned toward Senator Dan Inouye of Hawaii, who had supported him solidly and would have added a new dimension to the Presidential race. Putting a Japanese-American war hero with one arm (the other lost in combat in Europe) on the ticket was a ploy that appealed to Johnson's sense of drama, justice, and good politics.

But Johnson recognized Muskie as an able Senator and good campaigner and was satisfied with Humphrey's choice. One of the real "low spots" in Johnson's relationship with the campaign, however, involved a Muskie television program. It was a fifteen-minute film, depicting the qualifications of the Senator from Maine and his long association with the Democratic party. Here were movies of Muskie with Harry Truman . . . with Humphrey . . . with all three Kennedys . . . even with Adlai Stevenson. But no pictures of Johnson, no mention of Johnson, no evidence that Johnson existed. Accidental or not, it was the ultimate insult by the Humphrey-Muskie organization to the incumbent President who had obtained passage of nearly every Democratic program to be found in the deepest recesses of Congressional pigeonholes.

Johnson swallowed his pride and said of Humphrey and Muskie in a television broadcast just before the election: "Both of these men have the mark of a President in their character. That is where I have looked, into the heart, into the fiber, where Presidents are made or Presidents are broken."

Bitter though it was to accept, Johnson somehow reconciled himself to the fact that the Humphrey-Muskie campaign would be extremely wary in its praise for the Democratic President.

The short shrift given Johnson as a person in the campaign oratory was nettlesome, but not nearly so brutal as the tactics of dissident Democrats who gathered under the Humphrey banner after recovering from their disappointments during the pre-convention struggles. Well-placed Democrats in New Jersey and other states urged Humphrey to resign as Vice President, to denounce Johnson, and to otherwise repudiate Administration war policies. Several columnists speculated this was Humphrey's only hope.

In October some of Humphrey's people struck at Johnson on the issue of campaign funds. Many months before, some seven hundred thousand dollars had been raised by the party by selling program advertisements to corporations. Upon learning that it would be against the law to utilize funds raised from corporations for partisan purposes, the President ordered the money committed to a special fund so that it would not be spent by the Democratic

National Committee. There the money languished, and after Humphrey's nomination the President called it to his attention and suggested a means be found to spend it legally. One thought was to finance a voter registration drive, administered by a non-partisan committee. Otherwise, Johnson thought, the money should be returned to the donors.

Rumors circulated through Washington about this fund and finally found their way into print—notably in the Evans-Novak column. The picture presented was that Johnson was sitting on this money, refusing to turn it over to the Democratic candidate at a time when Humphrey was hurting for funds.

I probably overreacted, but was upset with the knowledge that someone in the Humphrey camp had deliberately leaked the story to put Johnson in a bad light. In my press briefing I used such terms as "poison pens" and "tommyrot" in denouncing the report, and the *Washington Star* bannered: "White House hits poison politics."

In short, the Vice President had ample internal problems and had to step gingerly around them.

He thought he should stake out his own position on Vietnam, somewhere to the dovish side of Johnson, but not too dovish to run off the Johnson people. He and George Ball tried valiantly to accomplish this, and seemed to pull it off well enough to satisfy some of the war-weary in the Democratic ranks. But Humphrey's Vietnam position alienated some of the Southern governors who had supported him in the convention, made Johnson unhappy, frightened Saigon, and helped him only a modicum with the hard-core McCarthy wing. To Johnson, his most cutting remarks were implications he would dismiss Dean Rusk. However, when Gene McCarthy finally gave his old colleague a faint endorsement on October 29—a week before the election—he complained that Humphrey's stand on Vietnam "falls far short of what I think it should be."

No matter what he said on Vietnam, Humphrey's problems with anti-war hecklers never ceased. He was at a loss to cope with them. He thought the press blew up heckling out of proportion.*

Union leaders volunteered to handle demonstrators "their way," but the Humphrey staff would not concur. The Vice President admitted later that he was tempted to turn the whole situation over to the union lads. Once in Youngstown, Ohio, the steelworkers, on their own volition, dealt with a demonstration. "They stepped on a few insteps and kneed a few groins, and it was over before the press people knew anything about it," one leading Democrat chortled afterwards. "All of those signs began coming down in the crowd, and we never saw them again."

Humphrey campaigners lived in fear of the "image" such fights would create, in view of the Chicago disaster. So in the main, both the Presidential nominee and his running mate endured the abuse, while wishing for a few voices to be rudely muzzled.

Demonstrations of this kind were even more of a factor in President Johnson's appearances. They added to the fear of bodily harm inflicted upon the President, and they demeaned the Presidency in the eyes of the world. Thus, they were to be avoided at all costs. The best way was limited public notice of a Presidential appearance; if the Students for a Democratic Society and other campus militants did not have time to organize a protest, all was serene. This became almost a game in the last year or two of the Johnson Administration. In some places, according to our FBI and Secret Service reports, the SDS chapters were poised to go into action on the basis of publicized invitations to the President, or just plain rumors. There were a lot of disappointed kids when the President did not show up. The standing rule of SDS was to go after Johnson if he was scheduled to appear within a hundred miles of a college chapter. A demonstration could be organized quickly and effectively, especially during the heat of the political campaign.

* Humphrey formed this view much earlier, when during a Vice Presidential trip to Europe certain editorial chiefs notified reporters to play up the demonstrations in news leads; this may have been a matter of news judgment, but it was not calculated to please a high American official who thought he was having a fairly successful goodwill trip in his country's interests.

Much has been written of the President's isolation from the public in his latter days because of these intimidations. That they were a very real problem cannot be disputed. There was no concern that a left-leaning college kid would try to shoot Johnson, but demonstrations collected far more dangerous characters than shaggy-haired SDS members. Nevertheless, even the President had to take acceptable risks, and he did, depending upon the Secret Service and local authorities to contain the demonstrators.

The worst demonstration against Johnson was almost lost to history because it occurred late at night on the West Coast and therefore received scant television coverage in the eastern half of the country. This was in Los Angeles in June 1967, halfway between Johnson's two meetings with Premier Kosygin at Glassboro, New Jersey. The President flew to California for a Democratic fund-raising dinner, and into the eye of a storm. Thousands of demonstrators clashed with police outside the hotel, led by a hard core of violent types and backed up by excitable leftists from miles around. Arrests were numerous, and it was a miracle no one was killed.

This was a forerunner of things to come in the winter of 1967–68. By then Johnson was being criticized for confining his out-of-Washington visits to military bases (yet there were threats on his life even at the Camp Pendleton Marine Corps base in California). Actually, the President moved about the country in civil situations as well, but his travels became even more secretive, giving supporters little or no time to rally crowds and providing ammunition for press complaints that he was no longer in touch with the people.

II · *The Secret Service Responds*

After the murder of Robert Kennedy, an unbelievable load was placed on the Secret Service, and they responded well. Johnson ordered protection for all candidates, securing Congressional authority later, and the Secret Service had to bring in dozens of men from the field to bolster their protective contingents. Senior agents from the President's own detail were assigned to the various candidates for the nomination of their parties, including Ronald Reagan who never really announced as a candidate but acted like one. When the field narrowed down to Humphrey, Muskie, Nixon, Agnew, Wallace, and LeMay, the workload was still unusual. The Secret Service received scant credit for helping the nation stage an election in a virtually normal manner despite unusually dangerous circumstances. The year 1968 will be remembered for the political murders of Martin Luther King Jr. and Robert F. Kennedy. It should be remembered also as the year that six candidates and the President made it through without one or more meeting a similar fate. The peril of politics in that year cannot be overestimated.

Lyndon Johnson's protection was never an easy assignment for Chief Jim Rowley's White House detail. Early in his Presidency, especially during the 1964 campaign, Johnson was exposed constantly to the public. He loved to plunge into crowds and "press the flesh." He talked through the fence with tourists standing outside the White House grounds, sometimes inviting them in for a walk with the President. He was mobbed by crowds everywhere he went in Asia and the Pacific. In Brooklyn in 1966, he and Bobby Kennedy, campaigning together for the last time, were surrounded by a crushing mob of shouting, seizing, surging humanity. In Honolulu that same year, he and Mrs. Johnson walked down the street in Chinatown and were so swamped by throngs of people that the Secret Service could barely clear a path.

This was Johnson's cup of tea: the crowds, the squealing, the outstretched hands reaching for both of his. So he resented it when he could no longer enjoy the crowds, which had always rejuvenated him in the past.

Crowds of friendly people do not bother Secret Service agents as much as walking into an unknown situation. This latter circumstance was more common in the waning months of the Administration, because frequently there was no time to properly "advance" a Presidential visit. At times the Secret Service nearly missed having transportation for Johnson at the airport because of inadequate notice of travel. "Some day we're not going to get a car there," was an oft-repeated and exasperated complaint. Once in New York the President was forced to ride in a crowded and uncomfortable police unit when a limousine could not be sped to LaGuardia Airport in time.

The President grew weary of the constant protection and the Secret Service pleas for more "lead time" to arrange his travels. Harry Truman had said that the Secret Service was the only "boss" the President had. Johnson did not like to be bossed, and he reacted.

One of his pet peeves was the police sirens leading a Presidential motorcade, especially in Washington. He wanted to move silently and unobtrusively, and not like a "circus." Unfortunately, if the District of Columbia police knew he was leaving the White House, they almost always sent a motorcycle escort. Johnson made known his feelings about this in plain terms, but the Secret Service had difficulty solving the problem. Once the President ordered his car to pull up to the curb while two motorcycle policemen plunged merrily on down the street, sirens wailing. When the policemen discovered this and turned back, Johnson ordered the driver to turn down a side street and go a different way, confounding the police department's plans for routing him to his destination.

Two months before he left office Johnson met with all of his agents on the South Lawn of the White House for a picture-taking session. There were a few tears and a good many tight throats among these spic-and-span, hard-muscled young men when he said with emotion:

> As long as I live I am going to have a very special memory of this extraordinary group of men and a sentimental, affectionate feeling for each of them. This may be a surprise to most of you because I don't express that sentiment through the days. I know that sometimes you are surprised at the way I react to your orders and sometimes I am surprised at the way you react to mine.

He went on to recall the time in Dallas on November 22, 1963, when a "husky roughneck from Georgia," Rufus Youngblood, pushed him to the floor of his car and yelled "Down!" when rifle shots fell on the motorcade. "There wasn't any place to go but down because he was on top of me," Johnson said.

He said one of his greatest comforts was the knowledge the Secret Service was protecting his wife and daughters. He recalled the scene in Melbourne, Australia, in 1966 when demonstrators threw red paint on his car, and "I just couldn't keep back the tears when I looked in the faces of Jerry Kivett, Dick Johnson, Jerry McKinney, Lem Johns, and Bob Heyn, and the dearest of all, Rufus Youngblood, with that paint streaming down their faces, splattered all over them, but their chins up and their President safe."

He recalled Agent Bob Taylor having his foot run over by the Presidential car when a crowd jammed him against it. And he remembered the integrity of Clint Hill, who a few days before had stepped forward to admit a mistake which had turned the President's wrath upon deputy press secretary Tom Johnson.

"A lot of things you have had to live through with me," the President told his agents. "If I could rewrite them, I would change a lot of them because I have abused you, I have criticized you, I have been inconsiderate of you, and all of those things that you know better than I do. I have spent more of my time telling you what you did wrong than what you have done right."

He said he had informed President-elect Nixon that the best friend he would have, "when you come in and when you go out," would be the Secret Service of the United States.

III · *Joining the Fray*

Prior to the Democratic Convention, the President laid down some hard and fast rules for his official family: Stay out of politics; it's our job to make certain this Administration continues to function and completes its tasks. Johnson told his Cabinet that if any of them wanted to get involved in the Presidential race, he should resign and let someone else carry on his duties. Postmaster General Larry O'Brien stepped aside to help Bobby Kennedy and moved effortlessly into the Humphrey camp after Kennedy's death. But most of the Cabinet stayed on, while searching for ways to accommodate the President's wishes without ignoring their political party.

Johnson made himself abundantly clear in a news conference months before the election.

> Every person has the right to state who he is going to vote for and to campaign for whomsoever he pleases. But I don't think he should do it as an appointee of the President while he is paid to perform a public service. I think he has plenty to occupy him. He ought to stay on the job and do that job well. Of course, he can vote for whomsoever he pleases, but if he desires to run up and down the country campaigning for any individual, I hope he will give me an opportunity to have someone else take over his job here in Washington.

The edict was easy enough for the pro-Humphrey people in the Administration—a vast majority—to obey prior to the Chicago Convention. Humphrey was not involved in state primaries, and that's where the visible action was. After Chicago, it was unrealistic to think that men like Orville Freeman, Secretary of Agriculture, Willard Wirtz, Secretary of Labor, and Wilbur Cohen, Secretary of Health, Education, and Welfare would sit on the sidelines in a Humphrey-Nixon-Wallace showdown. By early autumn Cabinet officers began appearing in political situations— State and Defense were exceptions, of course—and Johnson chose not to enforce his earlier order. Attorney General Ramsey Clark became such a Nixon target himself that he fought back with special vigor. Late in the campaign, it appeared that a sizable portion of the Executive branch of government was geared toward the election of Humphrey, as everyone knew it would be.

The White House staff enjoyed a warm relationship with the

Vice President, who was almost "one of the boys" to some of us. Gregarious, genuinely friendly, open minded and thoroughly decent, Humphrey never had the troubles with Presidential aides that other Vice Presidents—including Nixon—reportedly had. The older brother, younger brother relationship with Johnson could not have been easy for Humphrey, but he was accepted as a team member and friend by virtually everyone around the President.

Joe Califano, who shared Humphrey's burning desire to correct society's flaws through massive Federal efforts, worked closely with him on programs affecting the cities. Douglass Cater, who headed Johnson's health and education section, was so strongly pro-Humphrey that he finally resigned his post to work in the campaign. George Ball, onetime Under Secretary of State who had been recalled by Johnson to serve as United Nations ambassador, resigned to become Humphrey's foreign policy adviser.

Open evidence of White House activity in Humphrey's behalf was almost nonexistent at first. Johnson insisted that his aides devote their energies to the business of the Presidency, and most of them had little time for anything else. Between September and November, however, Califano's office was a funnel for information, ideas, and statistics used in the campaign. For those in the periphery of the White House, such as Dr. Edward Welsh of the Space Council and Endicott Peabody of the Office of Emergency Preparedness, it was less essential to cloak campaign activity. Some of these officials sent their wives into action as Humphrey organizers and campaign workers, and they themselves moonlighted in the Vice President's behalf.

The Humphrey-Muskie organization, with pros Larry O'Brien, Jim Rowe, and Bill Connell at the helm, recognized that Lyndon Johnson had an important role to play in the campaign. Apparently their dilemma was to settle upon what it was. It was suggested to the White House that the President could be useful in the Border states—West Virginia, Kentucky, and Maryland—and in states such as Texas and Tennessee which were thought to be toss-ups in the election. Some of this planning was done without

Johnson's knowledge, and he was irked when it leaked to the press with the implication that Humphrey wanted his help only in a few states, and not in the nation as a whole.

Johnson held the view that the most beneficial help he could give the Democrats was to stick to the helm of government and try to resolve existing problems, thereby providing the proper backdrop for the Democratic campaign. He had no intention of barnstorming the country but made clear he was available for spot duty. Ironically, some of the newsmen and columnists who had earlier made special note of Johnson's popularity problems were telling both the White House and the Humphrey group in October that an all-out Johnson campaign was essential to a Democratic victory.

In Texas the polls showed a close race, with Nixon the winner. Wallace was hurting Humphrey in labor areas and the "brass-collar Democrat" sections of the state. Only a unified campaign by liberal and conservative leaders could win for Humphrey, so Johnson's fine hand went to work. In the final analysis, Senator Ralph Yarborough and Governor John B. Connally—political foes of a most bitter kind—not only joined in support of the Democratic ticket, but also campaigned side by side. The Democratic establishment—legislators, state and local officials, precinct chairmen—swung in behind Humphrey, and he carried the state by a whisker. Johnson felt he owed this to his Vice President, and he delivered.

The President's first sally into election politics, aside from a union-sponsored radio broadcast, was more or less nonpartisan. He agreed to attend the annual dinner in New York of the Alfred E. Smith Memorial Foundation, at which both Humphrey and Nixon would also speak. His speech writers gave him some sparkling material, and he embellished it royally, upstaging the two candidates as well as Governor Nelson Rockefeller and Mayor John Lindsay. The crowd of wealthy New Yorkers in the Waldorf-Astoria ballroom was friendly and bedazzled by the display of political might. The head table was all-star: the two candidates, the governor, the mayor, former Governor Tom Dewey, former

Postmaster General Jim Farley, both New York senators, Archbishop Terence Cooke.

With an actor's sense of timing, Johnson pictured Al Smith in heaven, chuckling at the secret thoughts of the head table when they looked at the Archbishop.

Of Nixon: ". . . hoping that the Archbishop has come here to witness a resurrection. He appears to be so confident these days that he is already planning to change the name of Washington, D.C., to Resurrection City."

Of Humphrey: "He is sitting here hoping that the Archbishop perhaps will pass the collection plate a second time."

Of Rockefeller: ". . . sitting over their smiling and thinking, 'Well, they almost got me to the church on time'."

Of Lindsay: ". . . to his left and our left, always looking far ahead, is offering up a slightly different prayer—'Get me to the church; get me to the church next time'."

The President apologized to the Archbishop for Senator Eugene McCarthy's absence: "I think it is a shame, Your Excellency, that Gene McCarthy has refused to come to church. He has chosen to go off and fast in the desert instead."

Now looking down at Nixon, the President remarked he would not say he was sorry to be leaving the White House, "but I will say this: This could be my last press conference. Pretty soon you won't have Lyndon Johnson to kick around any more."

The audience roared; Nixon blushed and laughed heartily. Johnson commented later that it was the kind of laugh a man makes when he is trying to be a good sport, and that it was too brutal a dig to remind Nixon of his "last press conference" after being defeated in the California governor's race. But I thought Nixon took it in good graces.

In his more serious remarks, the President called for compassion for the poor, the black, and the culturally deprived. Their cause, he said, "is not a cause that can be abandoned or exploited or maligned by any man or party."

Afterward, the press photographers were accommodated with a picture session. It was difficult to pose so many political figures in one place, and Tom Dewey tried to slip away. "I'm in the wrong place," he said. "They're not interested in me."

In October, Johnson consented to tape radio and television speeches in Humphrey's behalf.

Two of these embraced a rather studied attack, without real rancor, on Republican policies of the past and present. He declared that the essential difference between the two parties was that "Democrats face problems, Republicans defer problems." He compared Humphrey's campaign to Truman's uphill climb in 1948 and referred to Nixon as "a man from the past—a veteran from the time when America's problems were deferred, when America's needs were ignored."

Johnson gave only brief, pungent attention to the Wallace campaign:

> His solutions to the country's problems are pretty simple. You line up a few thousand on the sidewalks of the city to preserve order. You throw those bureaucrats' briefcases into the Potomac, including, I suppose, the ones that contain help for the people of Alabama. You turn the most difficult diplomatic and military problems that this nation faces over to General LeMay, and you use the Presidential limousine to take care of the protest movement.

The President said that Humphrey, on the other hand, "began fighting for human rights before others began to pay even rhetorical tributes to freedom." Crediting Humphrey with offering "good, practical solutions that appeal to the best instincts of our people," Johnson said:

> I asked Hubert Humphrey to be my running mate in 1964 for one reason: because I believed that he was the best qualified man in America to be President in the event I did not finish out my term. The four years since then have convinced me that my judgment was right; that today in 1968 Hubert Humphrey is beyond question the American public servant who is now best prepared by intelligence, experience, compassion, and character to succeed to this highest office in the land.

In one of the radio talks—this sponsored by the International Ladies' Garment Workers Union—the President used the "Nixon-is-the-one" line already adopted by the Democratic campaign to assault the Republican candidate's record:

—Nixon is the one who cast the tie-breaking vote that killed aid to education back when he was Vice President.

—Nixon is the one who said that Medicare would do more harm than good.

—Nixon is the one who speaks for the Republican party that always opposes so much vital and progressive legislation.

In his final broadcast of the campaign, Johnson rose above even this restrained partisanship. The consensus at a White House staff meeting was that the President's swan song as a campaigner should be a memorable one, and that meant a full measure of statesmanship. We decided the tone should be above the grime of the 1968 election process. The President should issue to his countrymen a clear call to reason. There should be no bitter swipes at Nixon or Wallace, but just a gentle reminder that the country was better off in Democratic hands.

To Charles Maguire fell the task of writing the speech and coordinating its production. We decided to use both a speech and documentary material, and finally found use for a film about Johnson produced for the Democratic Convention but never used after order and decorum collapsed in Chicago. Maguire and a technical crew in New York skillfully edited the film, preserving a part of the Gregory Peck narration, and blended it into the most effective political broadcast I have ever observed. It was televised the Sunday evening before the election, and when Tom Johnson showed the hard-to-satisfy White House press a preview, the reporters burst into applause at the end.

The President was never more eloquent as he related how he and his family looked forward to private life, and how he had reflected "naturally and soberly" upon what type of man would occupy the White House when he left.

That man—the thirty-seventh President of the United States—will find, as I did, that all of the Presidents who have gone before have left something of themselves behind. He will discover, as I did, that this Oval Office—while a lonely place in many ways—is filled with the presence and the thoughts of men who bore the burden of national leadership in trying times.

That is the unseen Presidency. Its tradition, experience, judgment, and example speak across the centuries from one President to the next.

Johnson used the words of Hoover, John Adams, Jefferson, Lincoln, Theodore Roosevelt, and Eisenhower—a predominantly Republican list—to warn that the people should elect Presidents capable of serving the people as a whole, without partisanship and favoritism.

They say that you must select a man of conscience; they say you must select a man of conviction but never elect a man of narrow partisanship. He cannot be President of part of the people, he cannot be a spokesman for one race, or one faction, or the servant of one group of states, or one set of interests.

No man can come to the Presidency compromised in honor and lacking public trust. He will fail, and the people with him.

Johnson said his vote for Humphrey and Muskie would not be given lightly; "It is a heavy responsibility for the President ever to recommend his successor, but it *is* his responsibility—and from a vantage point of his experience in this office, he must meet that responsibility."

The documentary portion of the broadcast depicted the Democratic Presidencies, from Roosevelt to Johnson. FDR's voice provided nostalgia, and there was a poignant scene of John Kennedy shaking hands with a little boy in a crowd, and afterward the child seizing his wrist and staring thunderstruck at the hand which touched immortality.

How effective were the President's broadcasts in gaining votes for the ticket? I have to think they were highly effective, judging from the response. There was even a letter from two of Johnson's most persistent critics, the Smothers Brothers, who wrote:

> We saw the television broadcast you made last night in behalf of the Democratic party and Hubert Humphrey, and we were quite moved by your sincerity and by the content of the message. If the opportunity arose in this coming election to vote for you, we would.
>
> Often an emotional issue such as the war makes people tend to overreact. Please accept our apology on behalf of the *Smothers Brothers Comedy Hour* for our overreaction in some instances. Please know that we do admire what you have done for the country and particularly your dignity in accepting the abuses of so many people. We are now working for the election of Hubert Humphrey, and much of the enthusiasm we have for him is due to that broadcast of yours.

Johnson's one effort at barnstorming was designed to help Congressmen Carl Perkins, Ken Hechler, and Harley Staggers, and Kentucky Senatorial candidate Katherine Peden, as much as it was to aid the Humphrey-Muskie ticket.

On Saturday afternoon, October 26, the President flew to Huntington, West Virginia, to put in a good word for Hechler and other West Virginia Democrats in an airport speech, then boarded a helicopter for a long flight deep into the hills of Eastern Kentucky to dedicate Fishtrap Dam near Pikeville.

The dam is in the district of Carl Perkins, a Congressman known for his ability to recruit Federal dollars for his beautiful but poor Appalachian area. Months before Johnson had promised Perkins he would dedicate it, and a ceremony was set, but heavy rains made travel in the region so difficult that it had to be cancelled. Now, on a cool, sunny day in October, the President whirled into Fishtrap Dam in his chopper. The press helicopter we had borrowed from the Marine Corps belched black smoke just as it was landing and came to rest on a pad constructed high up on the mountainside near the dam, about a mile from the site of the dedication in the valley below. There it sat, while the crew wondered what to do with the stricken craft.

Looking up from the valley a little later, and realizing the press chopper would never fly out that day, Jim Jones and I reasoned that it could be made another monument to Carl Perkins: a genuine Marine Corps helicopter, perched forever on the mountainside.

In a more serious vein, I reminded Jones that Katherine Peden's Republican opponent, Judge Marlow Cook, would also be on the platform, so he should probably advise the President of this so he would avoid being overly partisan in the senate race. Jones did, and the President responded in his speech:

> What we have built together has been built on the enduring and honored principles of the Democratic Party. The Democratic Party is the party that believes in the greatest good for the greatest number. The Democratic Party is the party that acts on your problems instead of deferring your problems.
>
> And I want every one of you to remember that when you go to the polls on November 5 and vote the straight Democratic ticket from the White House to the courthouse. . . .
>
> And the more Democrats we have in the Congress, the better bills we are going to pass. That is why we want to be dead sure that you send us back Carl Perkins and you elect a Democratic Senator in Katherine Peden. . . .
>
> The surest way in the world that you can turn back the tide of progress in America is to go out and elect yourself a Republican President and give him a Republican Congress.

The crowd cheered lustily, and Judge Cook, who certainly knew what he was getting into, sat on the platform and smiled gamely.

It was now certain that I could never get the White House press out of the valley by chopper, so I put together a small "pool" to fly on the President's chopper since he was going on to Morgantown, West Virginia, for another speech. Fortunately, our trusted transportation experts—Jiggs Fauver, Ray Zook, and Bob Manning—seemed always to be prepared for such emergencies. Two busses had been chartered to carry us from the chopper pad to the dedication site, and Fauver quickly arranged for these to transport us back to the airport in Huntington, West Virginia.

I chose to stay with the main body of the press, and we bought hot dogs and coffee from the food stands local citizens had thoughtfully provided, and watched unhappily as the President's helicopter took off into the gathering gloom, leaving us with a three- to four-hour drive. The reporters, cameramen, and technicans accepted their fate with good grace, though we had to creep through the night at slow speed because of the narrow mountain roads.

On the Virginia border we pulled into a lonely service station and assaulted its vending machines, thankful for a few minutes' respite from the bus ride. A baffled young boy who was keeping the store did not know what to make of my question: "Have you heard any football scores?" He replied: "Yeah, we beat Russell, fourteen to seven."

While we were making our way through the hills, the President was delivering a rousing Democratic speech at a dinner honoring Congressman Harley Staggers in Morgantown. As reported later to the newsmen by "pooler" Bob Pierpont of CBS, Johnson went down the laundry list of Administration accomplishments, most of which were of special benefit to the people of West Virginia. He exhorted the crowd to remember that the Republicans always ran against something, not for it.

"I have never, in all my days, seen a slicker, more overorganized, trumped-up, misleading, now-you-see-it-now-you-don't political campaign than the one the Republicans are waging this year," cried old Democrat Johnson.

". . . They have fed the American people a steady diet of colored balloons and bass drums and cheerleaders and television commercials that don't even show the face of their candidate most of the time. They have run this campaign on a single principle: Don't make any waves."

As for the Democrats, Johnson described their program this way:

> We like this democracy so much, this freedom so much, this liberty so much, we want everybody to have a little taste of it. It is like the fellow who had a few too many drinks. He came home and woke up the middle of the night. His mouth was burning, and he said to his wife, "Get me some ice water." And she got the pitcher of ice water and brought it to him and he took a drink. Then he said, "Honey, this is so good, go wake up the kids and give them some of it."

Johnson arose Sunday with a blossoming cold. He had worn a light suit to Appalachia, with no top coat, and had gotten chilled. Also remember that the "crunch" was coming on his Vietnam bombing decision, and his anxiety over this was increasing. But the only fever he had was a slight dose of political fever, because the crowds and the cheers had been good in West Virginia and Kentucky, and it was almost like old times.

In addition, Richard Nixon had stepped up his campaign against the Administration. He accused the Democrats of creating a "security gap" by not maintaining a clear-cut military superiority over the Russians. Clark Clifford promptly denied it, and Humphrey claimed Nixon was "playing politics with our national security."

Sticking with his new attack, Nixon contended in Albany that the Democrats had "invariably forfeited any right to hold power in America." He asserted: "They helped to create the crises we face, they failed to resolve a single one of the major national crises in the four years they held power. The embittered and angry and squabbling crowd that the nation watched in Chicago is not qualified to lead Americans to peace at home and peace abroad."

Humphrey responded with a charge that the "real" Nixon was emerging at last in the campaign.

"I say if you've seen one Nixon, you've seen them all," he said at Akron. "The real Nixon has emerged right on schedule. So batten down the hatches—for the most desperate and cynical display of political irresponsibility ever seen in America. That's the real Nixon—and that's the Nixon we're going to beat."

Johnson did his best to help Humphrey fulfill that pledge, by flying to New York on October 27 to address a luncheon meeting of the All American Council of the Democratic National Committee. This was a conglomeration of the ethnic groups which the Democrats had always courted heavily in many parts of the North —Italians, Poles, Latin Americans, several others. It was a well-organized, enthusiastic political rally in the Waldorf. When Johnson arrived, toting young Lyn Nugent on his arm, the shouts and applause were deafening. The President had some prepared remarks, but in the face of such political fever he used them up and ad-libbed most of the speech.

Using his customary approach, Johnson traced Democratic ideals from the time of the party's first Roman Catholic candidate, Al Smith, through his own five years. And what of the recent Democratic accomplishments?

—Ninety-two months of unbroken prosperity;

—The unemployment rate cut in half;

—Real personal income up 32 per cent;

—A sharp decline in infant and maternal deaths, and in deaths from childhood diseases;

—Seventeen million children getting additional Federal help in school;

—A million and a half young people going to college with the help of the Federal government;

—The number of people in poverty down 38 per cent in five years; and

—Cash benefits under Social Security up 60 per cent, and more than twenty million people covered by Medicare.

Johnson pumped up Humphrey and Muskie as logical leaders to carry on the crusade. "Hubert Humphrey is going to wake up on the morning of November 6 as the new President-elect of the United States!" was one applause line. For the spice of low humor, it was the story that a reporter had asked the President which was his favorite poll, Gallup or Harris, and "I didn't have to hesitate for a second; I told him my favorite Pole is Muskie."

The speech in print does not look extremely partisan, merely Democratic pridefulness. In the heat of the crowded dining room, amid waving placards and banners and bunting, with cheers following nearly every time he increased the pitch of his voice, it gave the impression of Johnson of old, Johnson the mover, Johnson the conqueror.

Commented Forrest Boyd of Mutual News: "Richard Nixon said, 'Sock it to me.' Lyndon Johnson did."

Mrs. Johnson and Luci also made several campaign appearances during October. The President's final campaign appearance was in Houston's Astrodome on Sunday, November 3.

The Johnsons were at the ranch, where on Saturday they had entertained Apollo 7 astronauts Walter Schirra, Donn Eisele, and Walter Cunningham and had viewed the spectacular films taken on the recent flight. But Vietnam, not space travel, was very much on Johnson's mind—especially the persistent reports that South Vietnam was being persuaded by Republican contacts to delay the Paris peace talks for as long as possible. The Nixon camp was obviously reacting to the October 31 bombing halt with renewed nervousness over the help it afforded Humphrey. However, first Everett Dirksen and then Richard Nixon himself denied to Johnson that Nixon was taking overt steps to influence the South Vietnamese.

Humphrey made a strong appeal for Johnson to participate in the Astrodome rally, which was a combination political event and songfest (Frank Sinatra, his daughter Nancy, Trini Lopez, and others). The President was still plagued by his cold and reluctant to go but finally consented. While en route by Jetstar, the President was radioed by the Vice President with the request that Johnson's plane land first so that he could greet Humphrey when he arrived. This was not exactly protocol, but Johnson agreed.

The President was met at the cold and windy William P. Hobby Airport by Congressmen Bob Eckhardt and Bob Casey,

Houston's liberal and conservative Democrats in the House. Senator Ralph Yarborough would also be at the Astrodome, but on this occasion Governor Connally would not. Then the Vice President's airplane roared in, and a curious event transpired.

By all rules of procedure, Humphrey should have been the first off the plane to greet Johnson at the ramp. But virtually everyone else on the craft debarked first, including Orville Freeman, old LBJ staffer Jack Valenti, and a host of Humphrey aides. Like some local dignitary, Johnson dutifully stood in the cold and shook hands with each one, until finally Humphrey appeared at the airplane door for his official arrival in Houston. There was more than a little bitterness among Johnson staffers at the campaign advance men who had planned this procedure.

At the Astrodome things warmed up somewhat. The party arrived as Frank Sintara was completing his part of the musical program, and the giant dome was packed with fifty thousand people. Judge Roy Hofheinz likes to compare his magnificent entertainment hall with the Coliseum of Rome, and it took on this appearance indeed as Johnson and Humphrey walked side by side along the track encircling the artificial grass of the playing field. They grinned and waved, nodded and saluted, as thousands of voices roared as the ancient Roman citizens must have roared during the march of the gladiators. One newsman said later it was more like a bullring, with the dust rising from the track as the two matadors paraded, sans capes, before doing battle with the Republican bulls.

The huge Astrodome scoreboard was very much alive, flashing electronically a series of Humphrey-Muskie signs and cartoons of a snorting Texas longhorn. It helped to have Roy Hofheinz on your side.

The speeches could not match the entrance—or the musical show, for that matter—and a number of people began to drift away when the oratory began. But the vast majority stayed to hear speeches from Johnson and Humphrey which were a little too statesmanlike for a stadium crowd whipped up by popular singers and longhorns on the scoreboard.

The President called for national unity, for "union is good for Texas, for this region, and for our entire nation." He quoted Sam Rayburn's hope, in his maiden speech to the House in 1913, that America would become a country "that shall know no East, no West, no North, no South." Only in that way, said Johnson, could the South "rise again—as a vigorous, progressive part of America."

His speech, then, was directed at Texans' Southern instincts. But he attacked "divisive men on both sides . . . trying to play upon fear and grievances in this country." Behind much of this, he said, was hidden racism.

I say to you, my fellow Texans, for the sake of our American union, this man—Hubert Humphrey—should, and must, become the thirty-seventh President of the United States. . . .

Soon I shall be coming back to Texas, to live here after thirty-seven years in public life. I will come home as a private citizen.

In all my years in Washington, I have never ceased to be a Texan.

In all the Texas years ahead, I promise you that I shall never cease to be an American.

Johnson listened to a low-key speech by the candidate, citing a "confluence of three revolutions"—in technology, race, and "the individual against bigness." Humphrey said the next four years would be years of trial for the nation, but pledged to "call forth from America the best that lies within it." This was far from a political rouser.

The loudest cheers came when Humphrey said he had been proud to serve under Johnson. "I have been—at least I have tried to be—and will continue to be his faithful friend during these months of his Presidency—his loyal Vice President and proud of it."

IV · *Trail's End*

On the day before the Tuesday election, I released in San Antonio a memorandum to the President from Arthur M. Okun, chairman of the Council of Economic Advisers. It was a glowing report contending that "the economy is moving into better balance and . . . we have turned the corner toward price stability." Okun announced that we had an international trade surplus in September for the third consecutive month and there was improved confidence in the dollar.

"The prospects for continued progress and improved balance are encouraging," Okun asserted in his memo.

"Is there any significance in the timing of Dr. Okun's release today?" a cynical reporter asked me.

"Not particularly, no," I replied, pained at the implication.

"It has nothing to do with partisan politics?" another asked.

"Of course not," I replied.

Monday night the President told Tom Johnson to have the press at Johnson City between seven and seven-thirty in the morning if they wanted to watch him go to the Pedernales Electric Co-op to vote. So we all gathered at the modern brick building at the appointed time, then waited and wondered as Johnson failed to arrive. Once a white Continental drove up and the television newsmen rushed to the street, but a surprised rancher—an HHH-Muskie sticker on the bumper of his car—climbed out and went in to the polling place. The Johnsons finally arrived shortly before nine o'clock.

"Did you all vote absentee?" he asked the reporters as he walked past them. Inside, the President picked up his long paper ballot and asked an election judge how to properly mark the fourteen State Constitutional amendments.

Outside, Johnson declined to comment when the newsmen pressed him on how he voted. Mrs. Johnson volunteered that her vote was Democratic. After they had driven off, some of the reporters asked me why he was so brusque. I had no answer for that, but discovered later that his throat was so sore from his cold that he feared he would stir up stories of serious illness if he tried to converse at length. Later in the day he also ordered a television van removed from the ranch. It had been put there to provide live coverage of the astronauts' visit on Saturday, and I had permitted it to remain in the event the President wanted to make a statement on Tuesday's election. Johnson precluded any televised comments by sending it away, prompting press speculation that he was "moody."

"Nobody's going to know tonight how this election will come out," he predicted to me. "I'm not going to say a thing. I don't feel like it anyway."

That evening he called Humphrey to wish him well, then went to the home of his friend, A. W. Moursund, for dinner and watched the early returns on television. He went to bed with the knowledge that his candidate had lost, although there would be no formal concession forthcoming from Humphrey until the next day. As everyone had forecast, it was a squeaker.

Lyndon Johnson tried hard to prevent Wednesday from being one of those several "low days" since his decision not to run. But now it was certain: Richard Nixon would be the next President. The countdown to January 20 had begun in earnest. He was human, and he felt it.

In his congratulatory wire to Nixon, he voiced admiration for the "perseverance and determination you have displayed in achieving your victory." Then he said:

As you well know, the responsibilities of leadership today are probably heavier than they have ever been before. They are certainly too heavy, and too important to be also encumbered by narrow partisanship. I hope that our people will turn now from the divisive contentions of the political campaign to a united search for peace and social justice. You can be certain that I shall do everything in my power to make your burdens lighter on that day when you assume the responsibilities of the President.

To Hubert Humphrey he telegraphed:

You fought well and hard. You have carried your convictions and the standard of our party with eloquence and magnificent courage. In twenty years of national service, you have had no finer hours than those of the past few weeks—in which you awakened the support and interest of millions of our people.

Johnson suffered another painful blow. Senator Mike Monroney, one of his best friends in the Senate, had been defeated by Governor Henry Bellmon of Oklahoma. He called Monroney to express his condolences, then checked for other Democratic casualties. Not too good in the statehouses, not too bad in the Congress. Old friend and foe Wayne Morse was in deep trouble in Oregon; it would be several days, however, before his defeat was a certainty. Some of the other Democratic losses could not have been too sorrowful for the President, since numbered among them were two or three outspoken "doves."

A few days later in Washington, Humphrey and Muskie came by the White House for breakfast. Even the Vice President's natural ebullience was finally muted, and when the three of them walked out of the Family Dining Room it appeared to me they had been attending a wake. As they walked to the elevator, Johnson told them: "I want to help both of you as much as I can. You ran a great race. You've got a lot ahead of you."

When they had left, the President said to me: "Well, they almost did it."

FIVE

I · *The Care and Feeding of Crocodiles*

"Finally," said the *Newsweek* headline, "Nixon's the One."

For the White House press, this was certainly the case. Most of the regular correspondents—who had scattered to the winds with the candidates in September and October—settled now on perches in New York City and Key Biscayne to size up the "new Nixon" as the next President of the United States. Some others, like Herb Kaplow of NBC, were being groomed to take over the White House beat on January 20 (Ray Scherer would be assigned to London). It is not unusual for the news media to designate White House correspondents on the basis of their familiarity with the incumbent. Hopefully, they will have a rapport with him which might aid news coverage.

Few of the regulars lacked familiarity with Lyndon Johnson. The days of walking news conferences on the south grounds were

long over, but Johnson still saw them frequently, liked some and
disliked others, thought some were fair and some unfair, recognized their individual strengths and weaknesses, and even enjoyed
the dueling from time to time.

Yet the news media were something of a *presence* in the
Johnson White House—an alien force inside the moat, always
capable of mischief. And out there in the city were a thousand
more of the same, able to cross the drawbridge at will through the
magic of a press pass.

"I do not envy you your job," Al Mark of the Democratic
National Committee remarked to me one hectic day. "It is something like the care and feeding of crocodiles."

On many days the White House as a source of news is as dry
as a prune. The President is busy seeing people he does not want
the press to know about, the press secretary is preoccupied and
uncommunicative, and the handouts are such worthy items as
postmaster appointments and reports on the progress of data
processing in the government.

All of this may change in a flash. Bulletins move on the AP,
UPI, and Reuters tickers that a breakthrough has occurred in the
Paris peace talks. Or, a riot has broken out in Detroit. Newsmen
who have drifted off in boredom to their offices rush back to 1600
Pennsylvania Avenue. The atmosphere in the West Lobby comes
alive. The press secretary is seen charging in and out of the hall
leading to the President's office. His voice comes over the speaker
in the lobby: "The President will see the press in the Cabinet
Room. Photographers and correspondents in the corridor." All
move quickly to the narrow hallway leading to the inner sanctum
of the White House West Wing. A security door, which can be
opened only from the inside or by an electric button under a press
office desk, bars their way momentarily until an assistant press
secretary swings it open and leads them into the Cabinet Room
while a Secret Service agent scans the crowd to see if there are
any "ringers."

Now they gather on one side of the Cabinet table, the photographers in front. The President walks in, smiling or glum as the

occasion dictates. The cameras whir and snap for exactly one minute, while lighting technician Grover Cleveland Ryan holds a hand light as high as he can reach. Then the assistant press secretary says, "Lights!" That is the signal for Ryan to turn them out, and the cameras cease. The photographers file out, and the President, now seated at the Cabinet table looking across at an expectant platoon of newsmen, delivers the news it is his duty to deliver.

The reporters are rewarded for their patience in the lobby. The stories they file will be front-page news or lead bulletins on broadcasts all over America, and perhaps the world.

The White House regular is a breed unto himself, whether reporter or artisan.

Some, such as Merriman Smith of United Press International and Douglas Cornell of the Associated Press, date from the Roosevelt days. They knew every trick of the press secretary, every depression in the West Lobby sofa, every pace into the President's Oval Office. Like the fellow whose hobby is watching old war movies on television, they've been there and they've heard the dialogue before.

By and large, Washington newsmen become Washington newsmen because they are good at their business. Here the competition is fierce, and the unskilled fade fast unless they have the good fortune to be the editor's favorite and manage to cling to a working pension. Many are among the country's finest writers, and in fact contribute learned works in literary fields other than journalism. Fletcher Knebel and Charles W. Bailey, II (known to his colleagues as Chuck Bailey of the *Minneapolis Tribune*) utilized their intimate knowledge of the White House and the Pentagon to write *Seven Days in May*, a booming best seller during the Kennedy Administration. Other books by Washington correspondents and columnists are legion, for instant history and fictional plots abound here as nowhere else.*

---

* An exception to the *instant* historian is Jack Sutherland, White House correspondent for *U.S. News & World Report*, who wrote a painstakingly researched book about the battle of Waterloo.

There is a common suspicion, of course, that newsmen write a great deal of fiction that passes as fact. Journalists are quite aware of their own "credibility gap" with the public. It cannot be denied that some Washington newsmen do not specialize in accuracy, that some are lazy, and that some are prostitutes. A few, in the exercise of their journalistic power, become the "Anointed Ones." As critics of the government, they become—in their minds—more knowledgeable, more understanding, more clear-minded than the government itself. Free of the responsibility to govern, their decision-making is so obviously right that it is absurd the President and the Secretary of State do not always follow their advice. On the other side of the coin, the opinions of many leading journalists *do* count heavily in high places. Washington officialdom is so smothered in its own gobbledegook that it sometimes takes the clear interpretation of events by a competent newsman to give officials themselves the full picture.

Douglass Cater of the White House staff once wrote a book, while still a newsman, entitled *The Fourth Branch of Government*. His thesis, of course, was that the press constituted what in effect was a separate branch of government, equal in power to that of the executive, legislative, and judicial.

President Johnson felt that power often and was rarely insensitive to it. In this he was not unlike other Presidents.

There is a famous photograph of President John F. Kennedy, leaning over a small table with his back to the camera. The picture connotes much that is inherent in the Presidency: weariness, difficult tasks, lonely decisions.

A prominent Washington columnist told me he was in the Oval Office when that picture was taken and that Kennedy was reading a copy of the *New York Times*. He said the President exclaimed: "That damned Arthur Krock!"

That, too, connotes much that is inherent in the Presidency.

In Washington, *the press* has numerous definitions. The press is the working newsmen who cover their beats, including the White House. The press is the news magazines with their neatly packaged overview of complex issues. The press is the network newsmen, who have two minutes or less to explain these same issues on the air. The press is a handful of columnists, and interpretive writers and commentators, some more influential than others, but all equipped with sharp stingers. The press is the editorial policies of the *New York Times* and the *Washington Post*, both potent voices on the Potomac.

Lyndon Johnson tried to sift out some of these categories by referring to the "opinion makers." In this group he listed the two newspapers named, the three television networks, three or four columnists, and the magazines. His implication was that a politician who controlled them all would be almost invincible. He never had to worry how he would perform as a dictator, because he never came close to sacking up the opinion makers in one bag.

"Your boss has no idea whatever of the concept of the free press," a White House reporter friendly to Johnson told me at a bull session one day. A large group of his colleagues nodded in agreement. "Why does he pay so much attention to us?" I was asked. "He would be so much better off if he took us in his stride and stopped trying to sell us something all the time."

Johnson had a few close friends among the press, notably the columnist, William S. White. He had known Bill White for all the years he had been in Washington; from the time he was a Congressional secretary and White, a struggling AP reporter. Yet White treated Johnson as a friend, not as a source of news. He was one of the four or five people who were told by the President in 1967 that he was writing a statement of retirement, months before the actual decision on March 31. White and I discussed and analyzed the President's expressed attitude several times in the interim, but never once did White betray the confidence and write a line.

Close Presidential relationships with White House correspondents who covered him every day were not practical. There may be some "kept" newsmen in Washington, but I knew of none around the White House. Even those who enjoyed favors from Johnson and considered themselves friends respected the wall that existed between them. There was an adversary relationship, as there should have been.

But Johnson enjoyed talking with reporters, privately or in small groups. He could expand on the whole range of issues, calling up from memory more facts and figures than the average man can assimilate. He could talk about the thing with which he was most familiar: his job. And he would be discussing it with men and women who understood the issues—people you might win over if your debating points were sound.

These sessions were invariably billed as "off the record," but much of what he said found its way into print.

In some instances, this was an effective method of communicating Presidential views to those who portray such views to the public. There were also pitfalls. An unflattering Presidential comment about someone else in public life, especially a Congressman, would find its way to the offended party. Worse, the interview might take on the appearance of a high-pressure sales pitch, and a reporter who was suitably impressed at the time might decide later, when he was not under the spell of the office of the President, that he was being conned. It took some time for this to dawn on both Johnson and his press aides, and the President began to temper his enthusiasm to guard against this impression.

It was impossible for Johnson to maintain a distant relationship with the press as Eisenhower had done and as Nixon did during and after his election. He was fascinated by the news media. Realizing this, he sometimes attempted to kick the habit. Stories were common about his obsession with news, his overexposure, his testiness with reporters and photographers, his unorthodox press conferences. But he could not break habits formed in his youth. Until the day he left office, he was striving valiantly to improve his press relations. He counted this area as his biggest failure, and perhaps this fact alone made it more difficult for him to do better with the press. Even those in the news media who admired and defended him bewailed this.

The credibility issue was especially nettling and impossible to end once it began. Sensitive to charges about his own credibility, the President made frequent reference to "press credibility." This included everything from typographical errors to major misinterpretations. The Great Credibility War was a very real one in the Johnson years.

The President had a special liking for reporters who stuck to the "what, where, when, who" philosophy taught in sophomore journalism classes. When they wrote about the "why" they were in dangerous waters, he believed.

"If they write that I have big ears, that's a fact," he often said. "If they write that I mispronounced a word or two, that's a fact. But when they write what's in my mind, that's not usually the fact, unless they've asked me and I've told them."

Johnson's attitude toward interpretive reporting had a sounder base than one might imagine. He felt that most of the interpretations were not calculated to help him administer the business of the nation in the manner he thought best, and he resented it. To read abrasive editorials and columns every morning of the world does not help the digestion. It can also have a profound effect on the decision-making process of the President; the media can confine him within limits he does not want, and close options he prefers to remain open, or compound problems he already has with the Congress or a foreign nation. This is the negative power of the "opinion makers" as seen through the eyes of a Chief Executive.

"Our most tragic error may have been our inability to establish a rapport and a confidence with the press and television—with the communications media," Johnson told a reporter near the close of his Administration. "I don't think the press has understood me."

He believed that part of this was due to geography—"to where Mother was living when I was born." He felt a prejudice on the Eastern Seaboard toward anyone from Texas—magnified by the bitterness toward Dallas after the Kennedy assassination.

For some time after he succeeded Kennedy, there was almost universal praise in the press for Johnson the man, for taking up the torch and preserving the Union. But even then he told one newsman, "It will be a very short time until people in your profession will be pointing out the evils of Texans, the sins of personality and style."

But Johnson was willing to accept this as regional prejudice, which does exist in varying degrees.

He was unable to accept what he believed to be editorial influence upon news reporting. After the Vietnam effort began to decay, some in the news media could find little that was "right" with Johnson. Generally, these were the same individuals who backed him wholeheartedly in achieving the great social reforms earlier in his Administration. The use of Amercan military power in the Dominican Republic opened a wedge for criticism, and Vietnam made it a veritable canyon.

No less a literary personage than the late John Steinbeck complained, after an extended visit to Vietnam, that news coverage of the war was unfair. Steinbeck accused the news media of sending to the war zone too many young reporters "on the make," who were far more interested in finding critical angles than anything else, especially if they worked for editors who opposed the war.

His view was shared by the American civilian and military leadership in Vietnam. To some of them, the press was virtually a second enemy to whom everything in Vietnam was suspect: the body count, the M-16 rifle, the pacification statistics, Vietnamese government reforms, the ARVN.

Perhaps it is a reflection of the times that the U.S. government attempted to fight a war without press censorship, an accepted practice before, and that the U.S. press dwelled heavily on everything that was wrong with the war. In this age of the anti-hero, of cynicism toward authority, and of national guilt complexes, it is not difficult to understand these problems with war coverage. But it was still a constant irritant in Saigon and in Washington.

In fairness it should be noted that the coin had two sides. We— the Administration and the military—undoubtedly were guilty of casting a jaundiced eye at all unfavorable news stories on the war, regardless of the facts. We liked stories of success and disliked stories of failure, with little gray area between. From our point of view, with the national welfare at stake, we were not above feeling that the U.S. press should be a propaganda organ for the patriotic cause.

It is only when the pressure eases, and there is time for sober reflection, that one is forced to remember that this would be an unnatural and dangerous posture for the press.

While we were rarely pleased with press coverage of the war—and justifiably angry at occasional breaches in security—in our defense we never seriously considered drastic countermoves. Censorship was thought to be unworkable. A concerted propaganda campaign—all-out patriotic fervor with the President wrapping himself in the flag and waging a holy crusade—was likewise ignored. We spent a great deal of time answering criticism and trying to get our story across. We did not succeed very well.

Despite the admitted lack of affinity between President and press, the mutual suspicion, and the disagreements over war policy, the fact remains that Johnson's relations with the White House press corps itself were reasonably good. This relationship had its peaks and valleys, but it averaged out on the side of at least adequate understanding in both the Oval Office and the press room.

The reporters who covered Johnson on a regular basis were as much a part of the White House as the employees who worked there. The White House was their office, even if only a cubbyhole in the crowded press room off the West Lobby. Many of them never went to their own bureaus except to pick up their paychecks. From nine o'clock or so in the morning until the press secretary told them the business of the day was finished—which might be four-thirty in the evening or midnight—they lived in the environs of the West Lobby. Some had the habit of napping on the stuffed chairs and sofas in the lobby, which was the main entrance to the working West Wing of the White House. On occasion, the lobby took on the appearance of a genteel flop house.

Newsmen had the run of the press office. Unless I was involved in a particularly sensitive conspiracy, my door was always open. They came in singly and in groups, at all hours of the day, for questions or private conversations. I learned to sandwich other work around these visits, because nothing was more important than an open door policy.

It was almost impossible for the girls in my outer office to type or talk on the telephone in privacy. Reporters, photographers, and technicians hung around constantly, reading our newspapers, talking to the secretaries, or waiting for Tom Johnson, Loyd Hackler, or me to get free of some other visitor or come back from a meeting. When a crisis occurred that necessitated privacy in the outer office, Connie Gerrard or Rosemary McBride would tell the assembled throngs to scram, and they would obey without question. It was a satisfactory if hectic arrangement, and I resisted any suggestion to change it.

The White House reporters came in all types, sizes, and personalities.

Those who worked for the wire services generally practiced the old-time theory of journalism: Get it first, get it fast, get it in the early editions. Try to get it accurate. If you don't, get it corrected as soon as possible.

Merriman Smith, Georgia-born, had covered the White House for UP (later UPI) since 1941. He was at Warm Springs when Roosevelt died, at Potsdam with Truman, in Korea with Eisenhower, in Paris with Kennedy. He had a string of journalism honors, including a Pulitzer Prize, and there wasn't much new under the sun to Smitty. He was crusty, sarcastic, devious, intelligent, honest, fair-minded. When he looked at Lyndon Johnson, or any President, he tried to look with an objective eye. He could cut, but he did it with swift, clean strokes. On his last day in office Johnson awarded him the Medal of Freedom.

Smith's counterpart for AP was Frank Cormier, a towering Ivy Leaguer, expert economist, and classic wire service reporter. He had strong views on many issues; he was a dove on Vietnam, thinking it would serve the Communists right to have the place. But he never allowed personal opinions to affect his objectivity in filing a story on the wire. I often prayed for more like him.

Obviously, the relative power of publications and other media was quite evident to, and respected by, the President and his press secretary.

Washington is a local news beat for four daily newspapers: the morning *Post* and the afternoon *Star*, the *New York Times*, and the *Baltimore Sun*. The third Washington newspaper, the tabloid *Daily News*, makes no attempt to compete at the same level. Since most people in high places read the *Post*, *Times*, and *Star*, and many have access to the *Sun*, their news articles, editorials, and interpretive writers carry more weight in the nation's capital than do newspapers in other areas of the country. Therefore, it is especially important to any President that the policies he is advocating and articulating receive fair recognition in the Big Four. These are the papers read by members of Congress and just as importantly by the national columnists and other so-called "opinion makers."

Because the usual game is follow-the-leader, a good editorial or a good column by James Reston in the *Times* could be counted on to launch an Administration effort in grand style. Conversely, antagonistic comment in the *Times* and *Post* especially (because of their liberal approach) would more than likely result in similar criticism from those in Congress or the academic community who keep up with the world by reading one or both of these great newspapers.

When the *Times* turned all of its powers against the Vietnam War, President Johnson's forces worked overtime in a vain effort to stem the tide. Not only was the *Times* unmoved, but its policies also had a clear effect far beyond its own editorial rooms. It provided a prestigious voice for changes in war policy and a popular rallying point for Johnson's opponents.

It did not take me long to learn that the *Times* could not afford to make a mistake in covering a story. More than once a

Times error in interpretation was picked up by a wire service or a network and sent across the country before it could be corrected.

The *Post* was formerly run by one of Johnson's better friends in journalism, Philip Graham. After his death the newspaper remained essentially friendly on Great Society programs and was a beacon for the President's foreign policy in most cases. But its early support for the war faded somewhat during the last year of the Administration, and its tendency to be competitive with itself as well as the opposition was unsettling to those of us who liked to know whom and what we were dealing with. Jostling for position at the top brought similar jostling in the ranks, with younger newsmen trying to win their spurs at the expense of the older set. This type of activity may result in improved journalism, but from our standpoint, we were always more comfortable with familiar reporters who knew the ropes and who weren't surprised at every nuance in word and deed of the official they were covering.

A press secretary could talk more freely with a Carroll Kilpatrick of the *Post* or a Garnett (Jack) Horner of the *Star,* who were regular White House correspondents, than with a reporter he barely knew. He would learn quickly to spot a rookie or a climber —and act accordingly, in self-defense.

There was a great tendency in the Johnson government to judge the national sentiment by what one read in the New York and Washington press, since those were the newspapers delivered to one's door and timely to one's needs. Despite the power of these newspapers, one could be badly misled if he held to this view.

It was a source of annoyance on the part of the non-Eastern newspapers that the White House press office had a long tradition of special service to the Eastern media. "For Christ's sake, don't you guys know there's a place out there called Chicago?" Peter Lisagor demanded one day. Lisagor, the *Chicago Daily News* reporter-columnist and one of the best writers in Washington, had a valid point. Newspapers in Chicago, Los Angeles, Dallas, and Philadelphia covered the White House with aptitude on a par with the New York, Baltimore, and Washington press; we just rarely saw their copy.

I did attempt to break the habit of Eastern favoritism, by constantly reminding myself that Bob Baskin of the *Dallas News* and Bob Young of the *Chicago Tribune* did not exactly represent Eskimos in the Yukon. Their readers, too, were part of the American public.

Foreign correspondents also felt they were left out in many circumstances, and they were. Few of them covered the White House as closely as the regulars—with the exception of the British and French wire services—because they were not staffed well enough to assign a reporter full time to a beat as slow as our establishment. They concentrated on the State Department and came to the White House only when they believed something of special interest would be happening.

Pat Heffernan, the Reuters bureau chief, was a British gentleman with considerable power of persuasion. He won his point with me that Reuters should be treated as a domestic wire service. The Tass correspondents, who are trained in intelligence as well as journalism, got no such consideration.

Tass almost always had a man at my briefings, and once I may have caused a minor international flap with a wisecrack to a new Soviet correspondent during a State Department reception. When he asked me why there had been a delay in obtaining his White House credentials, I told him there was always a delay because of normal security checks on all accredited White House newsmen. "In your case," I added, "there's a particular problem because you haven't yet signed the non-Communist oath." I discovered quickly that some Russians do not have a sense of humor.

Women reporters must feel the same discrimination as the foreigners at times, but those who covered the White House— both the President's West Wing and the First Lady's East Wing —were among the best in the press corps. Muriel Dobbin of the *Baltimore Sun*, for example, was given top reportorial assignments by bureau chief Phil Potter, including the brutally tiring four-and-a-half-day Presidential trip around the world in late 1967 when the only bed rest for the press was a night in Australia and two hours in Thailand.

A man could spend a lifetime studying broadcast news and never complete the job. New electronic developments would keep his work outmoded, and he would never find his way through the human entanglements either.

Top television newsmen are not only far better paid than their counterparts in the print media, but they become national celebrities much more easily. The best reporter in America might remain relatively obscure throughout his career on a newspaper, but switch him to the evening news show and stardom is assured.

More often than not, we in the White House observed television news in horrible fascination, much as a condemned man might watch the hangman adjust the noose. Since networks operate under extreme pressure—not the least of which are the ratings— an uninteresting news show is *verboten*. Television news without action is vapid stuff indeed. This leads to instant news personalities —articulate student radicals, raging black militants, controversial churchmen, and the like. It also leads to a greater degree of subjective reporting than in newspapers or even on radio. Television newsmen often are forced to interpret a great event with little if any time for preparation. But even when this is not the case, they are expected to explain the background and the reason for a certain action and to do it briefly. It is not unusual for one newsman to report an item and immediately make editorial comment, thereby making personal opinion part and parcel of the news story.

"Interpretive reporting" of this nature is one of the sharpest thorns government leaders must endure. We were bowled over one Saturday evening when Frank McGee of NBC wound up his news program with a lengthy denunciation of the Vietnam War. On another occasion David Brinkley, after an account of an alleged peace feeler our State Department snubbed, commented wryly that it appeared the Administration did not want peace as badly as it said it did.

Television's effect on public opinion during and after the 1968 Democratic Convention will be debated for a long time. One fairly clear fact to emerge from the Chicago affair was that nominee Hubert Humphrey did not enjoy the usual upsurge in popular acceptance that a well-covered convention usually brings. The shouting contests between Mayor Daley and the McCarthy-ites, the squabbles between newsmen and security guards, the almost caricatured parade of "old politics" in the hall interspersed with the deliberate attempt by the New Left to shatter the Democratic Party in the streets, and some remarkably waspish comments by television anchormen combined to portray a party with diminishing capacity to lead.

Deliberately or not, television depicted the Humphrey majority as the villains of the piece and the dissident forces in the convention as heroes attacking the System. The Chicago police also came out second best. If one judges public opinion by an outpouring of calls, letters, and telegrams to the networks and the White House, then most Americans did not consider Democratic Convention coverage to be television's finest hour.

I thought the American Broadcasting Company showed the better part of wisdom by not attempting gavel-to-gavel coverage in the hall. The other two networks strove mightily to make things interesting, which often meant repeated interviews with actress Shirley MacLaine on the floor and a studied search for anyone who would say something daring.

There was also the disconcerting habit (to those interested in politics, at least) of switching the cameras away from the podium during fairly entertaining speeches, and inserting the commentary of the newsmen. When I challenged John Chancellor, the astute NBC reporter-analyst, on this point, he reminded me that very little news comes from convention speeches. I would have to admit that this is true, but it might follow that conventions are made up of politicians doing their thing, well or badly, and if the people are going to be subjected to long evenings of this dubious entertainment, perhaps they should at least be given more leeway to make their own judgments on the cast of characters.

Since a press secretary watches a lot of television news, it is easy to develop such personal opinions as: (a) the "straightest" war coverage was on ABC; (b) President Johnson was better understood and more fairly reported by network newscasters who had been White House correspondents, like Frank Reynolds of ABC and Harry Reasoner of CBS; (c) of the three evening news shows, only Reynold's *ABC News* and the *Walter Cronkite Show* regularly used direct reports from their White House correspondents, the *Huntley-Brinkley Report* preferring to cover the President by remote control, and therefore less effectively.

Above all, it was obvious that top network newsmen have become some of the nation's most powerful people. The persuasiveness of a Chet Huntley's stern directness, a Walter Cronkite's moral indignation, an Eric Sevareid's national soul-searching, a Howard Smith's gentle idealism and courage, a Harry Reasoner's humor without cynicism—who can truly judge their real impact on American public opinion? Since most Americans today look to television as their paramount source of news and interpretation, the burden of responsibility on television has become immense.

When Walter Cronkite, with his high rating for believability, raised serious questions about our effectiveness in Vietnam in several on-the-scene documentaries, it was not difficult to measure the doubt raised across the nation, and even in the government. As for the general television coverage of Vietnam, surely it dispelled all illusions that war is anything but brutal. Newsreel coverage of World War II and Korea could not avoid certain qualities of staged warfare as depicted in hundreds of movies from *What Price Glory?* to *Porkchop Hill*. Television coverage of Vietnam brought it all into the home just before the evening meal, with almost unbearable immediacy. Who will ever forget General Loan's pistol execution of the Vietcong prisoner, or the suicidal, gasoline-drenched monks bursting into flames?

Much has been written of television's equally profound effect on President-to-public communication. The televised news conference, the modern version of the fireside chat, the announcement of major events, and display of some of the pomp and ceremony of the Presidency are all commonplace in the day of the coaxial cable and video tape.

By the time of Eisenhower, the White House was scheduling news to take full advantage of television. Kennedy and Johnson refined the technique, and Nixon has given every indication that his Administration will refine it even more.

It is a simple art: The President makes major speeches at night, in prime viewing time; he arrives home from a successful overseas trip at night, in prime time; if something important is to be announced by the White House, the best time is shortly before the early evening news programs; if something distasteful must be reported, on the other hand, it is best to hold it until after those same programs.

If the Administration wants to "sell" a point to the public—progress in Vietnam, for example—the Secretaries of State and Defense are made available for the Sunday interview programs. If the Administration does not want to talk about something sensitive or momentarily embarrassing, the word is passed to stay off those shows.

At times we were able to hit the *Today* show on Friday and perhaps two out of the three network interview programs on Sunday with different Administration officials.

To me, this particular technique is not news management in its true sense. One of the toughest newsmen alive, Lawrence Spivak of *Meet the Press*, holds to the view that a high public official should appear on a nationwide question-and-answer session only when he feels it is in the national interest for him to do so. To expect him to appear for the convenience of the networks is naive, and they know it. But once a man consents to appear, no holds are barred on the program, and he had best be prepared to defend himself. And there is always the risk that an official who is urged to go on television will fail to express Administration policy with precision, as evidenced by Clark Clifford's remarks on the war after the bombing halt.

The nighttime televised news conference is an innovation of President Nixon's. President Johnson stuck to late morning or mid-afternoon, and even at that did not particularly like this type of news conference. He preferred to invite the press into his office or the Cabinet Room—on short notice—and take care of his news conference needs without the fanfare and pressure of television.

Newspaper and broadcasting organizations criticized this habit, partly because it eliminated live radio and television but mostly because it also eliminated all but the most regular White House newsmen. It forced the correspondents to guess when a news conference might occur and created an edgy situation for some. A "regular" such as Cliff Evans of *RKO General Broadcasting* or Saville Davis of the *Christian Science Monitor* might miss an important news conference simply because he was too short-staffed to stay at the White House all day and wait. I attempted to help matters by encouraging these impromptu news conferences near the time of my regular eleven o'clock briefing, when the highest number of regulars would be at the White House.

Johnson liked the informality of office news conferences, and he never entertained the thought of changing the habit. For some of the newsmen they were actually a better vehicle for asking questions, because a subject could be explored in greater depth and both parties were more at ease.

A televised news conference mobilized the entire White House and a number of agencies into various activities. The press office called around for anticipated questions and suggested answers, and contributions would come from several staff members and agency heads. These we edited, eliminating the least likely subjects, and Tom Johnson prepared a loose-leaf notebook for the President's night reading on the eve of the news conference. Johnson might skip through the book and he might not, but he wanted it regardless. More likely than not, his answers to the reporters' questions were off the top of his head, because he disliked referring to notes in front of the cameras.

In critical times he might call a special meeting of his foreign policy advisers in advance of the conference, to discuss his handling of key issues.

The special needs of television, in the meantime, were being met by a conglomerate of press aides, network producers and technicians, Signal Corps technicians, and custodial workers. The three television networks alternated each month as the "pool" representative, so the cameras of one would also serve the others.

The "pool" mobile van would be brought to the east driveway and cables strung into the East Room of the White House, which in a short time would be turned into a television studio complete with special lighting for the President and folding chairs for the correspondents.

Two or three hundred newsmen would attend the conference, all seated in an arc around the President's podium. A blue cloth hung behind the podium, to provide a proper backdrop for the color cameras. Still photographers were allowed to stand in front of the cameras, which were on a specially built platform, to record pictures for a minute or two when the news conference began.

One minute before the hour stipulated for the conference, the President would come down the elevator from the living quarters. Bob Fleming or later Glen Phillips would be at the door to hand him a special pair of eyeglasses which reflected a minimum of light from the dazzling television bulbs. Johnson would stride down the hall to the East Room, arriving at the door after giving the networks their precise amount of time for an announcer to say, "Ladies and gentlemen, the President of the United States."

To the Associated Press always fell the honor of the first question. Then United Press International. Then twelve to fifteen additional questions, sufficient to fill the half-hour. At the proper time, Merriman Smith of UPI would bark, "Thank you, Mr. President!" Another formal news conference would be history.

Small wonder that Johnson preferred to call the regulars into his office or the Cabinet Room and take their questions with little pressure and fanfare.

The more ordinary way of dispensing White House news was through the press officer's briefings. These regularly scheduled events were a necessary evil, designed to put out the news items you wanted to put out, explain them if necessary, and allow the reporters an opportunity to get questions off their minds.

Richard Harwood of the *Washington Post* wrote a column one time referring to the briefings as "feeding the goats." Some of his colleagues resented the implication.

Briefings always reminded me of reservation Indians coming

into the agency wrapped in their blankets, to draw their rations. Most of the time they were relatively civil, but occasionally they became hostile. I jokingly used this analogy one day in a briefing, and it baffled the Easterners until they discovered what I meant. When I departed the White House, the regulars gave me a small silver tray, and they inscribed it: "To George Christian—from his blanket Indians."

When I briefed in my office, or in the Fish Room next door, I always studied the room for a moment to get the lay of the land. If I spotted certain reporters, I knew I was in for regional or specialized questions to which I probably did not know the answer. Others would mean a testy line of questioning on some pet peeve. The ones I hated to see the most were the show-offs who liked to bait press secretaries for pleasure. All of the network correspondents would have a sackful of inquiries most of the time. Carl Stern of NBC, a lawyer, tried to grill me like a witness. I called him Mr. District Attorney and reminded him I was not on trial, but it did not hinder him. Bob Pierpont of CBS, a dear friend after hours, was a leader of the incredulous group always looking for a slip-up.

Thankfully, most of the time I remained calm. Occasionally Sarah McClendon, a President-baiter *par excellence*, would get me rattled, such as the time she demanded to know why Johnson would take the advice of a ninety-two-year-old man, Senator Hayden, or the time she insisted that we do something immediately about crime in Washington, "where all of these women are getting raped, more than once." Bill McGaffin of the *Chicago Daily News*, who wrote a book about the White House called *Anything but the Truth*, was constantly searching for credibility gaps, which could be certain to bring an argument.

My favorite villain was Jim Deakin. As correspondent for the *St. Louis Post-Dispatch*, which was highly critical of Johnson, he made no bones about his dislike for the President. He also loved his role of chief baiter of press secretaries and was the master of lengthy, involved questions almost impossible to decipher. I sometimes tried to filibuster him, without much success. But when he went to Italy on a sabbatical, I actually missed his presence at the briefings.

At the end of the Administration the regulars gave me a luncheon to say goodbye to "Old Blabbermouth." I told them I would have difficulty in adjusting to private life and had therefore set twice-a-day briefings for my children. I had renamed one of my sons "Jim Deakin." He, I reported, was the son who pulled wings off flies.

Nothing could have pleased Jim Deakin more.

Dealing with interpretive writers—the six hundred newspaper columnists like Drew Pearson or the single-shot in-depth writers like Chalmers Roberts of the *Washington Post*—was a quite different matter than handling the needs of the regulars.

Columnists with a strong record of hostility to Johnson rarely called and almost never visited the press office. Whatever information they could glean was picked up on the cocktail circuit or from private contact with some friend or semi-friend on the White House staff. Johnson's door was closed to them. His celebrated feud with Walter Lippmann, once a friend of sorts, overshadowed a similar coldness toward Joe Kraft, Evans and Novak, and several others.

The President had a wary relationship with many columnists. I counted it an achievement when I could break the ice between Johnson and a man like Charles Bartlett, who was too perceptive a writer to be barred from the Oval Office. But some columnists never received Presidential forgiveness for bitter criticisms, uncorrected errors, and occasional pieces of fiction which hurt Johnson. Some, in fact, never sought it. If there was anything good about Lyndon Johnson, they preferred not to know about it.

Johnson had trust in several of the interpretive writers and broadcasters. Crosby Noyes of the *Star* and Richard Wilson were respected, even when they fired harpoons. When Noyes wrote that a Johnson-Kosygin summit meeting near the end of the Administration would be an exercise in futility, it was well noted in the White House. Roscoe Drummond, Joe Alsop, and Marianne Means could see the President on request, as could Ken Crawford of *Newsweek*, who believed in our Vietnam policy regardless of the prevailing view on his editorial staff.

There were others in both categories—the trusted and the untrusted—and Johnson attached great importance to their writings and their contacts within government. When he knew an official in the Administration had a relationship with one of the writers that he considered hostile, he did not like it. "You've got to remember that those people are smarter than you are," he warned his staff. "They will pick your brain before you know it's happened to you, and I'm the one who suffers, not you."

We tried without success to keep certain staffers away from the press. At times, the White House was like a sieve.

Of the propensity to talk too much, Johnson once said with total exasperation: "I have enough trouble with myself. I ought not to have to put up with everybody else, too."

The President also had a theory that the aide who talked the most knew the least. "They have to talk big to prove they know something they don't," he said.

These leaks, unauthorized backgrounders, and occasional acts of overt disloyalty were constant annoyances. Furthermore, they affected the President's actions, colored his judgment of individuals around him, and helped make *credibility* an overused word in his Administration.

We were accused of plugging legitimate sources of news and evading answers to legitimate inquiries. Neither charge, of course, was peculiar to the Johnson Administration. But I doubt if any administration was more gun-shy of possible credibility lapses, thanks to publicity on alleged lies in high places, and in the latter days government spokesmen tended to be extra cautious. Too often we took the easy way out by refusing to comment on sticky problems. I am not sure this defense mechanism should have gone into play as much as it did.

Public officials can be made and public officials can be broken by the attentions of the American press. Lyndon Johnson was neither made nor broken, but he was helped at crucial times and badly scarred at others.

We often asked ourselves in those latter days: What went wrong with Johnson and the press? Our answers to ourselves were not wholly satisfactory.

It is perhaps too simplistic to say that the President did not understand the nature of an aggressive, critical press and therefore could not respond to it nor learn to live with it, while at the same time a segment of the press never really accepted the man in the White House as anything more than an "accidental President" to be endured rather than respected.

The probable answer is somewhere in between, with the Vietnam War a complicating factor.

Much of the press treated the President as something of a curiosity, making much of his freewheeling energy, alleged impulsiveness, grandiose behavior, and populist instincts mixed with outmoded chauvinism and saberrattling.

Newsmen were fascinated by his complex personality, and half the press in Washington considered themselves to be "Lyndonologists," the term they used to describe their amateur analysis of the President's character. It was difficult to accept him as he was, especially when it was much more fun to dissect his every shortcoming and question his every motive.

"He is a man larger than life," an early White House aide once said. "So all of his attributes are larger than life, and all of his faults are larger than life."

The picture of Lyndon Johnson as drawn by writers of his period has more than a few inconsistencies:

He was depicted as the super-politician, but blamed on the other hand for neglecting the Democratic Party and being blind to dramatic changes in American life.

He was said to be a demon to those around him, yet accused of having a sizable band of loyal "cronies" always ready to answer his beck and call.

He was painted as a power-mad President with the instincts of a dictator, yet he voluntarily stepped aside for the avowed purpose of unifying the country, leaving the press in such total confusion that they half-suspected a monstrous trick.

He was labeled a man who always sought "consensus," and he did like to please the people as much as he could, but his greatest decisions involved principle over public opinion. Witness his determination to pass the open housing law in 1968, against all of the backlash in Congress, and his commitment of American soldiers to a limited war in Asia, against all of the rules of maintaining popularity (as Harry Truman could attest).

These contrasts emerged because Lyndon Johnson was never a predictable politician. Few of his Texas supporters dreamed he would accept the Vice Presidential nomination in 1960. Few of his staunchest backers believed he would retain the Kennedy Cabinet after he became President on his own. Few Negroes believed he would take up the crusade for civil rights with such zeal. Few union leaders thought a supporter of the Taft-Hartley Act could become one of labor's staunchest friends.

Well, his detractors would argue, all of these actions were for the sake of expediency. He was not high-minded enough to act out of conscience, or principle, or a desire to do right. He was an insensitive, vainglorious man interested only in how he would appear to history. He was anti-intellectual, anti-Kennedy, anti-everything that did not bear the LBJ brand.

That was the judgment of some of Johnson's contemporaries, and it was reflected in the writing of the period. There was yet another layer of paint: The accusation that he constantly twisted the truth, misrepresented facts, and lied to the press and the American public.

Lyndon Johnson went a long way on the American political scene because he was willing to work when others were resting and willing to compromise where others were inflexible. He was hagridden by the desire to accomplish; he was the eternal salesman of his point of view. He created jealousies in the Congress which came back to roost during his Presidency, and he could never come to terms with the government-intellectual complex, that powerful body of men who migrate between college campus and Federal agency. He was always the last man to admit defeat, and the first to come up with a scheme to succeed the next time.

He was essentially a legislator who became an executive; a man who knew where he wanted to go in the narrow confines of Congress and how to get there and knew where he wanted to go as President but failed somehow to communicate it to his expanded constituency once his opposition found voice and direction.

There was nothing weak about his leadership, despite his tendency to doubt himself, but there was something woefully amiss in his handling of the powers of persuasion and communication so desperately needed by national leaders.

At least some of this was due to his inability—our inability—to communicate successfully to the news media and through the news media.

Perhaps God saves the Republic from dictators by giving all of its leaders an Achilles heel. A combination of the Johnson drive and ability with the Kennedy charm and youthful appeal would have been devastating.

Lyndon Johnson had four press secretaries and all of us had our failings. My reputation was one of being too close-mouthed, not daring enough, and overly protective of the President. But I also survived the job longer than anyone else, for which I am grateful and a little proud.

Johnson was always thought to be his own press secretary, and this was a safe assumption. A President so news oriented, so mindful of press coverage, so active in all phases of government and foreign policy cannot really be anything but his own negotiator and debater with the news media. This exposed Johnson to a good share of the fish hooks when the reporters threw out their lines. He bared his breast so often that he was bound to receive more wounds than a reticent Chief Executive.

Jim Hagerty, President Eisenhower's much-respected press secretary for eight years, believes firmly that a press secretary is asking for trouble if he tries to be a policy maker. "He is the President's spokesman when the President is not speaking himself, and as such he should say exactly what the President wants him to say—nothing more and nothing less," Hagerty has said.

Obviously, he does not mean that the press secretary must be a robot. A Presidential spokesman must respond to the give and take of press relations. But he should confine his sermons within the limitations of policy spelled out by the President. That is what he was hired to do, and he won't last if he does not.

He must try to strike a balance between the President and the press—an impossible task.

He must try to be totally fair—an unnatural trait.

And he must protect himself, or he will become ineffective in carrying out his duty, if not destroyed.

The Washington press is voracious, so much so that it even feeds upon itself. It does not take a rumor long to become an established "fact," and once it finds its way into print there is no feasible way to alter it with truth. Too many people have already accepted it in its incomplete form.

In Washington the press talks to itself a very great deal. As I have noted, an incorrect interpretation in the *New York Times* may be picked up by a dozen other papers and all three television networks by nightfall. It is assumed by most reporters that a columnist with a sensational disclosure is bound to have inside information, when he may have nothing more than a garbled rumor and a lively imagination. An honest mistake by a government official is likely to become a vicious lie, a wider opening in the credibility gap.

But the press in the Capital operates in a pressure cooker, and when allowances are made for this I must say that it does a remarkably good job. Most newsmen want to do right, just as most Presidents want to do right. Unfortunately, the twain does not often meet.

It is not difficult for a press secretary and even a President to become personally attached to newsmen. This is admirable, so long as it is remembered that they bite.

II · *Educating a Press Secretary*

When I was summoned to Washington in the spring of 1966, I had had no more than three or four conversations with Lyndon Johnson during my lifetime, even though I lived in his Congressional district and had supported him politically. He knew me only through two governors he respected—John Connally and Price Daniel—and as the son of the district attorney in the hill country when he was a boy. "All of us were scared to death of George Christian," he said of my father. I was tempted to respond that the shoe was now on the other foot.

"I see that you served in the Marines during the war," Johnson told me when I sat down in his office for the first time. "That was your patriotic duty. Now you have another patriotic duty. Will you accept it?"

I did, of course, and was assigned to Walt Rostow's office to become better acquainted with national security affairs. I read position papers and intelligence reports until I was nearly blind. One reporter opined that my assignment for the President was to "translate State Department papers into Texan."

In the summer I was ordered to pinch-hit on occasion for Bill Moyers, the press secretary, and to learn the ropes in the press office. Moyers was already talking of leaving, and he was quite happy to begin the indoctrination of a possible replacement. I briefed the press for the first time in San Antonio, without incident. The first time I briefed them in the White House press office, with what looked to me like a sea of sharks before me, I botched up a question or two and ABC's Bill Lawrence, smelling blood, lunged in for the kill. He had fun and I learned a lesson: not to speak unless I was confident of my information.

Shortly after the President named me press secretary in December 1966, I underwent back surgery to correct an old ailment. Since this followed on the heels of various ailments of previous press secretaries—George Reedy's feet and Bill Moyers' ulcer— the reporters suspected I was getting a head start on infirmities which went with the title. Several suggested that I had cashed in my chips earlier than anyone else in the job.

While resting in the hospital, I was confronted one day by Dan Rather and a couple of his CBS colleagues, wheeling into my room what looked to be a body under a sheet. It turned out to be a hideous cement totem pole they had discovered in the country and allegedly purchased as an appropriate guardian spirit for the new press secretary. "You're going to need all of the help you can get," Rather told me.

The President was determined that I inform myself on everything he touched. This meant an early call in his living quarters each morning to go through the assorted memoranda and reports he received. He lectured me while shaving, while eating, while dressing, while watching the news on television. Where he went, I followed.

"If I'm meeting with more than one person, you come in and sit down," he directed me. "If I don't want you there, I'll throw you out. But I don't want to have to call you to come. You just come."

I went, and rarely got thrown out. Sometimes I dozed while Treasury chieftains Joe Fowler and Joe Barr were explaining an international money crisis (forgive me, Joes), and discussions of foreign trade left me cold. But most of it was a fascinating study of a President in action.

Johnson delegated a great deal of authority in fields outside his normal purview. He had total confidence in his Secretary of the Treasury on money matters, and a healthy respect for his Council of Economic Advisers. Jim Webb of NASA and Bill Driver of the Veterans Administration were particular favorites among the agency heads; he did not like to second guess them. He avoided meddling with the independent regulatory agencies and rarely bothered any administrator short of an emergency. He relied heavily on John Macy, his talent scout for Presidential appointments.

He lived in constant fear that some scandal would taint his Administration, and this anxiety grew in the final months of the

Administration when investigative reporters were combing Washington for anything they could turn up.

His greatest concern was that someone on his immediate staff would be guilty of influence peddling, and most of us got frequent lectures on the need to watch our telephone calls and visitors. Some individuals, in fact, were barred access to the White House simply because the President was suspicious of their missions. I know of one close friend he avoided for months because he feared the man would say something to him about the trans-Pacific airline route case.

This particular issue, involving new routes to the Orient worth fortunes to the successful applicants, was the touchiest question the President faced at the close of his Administration. Several former White House aides and others thought to be friendly to the President were employed in one capacity or another by various airlines. The press made much of this fact, causing Johnson to be all the more skittish about influence and reluctant to make the decision. Finally he did, and a short time later the new President reversed part of his actions.

During this period the press showed its imagination by coining a new word for influence peddling. The word was *rainmaking,* which was said to be a common expression in· the government. One interested government employee ran a check in the agencies on the origin of the term, and could find no one who had ever heard it used except in the newspapers.

If there was much "rainmaking" around the White House, it must have been carefully hidden from me. It is difficult for the democratic system to function without a certain amount of favoritism and partisanship, especially in appointments to public office. But I believe Johnson's record in this regard will compare favorably with any other President's.

On this matter of delegating authority, Johnson wanted to be personally involved in virtually everything that interested him. Debating both sides of a question was one of his richest pleasures. Another was the extended detail work on the budget; he enjoyed thrashing over the arithmetic with his budget director, who was

Charles Zwick in the latter days. On most matters important enough to reach the White House, he wanted to be fully informed and briefed before making up his mind on a proper course. And once that course was set, he wanted no Monday morning quarterbacking from anyone around him.

No matter how well informed a press secretary is determined to be, he is going to be caught short on numerous occasions. One problem with no solution involves the receipt of incorrect information from a government department or someone in the White House itself. It is possible to earn a handsome credibility gap by merely reciting what you believe to be the truth.

I established a system of constant checking with government agencies to be sure we were on the same wavelength. Walt Rostow supplied one of his aides, at first Richard Moose and later Lou Schwartz, to stay in contact with the State Department and Pentagon and relay information directly to me. Each morning Moose or Schwartz would consult appropriate officers in the two departments on the "party line" to be taken on issues of the day. Loyd Hackler, the assistant press secretary, performed the same chore with the domestic agencies. I maintained especially close touch with Dixon Donnelly and Bob McCloskey, the State Department press spokesmen, and with Phil Goulding, top public information official of the Defense Department.

After my eleven o'clock briefing, McCloskey was given a complete rundown in preparation for his regular noon briefing. Transcripts of the briefings were sent around as quickly as possible to White House aides so they would know how questions were being handled.

Even with these precautions, blunders occurred. But we held them to a minimum. After Richard Nixon's election he carried this process one step further by separating the White House press office from the task of coordinating public information for the government. Herbert Klein became "communications director" in a system I admired. I told him early in the game that shaky coordination is a cross for any Administration to bear, and any new step would be an improvement. An Administration should have a general policy that the Executive Branch should attempt to follow. Like everything else, the system needs a traffic cop.

Perhaps the worst blunder of my tenure involving lack of communication between agencies concerned the much-debated anti-infiltration "barrier" in the northern part of South Vietnam. This was the defense system known as "McNamara's Wall," and it consisted, among other things, of highly secret electronic devices for the detection of men and motor traffic on the infiltration routes from North Vietnam.

By mid-1967 it was well known that U.S. forces had cleared a strip of land with bulldozers as part of the effort to maintain a barrier. Press speculation began as to when the final determinations would be made on the extent of the barrier—the installation of the electronic devices and other costly hardware, as well as the more common fortifications.

At the height of this speculation, Dan Rather of CBS came to my outer office late one afternoon and asked the receptionist, Rosemary McBride, if he could see me immediately because he had to tape a report on the barrier for the Cronkite program. I was in the Situation Room in the basement, attending a meeting of the Vietnam information committee which Walt Rostow and I headed. Rosemary sent me a note, and I went to my office promptly to see Rather.

He told me that he had good information that a major decision had been made on the barrier. We discussed the admitted fact of the land clearing, but told him I knew of no further decisions on the matter, that recent stories out of Saigon were speculative and premature.

"Are you absolutely sure?" Rather asked, indicating that he thought his sources were usually reliable.

"Well, let me go check something to make double sure," I replied, and went out my back door and down the stairs to the Situation Room to talk to Phil Goulding of the Defense Department, who had been attending the Vietnam meeting with me.

I told Goulding about Rather's inquiry and asked him if there was some new development of which I was not aware. "No, nothing's happened," he said. "Something might be in the wind, so be careful. But there haven't been any decisions by my boss that you don't know about."

With renewed confidence, I returned to my office and told Rather I was now certain there had been no decision beyond the activity on the barrier with which he was familiar. I told him I would watch the situation and try to alert him if anything looked imminent since he was good enough to check out his rumors.

When I watched all three network shows a little later, I was surprised to hear Cronkite lead off with a White House denial that a decision had been made to erect a barrier. There was no qualification in his account that the military had been working on a barrier for some time. The NBC and ABC news programs both carried speculative stories about new decisions coming on the barrier.

Some ten days later, when the President was in Texas, one of my assistants handed me a wire service bulletin reporting that Secretary McNamara at a news conference had announced a decision to go ahead with the barrier. My first impulse was that I had let Rather down by not giving him some warning as I had promised. When I called Rather, who was also in Texas, he was miffed at this but also upset that he had not used the story originally. Apparently the CBS brass higher up were also provoked, feeling the White House had misled their reporter.

I called Phil Goulding to complain about lack of notice to me that McNamara was about to announce something. He apologized and said the Secretary had made a final check of devices a few days earlier and had decided to go ahead. Public announcement was made, Goulding said, because of speculative stories appearing in the press that morning. I also talked to McNamara, who was chagrined when I told him we might have the beginning of a new credibility gap. If the Pentagon had only warned me, I said, I could have tipped Rather and the question of credibility would not have arisen.

Later in the morning I telephoned the ranch and told the President about the incident, suspecting that he had also let me down by not advising me of a decision. "I didn't have anything to do with it," Johnson retorted. "McNamara had the authority to proceed as he thought he should on the barrier, but they should have told you about the announcement. I do everything I know how to keep you informed, but I can't help what the Pentagon does."

Word of mouth repetition of the barrier story in CBS circles kept it alive, and a few weeks later Richard Rovere of the *New Yorker* wrote an incredible story that brought me out of my chair when I read it.

Rovere recited the case of a correspondent named Network who asked George Christian if it were true, as a U.S. Senator had told him, that the government was planning to build "some kind of anti-infiltration barrier across South Vietnam." According to Rovere, Christian said there was "no element of truth in it."

Later, according to Rovere's account, Network obtained solid confirmation of his story from the same Senate source, and this time did not consult Christian but went ahead with the story in a taping session on the White House lawn. Forthwith, Network was "summoned by Christian" and conceded under questioning that he had made a taped report on the barrier.

Rovere went on to recount that Christian, "sounding as if he had no interest higher than a solicitude for Network's reputation," said that anyone who reported the construction of a barrier in South Vietnam was "simply purveying misinformation." And furthermore, Rovere related, "he went on to say that the whole idea of a barrier was one that had never at any time been given serious consideration by the Johnson Administration." (I jumped out of my skin when I read that.)

The story did not end there. Rovere told how Christian had left the room to check his own source again, and returned to "say categorically, on the highest authority, that there would be no barrier." Rovere said Network knew Christian had checked with the President himself, although Christian did not tell him this, and so he had the taped report killed.

In addition to garbling what I told Rather, the story by Rovere left the implication that I was somehow able to "tune in" on network taping sessions on the White House lawn, and that the President himself had lied to Rather, through me.

Despite a letter to Rovere and a later conversation with him, I never caught up with the story. The *New Yorker* made no effort to sort out fact from fancy, and the incident became one more example of White House "incredibility."

"We live and learn, in the White House press office as well as in the news departments," I wrote Rovere.

Rather and I remained friends, although I imagine I brought the unhappy incident to mind every time I referred to him as Network.

This was not my only brush with the credibility question, which was a burning issue with the press before I went to Washington and never really died out thanks to several unfortunate incidents, a number of sensationalized essays on the subject, and our continuing problem in communicating on Vietnam.

To explore the entire issue would require a lengthy volume of its own, and it is an assignment I would not relish. By the time I became press secretary I preferred to think of it as a "believability gap" rather than its more common name, because I discovered that the unvarnished truth was difficult to sell to a skeptical White House press always wary of being lied to.

A minor incident, for example. The governor of Pennsylvania asked to see the President, and when I announced the appointment schedule I so reported. Only the governor of Pennsylvania announced that the President had asked to see him, which was duly brought to my attention by the press. Who did they believe? It's not difficult to guess.

When the President went to church in Texas one morning, a slightly more celebrated incident occurred.

A couple of photographers were waiting at the ranch gate, outside their car and standing by the fence, when the President and Mrs. Johnson turned out on the highway, the President behind the wheel of his Lincoln Continental. The Secret Service car followed a safe distance behind.

After a delayed reaction, the photographers rushed to their car and drove after the two-car procession, which was now well down the somewhat foggy highway. Johnson was obviously driving the nineteen miles to Fredericksburg to attend Mrs. Johnson's Episcopal church, although the press office had put out no prior announcement.

The big story out of Texas that morning was the wire service accounts that photographers had driven eighty-five miles per hour in an effort to catch the President's car. Remember that the photographer's drove at this speed—not the President—and they were some distance behind him, endeavoring to catch up.

I called the Secret Service to get as much information as I could and was told that Johnson had not exceeded the seventy miles per hour speed limit on the trip to Fredericksburg. The Secret Service calculated his *average* speed from the total amount of time the trip took and the distance travelled. The average was something over forty-two miles per hour.

This I reported to the press. I should have saved myself the trouble. By now the stories were that the President had driven eighty-five miles per hour (not the photographers), and it was naive to think the press would believe anything different. *Newsweek* used this to point out that "as many White House reporters were willing to believe the AP as the White House on the speeding story." *Newsweek's* account, however, referred to Johnson being "accused by the Associated Press of driving eighty-five miles an hour through the fog" when he was "clocked by the U.S. Secret Service at forty-two miles per hour." Of course, the AP "accused" the President of nothing, and the Secret Service did not "clock" him at forty-two miles per hour, but merely reported an average speed. These facts eluded *Newsweek* and other publications, all delighted with the story.

One postscript will conclude the tale. A New York reporter, holed up in his San Antonio hotel room after an evening of fun, was awakened by an irate editor at the home office, wanting to know why he had not filed a story on Lyndon Johnson's speeding to church. The reporter who had no knowledge of the event should have won a Pulitzer for quick thinking.

"Hell, the story isn't true," he told the editor.

"How do you know it isn't true?"

"Because I was in the back seat."

"Oh."

That settled that.

There are several ways credibility problems can arise. One is overoptimism on the part of official Washington, a charge leveled especially at Bob McNamara during the early part of the Vietnam War. Another is overexuberance, for which the President was sometimes accused and which afflicted some of our military leaders who used too much "smashing" language in reporting our progress on the battlefield. Another persistent problem is that high officials and the press look at many situations from quite different perspectives. It is entirely possible for a man to tell the truth as he believes it to be and then be caught in what appears to be a lie because of subsequent developments or even current facts about which he is not familiar.

To me, some of President Johnson's more prominent credibility indictments could have been avoided simply by a better choice of words in answering questions of reporters and less reaction to press stories we did not like. I will illustrate by the account of Henry Cabot Lodge's successor as ambassador to South Vietnam.

A *New York Times* dispatch from Saigon, signed by R. W. Apple, Jr., quoted friends of Lodge and "informed sources" as saying Lodge wanted to be relieved of his post and that "the White House was conducting an intensive search for a successor." Apple reported that the search was more difficult than expected and quoted "a visitor from Washington" as saying: "We've looked at about everyone you could mention. A surprising number weren't interested."

Apple's list of possible replacements included Deputy Ambassador William J. Porter, General Westmoreland, Secretary McNamara, Cyrus Vance, Orville Freeman, John W. Gardner,

Arthur Goldberg, Robert F. Kennedy, McGeorge Bundy, and William W. Scranton.

When the President looked at that shopping list in his morning *Times*, his reaction was about as expected. He had never thought of most of them as a replacement and as a matter of fact had Ambassador-at-large Ellsworth Bunker standing in the wings ready to go to Saigon when Lodge passed the final word that he was ready to come home.

At a news conference later, Johnson was asked: "Mr. President, there are reports that Ambassador Lodge would like to be relieved of his post and that you are looking for a successor. Is there any truth to these reports?"

With the *New York Times* story firmly in mind, Johnson replied:

> No, there is no truth that I am looking for a successor. Ambassador Lodge has talked to me on several occasions [and said] that he, in due time, would leave his post. He left it on one other occasion, took a rest and went back and served a tour of duty.
>
> There is no definite date set at this moment for his departure. I do expect to be visiting with Ambassador Lodge and with General Westmoreland, as we do from time to time. We will fully explore his future in Vietnam, or elsewhere, if he cares to do that.

A few days later, Lodge asked to be relieved and Bunker was appointed to succeed him. Lodge simply swapped jobs with Bunker, becoming Ambassador-at-large himself.

"Credibility gap!" the press exclaimed almost to a man, and in my briefing I was asked:

"George, could you explain the President's comment at last week's news conference that he was not looking for a successor? Did that mean he had already found one?"

I replied: "That means he already had a successor. Mr. Bunker had been his candidate to succeed Ambassador Lodge. As you know, Ambassador Lodge has indicated numerous times that he did want to return when he could."

Johnson stated the fact at his news conference the week before. I stated the fact at my briefing. When the press put the two together, however, the whole incident was listed as a prime example of White House lying, and much has been made of it in print. Bill McGaffin and Erwin Knoll wrote in *Anything But the Truth* that I had "smugly" explained to reporters that the President's news conference reply had been "absolutely accurate." Hugh Sidey of Time-Life was a little kinder in his book, *A Very Personal Presidency*. He wrote I had "sickly" explained. Regardless of whether I was smug or sick, Johnson did not lie to the press in his news conference, although we might be accused of reacting too bluntly to an incorrect news story which started it all. A softer answer would have saved us a lot of grief. But he was anxious to knock down the *Times* story with the words *no truth*.

Perhaps the President's most famous gaffe in a public speech was at Camp Stanley, Korea, during his first trip to Asia. He was in an army mess hall near the demilitarized zone and was visibly moved by the enthusiasm of the soldiers who cheered him. He spoke emotionally of his pride in the work they were doing for freedom, together with their brothers in Vietnam. Recalling Texas history and the part his family had played in it, he said: "My great-great grandfather died at the Alamo. There was the battle of San Jacinto or Texas wouldn't have had its independence."

The two sentences were rather disjointed, because as a matter of fact Johnson had no relative at the Alamo, but did have a great-great uncle at the battle of San Jacinto—John W. Bunton—who was one of the seven men who captured Mexican General Santa Anna. He had mentioned Bunton many times, and his ancestor's part at San Jacinto was commonly known in Texas. In the Camp Stanley speech he got his tongue twisted in the emotion of the moment.

When I told him what he had said, he denied it vigorously. "I said no such thing. I didn't have any grandfather at the Alamo." I told him I had heard him say it and that the press was going to have a field day with it, but still he refused to believe it, insisting that I listen to the tape of his speech.

Bob Baskin of the *Dallas News*, who was travelling with us, was the first to ask me about the statement. Later Richard Dudman of the *St. Louis Post-Dispatch*, which loved to needle Johnson, went to the Texas Historical Society research files to "expose" the President's embellishment of history.

We were back in Washington before Johnson was convinced he had made a misstatement. He admitted to reporters he had gotten carried away and said something he did not realize he had said.

At any rate, our low believability rating forced me as press secretary to be perhaps too cautious, and the President was concerned constantly about accusations against his truthfulness. He would say: "If we do that they'll claim later we were incredible," or, "Let's be careful not to be incredible about this."

I insisted to other members of the staff to keep me fully informed or risk constant trouble for the President, but occasionally the system broke down.

During the 1967 Governor's Conference on a ship en route to the Virgin Islands, the issue became one of support of the President's position on Vietnam. I denied to the press that Johnson had asked for a resolution supporting his war stance, and in this I was correct. I also told them the White House was not meddling in the fight, which I believed to be the fact but it was not quite.

Price Daniel, the President's liaison with the governors, was on the ship, and the press was convinced Daniel was hard at work twisting arms for the President. But Marvin Watson told me Daniel was keeping the controversy at bay, and merely furnishing whatever information was desired. Watson said neither Johnson nor he was calling the shots for Daniel.

Late at night I received two enraged telephone calls from Merriman Smith of UPI and Frank Cormier of AP. I had lied to them, they said. Governor Ronald Reagan of California had intercepted a cablegram from Watson to Daniel, advising Daniel on how to round up votes for the pro-Vietnam resolution.

I called Watson, and my report gave him what sounded on the telephone like a sinking spell. He told me that some of the Democratic governors had asked Daniels for copies of Vietnam resolutions passed at previous meetings, and that Daniel had relayed the request to him. Accordingly, he dug up the old resolutions and telegraphed them to the ship. Relieved that it was no more than that, I gave this information to Smith and Cormier, who agreed that perhaps I wasn't as big a liar as they first thought.

However, the story does not end there. At the end of the long cablegram transcribing the resolutions, Watson had added a couple of sentences pointing out that two Republican governors reportedly opposing the new proposal would be changing their previous positions. This bit of information for Daniel put the whole matter in the context of Presidential advice to his liaison, and the press duly reported this, with abundant help from Reagan's staff.

The press attacked me with a mixture of bitterness and delight at my morning briefing. I attacked Watson for getting me into the mess in the first place. The President . . . reacted.

In the meantime, much ado was being made on the ship about the purloined telegram, and Reagan was beginning to look something less than honorable. Poetic justice. But Johnson, of course, was now firmly believed to be calling all of the signals for his Democratic friends on the ship and begging for support of his Vietnam policies.

Later, I asked Daniel if the President had ever talked to him directly during the voyage or after they reached the Virgin Islands.

"Yes, he did," the former Texas governor admitted, grinning.

"What did he say?"

"He said, 'Keep up the good work'."

Some reporters wrote in the latter days that I had closed the credibility gap. Naturally, I was grateful for such items as the one by Pat Furgurson of the *Baltimore Sun:* "[He] came to Washington from Austin when Mr. Johnson's press relations were near an all-time low, and with deadpan straight talk lifted them so that now you can sit around the West Lobby all afternoon and not hear the words 'credibility gap'."

And then one day Max Frankel of the *Times* pointed out a paragraph in *Gulliver's Travels* which he said should be my swan song. In a letter from Captain Gulliver to his Cousin Sympson, he wrote:

> Do these miserable animals presume to think that I am so far degenerated as to defend my veracity? Yahoo as I am, it is well known . . . that by the instructions and examples of my illustrious master I was able in the compass of two years (although I confess with the utmost difficulty) to remove that infernal habit of lying, shuffling, deceiving and equivocating, so deeply rooted in the very souls of all my species.

III · *Irritants*

Credibility was not the only irritant between press and President.

The most constant grating effect, like hard chalk on a slick blackboard, concerned White House travel arrangements.

Whenever Johnson travelled any distance, a good-sized contingent of newsmen and technicians followed him on a chartered airplane. If he moved about Washington, the wire services and networks sought to dog his tracks even if it were only a visit to church or to a wedding. Camp David was off-limits to the press, but the wire services stationed reporters at Thurmont, Maryland, to be within immediate range if he ventured away from the camp.

All of this was expected and had been the habit of press coverage of the President for many years. But Lyndon Johnson early in his term earned a reputation for sudden decisions on travel plans, or at least sudden announcements to the hapless press which might not be fully prepared to go with him. As antiwar demonstrations increased, the custom became more entrenched, and the press more irritated. Contrary to popular belief, however, during my time we never took the press on an overnight trip without luggage.

As far as domestic travel was concerned, the newsmen put up with their inconveniences with resigned bitterness. However, on one of our last trips to New York the press office was given such short notice that the only transportation I could charter for the press was an ancient Air Force Convair even below the standards of the government aircraft we occasionally had to lease when it was too late to acquire a commercial plane. This particular Convair had faulty radar, which was bad enough, but to top it off the stewards served sardines fresh out of the can as the only supper for the travelling press.

From then on I could always get a rise out of Sid Davis, the Westinghouse correspondent who was particularly vocal about our preparations, by telling him I had arranged for a nice sardine dinner on our next coast-to-coast trip.

"Sardines we can live with, radar we can't," was his usual rejoinder.

An all-time low in press relations—and in the spirit of the press secretary—came on a trip to Montreal to see Expo 67 and a subsequent visit with Prime Minister Lester Pearson at his lakeside retreat near Ottawa. This was at the height of the pre-war Middle East tensions, and Johnson—already being pushed by U.S. Information Agency Director Leonard Marks to visit Expo—thought it would have a salutary effect on world tensions if he conferred with Pearson, a Middle East peacemaker of renown. But the two of them could not make satisfactory connections, there was the threat of a demonstration in Montreal and other complications. So Johnson decided late at night that he would not go. Instinctively, I did not release a press airplane we had chartered that evening, but I was convinced the trip was off. The next morning Johnson called me about six-thirty and said he was thinking about going, but would talk to Arthur Goldberg—then our United Nations ambassador—and study the Middle East intelligence reports before deciding.

Goldberg urged Johnson to go, Johnson decided he would and advised me after seven o'clock that we would leave about nine o'clock from Andrews Air Force Base. I started alerting my office girls, and they began calling the newsmen, but the last ones were not reached until only thirty minutes or so before departure. The scene at Andrews was one of a raging volcano. My assistant, Tom Johnson, and Carroll Kilpatrick of the *Washington Post* had bitter words, and throughout the day I had periodic clashes with irate newsmen who had battled rush-hour traffic to reach the airport on time and had inadequate facilities for filing stories in Canada.

I also got some complaints from the Prime Minister's aides, who said we were treating the Canadian government like some inferior lackey by rushing off to see Pearson without any prior arrangements and amenities.

All in all, it was a forgettable trip.

In terms of secrecy on arrangements, though, it could not compare with the President's trip around the world just before Christmas 1967.

When Prime Minister Harold Holt of Australia was lost at sea on a swimming excursion, Johnson decided immediately that he would attend the memorial service in Melbourne for his devoted friend. I announced this to the press and told them that while there might be further travel after Australia, there would be no advance notice. Naturally, everyone suspected Johnson would visit Vietnam, or at least Thailand, during his Pacific trip, and they understood the need for secrecy.

When we departed Melbourne after the service, the press did not know our next destination. It was Darwin, in the northern, tropical section of Australia, and if this were publicized, it would be obvious we were heading north toward the war zone. Harold Pachios, a former press office assistant who excelled at overseas trips, had been recruited to help me on this one and was on the press plane while Tom Johnson and I flew on Air Force One. Pachios, a dedicated young man and tough as an acorn, had been told the press was not to file any copy when we landed at Darwin.

Lo and behold, we were greeted at the Darwin airport by Australian newsmen, and our own advance party had thoughtfully provided cable facilities for the American press. All of Australia, and therefore the world, knew Lyndon Johnson was landing in Darwin—everyone but the White House press travelling with him.

Pachios, true to the end, told the press it could not file stories. They attempted to devour him. He radioed me, some three hundred yards away, and with great compassion I told him he could step aside while still alive and allow them to reach their filing facilities.

The pattern continued that night when we reached Korat, an air base of the Royal Thai Air Force. It was populated by a few Thai workers and hundreds of American planes and airmen, of course.

My assistant, Loyd Hackler, had flown in only three or four hours ahead of us, and had been unable in that length of time to arrange telephones or other facilities. We had decided we would not allow stories to be filed from Korat until our departure, to keep the Communists in doubt as to our whereabouts for as long as possible and therefore protect the President on his next stop: Cam Ranh Bay, Vietnam. Even at that, filing would be difficult due to inadequate facilities.

Hackler had arranged quarters for the press in a string of new brick officers' huts, and we were settling down for a few hours' sleep at about one o'clock in the morning when Erwin Knoll of Newhouse Newspapers informed me indignantly that Armed Forces Radio was broadcasting the fact of the President's presence at Korat. Sure enough, the world was now aware of our location, without help from the White House press. I learned later that enterprising wire service reporters in Bangkok, knowing Johnson was bound to be heading for Thailand, had called around to the airfields, asking, "Has the President arrived yet?" and an operator at Korat replied, "No, not yet."

I flushed the bedraggled press out of their huts and held a briefing in the sandy yard, while they stood around in various states of dress and undress raising unshirted hell at being scooped on their own story. Hackler said there were a few telephones in a headquarters building some distance away, so the reporters scrambled in that general direction. Some of them commandeered an army truck; they got there late and had to stand in line for a telephone. The wise ones struck out across field and stream, risking cobras lurking in the bushes and decapitation by clotheslines, but they got there first.

Fortunately, Jack Horner of the *Washington Star* got a clear connection to his paper, and when he was finished he allowed numerous other reporters to file their stories through his switchboard. That did a great deal for Horner's image, but not much for mine.

After Thailand and Vietnam, the trip grew even more hectic. The President had intended from the start to visit the Pope if he could do it without instigating a Communist riot in Rome. Although the Vatican visit had been rumored in the press, we had kept its possibility a tight secret.

The advance team from Washington had been dispatched only as far as Madrid, with orders to stay there unless it became certain Johnson could go to Rome in safety. When Air Force One struck out westward from Cam Ranh Bay and stopped for refueling in Pakistan, we imposed a clumsy press secrecy on our destination in hopes of confusing the Roman Reds who were sure Johnson would visit the Pope on Christmas Eve. This was one of the President's alternatives—to spend the night in Madrid, and then backtrack to Rome on December 24. The other alternative was to fly directly to Rome on December 23, see the Pope at night, and bypass Madrid entirely. The first alternative, of course, was just a feint to confuse Communist timing. It was sealed when Air Force One radioed the embassy in Madrid to reserve hotel rooms. So when Johnson landed in Rome on the night of December 23, hundreds of thousands of demonstrators were enjoying their wine and their intrigues, planning for the big bash on December 24.

Naturally, press facilities for covering the historic visit to the Vatican were negligible. Most of the newsmen who had flown around the world with the President cooled their heels at the airport while a press "pool" followed him in a rickety helicopter in the inky darkness. Advance arrangements were so limited, due to the secrecy, that the President's chopper was a military hand-me-down from Verona piloted by an officer unfamiliar with Rome.

The Vatican visit was a diplomatic success and Johnson was elated as he flew home to Washington in time for Christmas. But the four and a half day trip around the world was promptly dubbed by the press to be a fiasco, a circus, a Presidential whim. Even later, when the newsmen who made the trip had had time to mellow, it was deemed universally to be the prime example of mercurial decision-making by the President.

A *Newsweek* report from Rome, after our return to the United States, added insult to injury by reporting that the President's visit with the Pope was irritable and unhappy. Nothing could have been further from the truth, but denials by the Vatican and a call from Dean Rusk to the publisher were not sufficient to bring a retraction. By then, our believability rating was too low.

Regardless of the diplomatic success of a trip like this, or the political worth of a trip to Kentucky and West Virginia, uncertainty on the part of the press blunted the news coverage to some extent and caused relations with the newsmen to be chronically unstable. Some of this was unavoidable because of the times. Johnson also argued that he did not like to make definite decisions on travel until he was certain he could go, because cancellations for reasons not clearly obvious to the public created a crisis atmosphere when none existed. The press scoffed at his reasoning on this point.

Aware of the problem Johnson had had, President Nixon promptly instituted a policy of travel notification far in advance. It was a sound move for his press relations.

Near the administration's end, a former Johnson official circulated an excerpt from a twelfth century biography of Henry II, saying that it reminded him of a mutual friend. I quote it *in toto*:

If the king had promised to remain in a place for that day—and especially when he has announced his intention publicly by the mouth of a herald—he is sure to upset all the arrangements by departing early in the morning. As a result, you see men dashing around as if they were mad, beating their packhorses, running their carts into one another—in short, giving a lively imitation of Hell. If, on the other hand, the king orders an early start, he is certain to change his mind, and you can take it for granted that he will sleep until midday. Then you will see the packhorses loaded and waiting, the carts prepared, the courtiers dozing, traders fretting, and everyone grumbling. . . . When our couriers had gone ahead almost the whole day's ride, the king would turn aside some other place where he had, it might be, just a single house with accommodation for himself and no one else. I hardly dare say it, but I believe that in truth he took a delight in seeing what a fix he put us in.

There were other irritants between Johnson and the press.

For his part, he grew weary of their tracking him to church on Sunday, both in Washington and in Texas. He did not like the photographers "running over people" trying to take his picture at church, and he finally stopped telling the press office where he was going to church. When we were in Texas this caused a big chase through the hill country each Sunday—one he helped bring on himself by occasionally inviting stray reporters to the ranch for a cup of coffee if they happened to find him on Sunday morning. Sometimes he confused the press by going to church in out-of-the-way places like Cypress Mill, hideouts they never discovered.

When Johnson was at home he wanted to be left alone on his trips to Johnson City, Fredericksburg, and other nearby towns. He liked to be able to slip away to Austin to visit the Nugents or to Lake LBJ for a boat ride. The wire services maintained close surveillance on the ranch, despite the guarded roadways, and I discovered that they had learned to monitor the ranch radio network, a highly valuable method of keeping track of Johnson's movements.

One day late in the Administration, the President decided he would accompany Mrs. Johnson and Lynda on a brief flying trip from the ranch to East Texas, to visit some of his wife's relatives and watch her plant a tree in a family park. When I told him that it would be impossible for him to fly that far without telling the press and arranging for coverage and that they would be justifiably indignant if he tried it, he abandoned his plans with considerable irritation.

Mrs. Johnson and Lynda went ahead, and they had no sooner left than Helen Thomas of UPI called me to ask why they were going aboard their private airplane "with a tree." I was astounded that they were discovered so quickly, not knowing at the time that the radio waves were not sacred.*

Secrecy, deviousness, news management, misleading statements —all of these are like poison to the press and plague every Administration. Johnson's problems were compounded because he did not like premature disclosure of his plans and might change them if it occurred. This kept the press off balance and made their predictions risky; often they became poor prophets if they tried to anticipate what the President would do.

Contrary to popular opinion, we made no effort at massive news management. My sins were generally no worse than slipping out a touchy announcement at a time when it would be covered up by other news events, or get poor coverage because of my timing. I avoided difficult issues in my briefings if I possibly could, preferring to let the departments handle controversies. Most military questions were shunted to the Pentagon and most foreign policy questions to the State Department unless the President was involved in a specific action.

For nearly a year, it was shameful the way I avoided answering questions about the crew of the Pueblo, referring everything to

---

* Ironically, some newsmen suspected Johnson of "bugging" the news briefings in the press office. Sometimes the President would ring me on the POTUS line during a briefing, which heightened the suspicion. The truth is he lacked the time or inclination to listen in on briefings, although he did read the transcripts. John Pierson of the *Wall Street Journal* also charged that the press office had some secret arrangement with Western Union to snoop on reporters' copy filed during our Texas visits. This was ridiculous, but it was difficult to dispel such fantasies.

the State Department. The intent was to keep everything on the subject away from the White House; there was little or nothing we could say that would help matters.

One thing the press really resented was Johnson's penchant for correcting their mistakes. Because he monitored the AP and UPI tickers in his office, he spotted errors quickly and had me correct them if I could. Frequently I spotted them first and called the wire services on my own, but his practice was so well known that he was blamed for these calls, too. Occasionally Johnson called a newsman directly when an interpretation was especially bad, and it became a mark of distinction among the reporters to be chewed out by the President. Such happenings added to one's prestige as an independent reporter, untarnished by favoritism to the President or anyone else.

Irritations aside, Johnson had some credits with the press, especially the White House press. He could be generous of his time with them, and he always included them in social activities—state dinners and the like—on a personal basis. He occasionally walked into the press lobby between appointments just to say hello and tell a yarn, and he loved to joke with reporters when he carried them somewhere in his car or took a few of them walking.

The press in general had much affection for Lady Bird Johnson. If she ever treated any of them unkindly, I was unaware of it. Liz Carpenter's skill meshed perfectly with Mrs. Johnson's humanity and unassuming gentility. The girls were also reasonably popular with the women reporters who covered them.

Johnson had another advantage. Unlike Republican Presidents, he could be sure that most of the reporters were on his side politically.

The American reporters in Washington are mostly liberal Democrats. Some were bitten by the Kennedy bug in 1960, accepted his martyrdom in 1963, and longed for him every day after that. Some admired Johnson for his ability and his basic philosophy. Some may have resented these qualities because they disliked giving him credit for anything. But some were blatantly pro-Johnson, not only and not necessarily because they liked him but because they saw in him a national purpose in which they believed.

As Johnson's days played out, many in the press began to get sentimental.

Art Buchwald, who used his sure little penknife on the President and everyone else, wrote a column on how Johnson's enemies of the year before were changing their tune. After relating how they had decided he had more strengths than faults, stood for important issues, had a nice free-wheeling style and a good family, Buchwald said he began to choke up and cried, "I don't want him to go."

On January 17, three days before he was to leave the White House, Johnson went dutifully to the National Press Club to talk to his old antagonists. He was well prepared with pertinent one-liners.

He said quietly that he wanted to acknowledge the close and frank relationship between press and President. "You were frank, and I was close."

He said he understood the press had complained about the way he treated them, but "why didn't you mention it sooner?"

He had his own complaints because the press misquoted him on occasion. Remember the Peter Hurd painting? "I never said it was ugly. I thought it was a pretty good likeness except for one little detail. He left out the halo."

As for his credibility gaffe on grandpa at the Alamo, the press "didn't let me explain . . . it was at the Alamo Hotel, in Eagle Pass, Texas."

A memorable picture of Johnson depicted him showing his scar after an operation. Said the President: "You all criticized me for showing my scar. That was only after a question from Sarah McClendon. I remember her popping up from the bushes and asking, 'You've been in office for almost two years, and what do you have to show for it?' "

As for his many other friends in the press, the President commented: "Today, all is forgotten. I have never doubted your energy or your courage or your patriotism. That is why I asked General Hershey to get in touch immediately with each of you."

It was a fitting climax to what he himself called "a lover's quarrel."

For while Lyndon Johnson was seldom happy with them, he would have been miserable without them.

SIX

I · *Passing the Torch, Deftly*

The Presidential Transition Act of 1963 states: "The national interest requires that such transitions in the office of the President be accomplished so as to assure continuity in the faithful execution of the laws and in the conduct of the affairs of the Federal government, both domestic and foreign."

President Johnson took this quite seriously, and shortly after the party conventions he set in motion the procedures for vacating office in an orderly manner. To oversee the operation he selected Charles S. Murphy, a former Truman aide and recently resigned chairman of the Civil Aeronautics Board.

Murphy, a laconic, fifty-nine-year-old North Carolina lawyer, had been in and around the bureaucracy for twenty years and knew that a good part of a successful transition was pure nuts and bolts. Transition to Humphrey would be easy. Transition to

Nixon would be more difficult; for the incoming Republicans would have a hazy view of the government establishment, at best. As early as September, two months before the election, Murphy knuckled down to his task. At the President's request, Humphrey, Nixon, and George Wallace designated individuals to work with Murphy. It was all rather academic, of course, until November 5.

Johnson's principal concern was not that the transition would be anything but smooth. For his part, he would see that it was, and it was unlikely that an incoming President would reject an open-handed offer of assistance and cooperation. He worried instead that his Administration—so keyed up with Great Society programs that it was difficult to tune down—would act like a petulant ass if Nixon were elected, and set out to embarrass the President-elect.

Long before the election, we began to pass the word to the government and the press that the Administration would make no dramatic new domestic moves unless they were absolutely necessary. The President did not want to limit the options of his successor, whoever he might be. In early October, Johnson instructed Budget Director Charles Zwick to formalize this in a memorandum to all agencies. The mandate was directed especially against "unusual one-time actions which are unnecessary, avoidable, or postponable, or which might prejudice the new Administration's plans or actions."

A number of plans and programs in the agencies, some of them dealing with reorganization, were in the works when the edict was issued. Most died aborning. One which enjoyed longer life was a major reorganization within the Labor Department which had been under study for several months, without the knowledge of the President, and which was worked out before Zwick sent his memorandum.

The story actually began in late 1967 when Johnson met with the nation's governors in an effort to establish better relations with the states. One of his pledges was that there would be no major reorganization or realignment of the Federal agencies which would affect the states unless the governors were consulted in advance.

One of the bones of contention was the employment service, administered by the states under Labor Department guidelines. Efforts to standardize these state programs and to bring them under closer Federal control had been bitterly resisted for years.

Not long after the meeting with the governors, discussions on Labor Department reorganization were begun. The principals were Secretary Willard Wirtz, Undersecretary Jim Reynolds, Joe Califano and Jim Gaither of the White House, and officials of the Bureau of the Budget. The discussions related especially to Assistant Secretary Stanley Ruttenberg's manpower administration. The reorganization plan would change substantially the way states operated their employment service programs.

While Labor Department officials talked with several state authorities known to be friendly to reorganization, the National Governors Conference was not consulted.

Wirtz later contended he had the authority to reorganize the department without Presidential approval. Be that as it may, on October 12, Califano sent the President a memorandum on the plan and asked for his approval. Johnson rejected it.

A few days later Califano tried again and asked that the President let Reynolds explain to him the necessity of the plan. For the second time Johnson turned it down, without seeing Reynolds.

On October 21 Wirtz announced the reorganization plan. Califano and Gaither were caught off guard and learned about it from the *Washington Post*. Johnson called Reynolds, who acknowledged that he had received the President's rejection from Califano and had understood it clearly. Reynolds added, however, that Secretary Wirtz had ordered the action taken anyway.

When Johnson confronted Wirtz face to face in a private meeting in the Cabinet Room, the Secretary at first contended the answers he received from the White House on the issue were "indirect, mixed up, and confused." Regardless, he added, he had authority to take action without Presidential approval and had sent the plan to the White House only in order that Johnson could get the credit for the reorganization.

The President said the action violated not only his agreement with the governors to consult with them, but his "loud and clear" directive that he wanted no major changes in the departments at the end of his Administration. He told Wirtz that messages of protest from various governors were already coming in and that Governor Ellington of Tennessee, chairman of the National Governors Conference, had urged Johnson to rescind the order until the governors could be consulted.

The question, Johnson said, was "how do we get back where we were before October 21?" He added grimly, "I don't care how this is corrected, but I want it done."

Wirtz did not blink. "I have taken action that cannot be overruled," he said, explaining that the Bureau of Employment Security would be destroyed if the states could overrule the Secretary of Labor.

"The state people are not overruling anything," Johnson retorted. "The President is the one with the authority, and I disapprove. I am not going to have this stand. You will have to work it out."

And again Wirtz refused: "I am not prepared to issue a different order."

"I am—to you or to someone else," the President said, adding that he did not want something like this "in the twilight of my Administration" and that the Labor Department could put the blame on him for disapproving the reorganization.

For the third time Wirtz declined.

Now it was a battle of wills as they stared across the Cabinet table at one another, a hard-headed but sensitive Labor Secretary who thought he was right, and a hard-headed President who was not debating the merits but felt he had been wronged.

"You cannot do what the President said not to do," Johnson said firmly. "I want you to carry out my instruction. If you refuse to, then I will get someone who can and will."

"I will not be able to take action to countermand what I have done."

"Does that mean you resign?"

"I will not make further comment."

"I want this done or your resignation."

"It will not be forthcoming."

"I want this done. You carry it out, you designate someone to carry it out, or then I want your resignation."

"My position won't change."

"You can't have a government where the President's orders are not carried out. I want them carried out or your resignation."

"You technically have it, don't you? Don't you have a letter of resignation I submitted when I came into office?"

"I don't know. If so, it is accepted. If not, I hope you will send me one."

"You have the right to remove me."

"I don't want to remove anyone. I just want my orders carried out. There are those who think you have been trying to put yourself in a position to be removed for some time."

"I hope you know that is not true."

The reference was to Wirtz' views on Vietnam, which in recent months he had not been shy about expressing. His vocal opposition to the war led Johnson to believe he was trying to force the President to remove him, in order to demonstrate a breakdown within the Administration.

"I don't know," the President said. "I just know I want my orders carried out. If you can't do it, I'll get someone who can."

"My position won't change. You have my letter of resignation if you want it."

"If I do, it's accepted. If I don't, I hope I'll have one later today."

Abruptly, the President got up and left the room. It was the worst flare-up he had ever had with a Cabinet officer, or probably with any other subordinate. He was left with a predicament over what to do with a man who would not obey his orders but would not resign.

Later in the day, however, Wirtz changed his mind and sent a formal resignation to the White House. It noted briefly that he had issued an order which the President asked him to retract. Since he did not feel he could retract the order, he had decided to resign.

Now Johnson began to grow concerned about the effect of the blow-up on the Humphrey campaign. At the President's request, both Clark Clifford and Deputy Attorney General Warren Christopher talked to Wirtz, urging him to retract the order and withdraw his letter of resignation rather than damage Humphrey.

Finally, late in the day of October 24, Wirtz capitulated. He requested that his letter of resignation be returned, and he rescinded the October 21 order. Governor Ellington was advised that the status quo would be maintained and that Wirtz would be glad to meet with the governors on the reorganization plan.

Johnson and Wirtz never discussed the matter again. Wirtz told several friends that he had taken the action only to avoid harm to Humphrey, and that he intended to resign immediately after the November 5 election. He did not, and the reorganization order was never reinstated.

Newsmen did not learn of the dispute until after Johnson left office. Then Wirtz confirmed that he had tried to resign.

At the last meeting of the Cabinet in January, the relationship between Johnson and Wirtz warmed somewhat when the Labor Secretary noted that discontent in the nation had risen largely from the fact "that in the last five years it has been discovered that this country can do anything that it sets out to do."

He recalled that once a member of the Cabinet had told Johnson, "I am not sure we can do that," and the President replied, " 'Can do,' the only two words that I know much of anything about." Wirtz went on to say: "I believe it is true that in your personal capacity you have contributed more to arousing this country to a sense of its human capacity and to a clarity about the human purpose than anybody else has ever done. Therefore, I am grateful."

Some of Wirtz' troubles with the White House may have emanated from his antipathy toward Joe Califano, the Presidential assistant assigned to serve as liaison with the Labor Department.

Wirtz disliked taking orders from anyone in the White House except the President himself.

The Secretary of Housing and Urban Development, Robert Weaver, had a similar relationship with Califano's staff, but serious disputes were avoided and Weaver finally departed a few weeks before January 20, giving Johnson the opportunity to elevate his deputy, Bob Wood, to Cabinet status.

Richard Nixon accused Johnson during the campaign of having only "yes men" around him. This was a strange charge, in view of the independent nature of several of the Cabinet officers.

Most independent of all was Attorney General Ramsey Clark. If he thought he was right, no one could persuade him to change his position, up to and including the President. Clark merely overlooked White House objection to some of his decisions and went on his merry way. Had Johnson not been completing his term, I have little doubt that these two strong-willed Texans would have had a bitter clash.

Alan Boyd, the able, no-nonsense Secretary of Transportation, did not always see eye to eye with the White House but remained one of the President's closer friends in the Cabinet. Orville Freeman, who served the full eight years of the Kennedy and Johnson Administrations, took a great deal of heat on the farm program, fought back like a bear, and had the President's full confidence. "That guy had half his jaw shot off at Bougainville, and it didn't take any of the fight out of him," Johnson said admiringly.

Postmaster General Marvin Watson and Commerce Secretary C. R. Smith were conservative-minded Texans who never exhibited anything less than the trait Johnson admired the most: unbending loyalty. Former Sergeant Watson of the Marines and former Major General Smith of the Army Air Forces knew how to follow the leader.

Wilbur Cohen kept his lines to the White House open and jangling. He and Douglass Cater had a close relationship, and he won the President's ear any time he needed it. The irrepressible Secretary of Health, Education, and Welfare had the advantage of talking Johnson's language: more and better services for the poor, the uneducated, the ill, and the hungry. A wit as well as a worker, Cohen once told his Cabinet colleagues: "We're not interested in helping people from the cradle to the grave. We're going to help them from conception to resurrection."

Late in the Administration, Cohen plugged for several programs which some interpreted as contradicting the President's order against major proposals. His favorite was called Kiddiecare which would extend medical aid to expectant mothers and small children. He also wanted a Social Security increase and other refinements of Great Society programs. Johnson whittled down his requests, but gently. He was happy to work with Cohen on modest programs that would plant acorns for great oak trees of the future. Cohen had a few acorns he wanted to plant before the Republicans came to power.

Interior Secretary Stewart Udall had an acorn, too, but it would not be planted quite as he had hoped.

Some months before January 20, Udall submitted to Johnson a proposal that seven and a half million acres of government-owned lands in Alaska, Arizona, and Utah be added to the national park system, thereby protecting them from encroachment. Johnson was concerned about the ambitious idea at the time, believing it to be a precipitous move by a President about to leave office, although he favored protecting the land. I was one of several assistants who expressed opposition to the move, arguing that the President had been warning Cabinet officers against revolutionary decisions, and his credibility would be attacked if he himself took action of such magnitude without Congressional action.

Johnson put the matter aside, but later expressed greater interest and told Udall to brief appropriate Congressional leaders on the plan and get their reaction. House Interior Committee Chairman Wayne Aspinall of Colorado was already known to be against the whole idea as a matter of principle.

On the Friday before Inauguration Day, Interior Department press officer Charles Boatner alerted the press that an announcement would be made on Saturday. Interior reporters were already familiar with Udall's proposal and were expecting a Presidential decision. Udall had received word from the White House that the President would see him at midday Saturday for a final decision. He had no doubt that Johnson would go along with the entire plan, so the wheels were greased at Interior.

As it turned out, they were far from greased at the White House.

Udall had failed to do his Congressional homework, and Aspinall especially remained outspoken against Presidential action. Furthermore, Udall had met with the District of Columbia Armory Board and renamed D.C. Stadium, home of the Washington Senators baseball team and the Washington Redskins football team, after the late Robert F. Kennedy. The Interior Secretary did not consult Johnson on the matter of honoring his most vocal political foe two days before a Republican President was to take office. Predictably, Republican complaints bloomed quickly as news of the surprise action got around.

On Saturday afternoon—with Udall still awaiting his conference with the President—the Interior Department announced that Johnson had signed orders under authority of the Antiquities Act to create four new national monuments and enlarge three others. Udall ordered the announcement, yet the fact was that the President had neither signed the orders nor indicated final approval of the move.

Johnson, already badly harassed that Saturday trying to wind up his business, was astonished to read the news ticker stories on the national monuments and on Robert F. Kennedy Stadium. He had no power over the naming of the stadium, but he did on the park lands. He called Udall and ordered him to retract the announcement about the national monuments; he had taken no action, the premature release of the story was outrageous, he would not react to such pressure. Udall was angry, then depressed. He offered to resign. Later he told a White House aide, "I'm fed up."

Udall retracted the news story and made no public statement about the controversy. On Sunday the President, cooled off somewhat, looked over the proposal again with his assistant, DeVier Pierson. Udall was reportedly on a hike, probably getting his own blood pressure in balance.

It was not until Monday morning, only minutes before the Inauguration, that Johnson signed orders committing three hundred and eighty-four thousand five hundred acres of land to the park system. This was quite a comedown from seven and a half million acres. It took no great ingenuity for the press to uncover the split between the conservation-minded Secretary and the conservation-minded President; while Udall tried to defend himself, he did attempt to play down the dispute. He could never explain, however, why the Interior Department made a public announcement of an action that had not taken place.

Perhaps the person most regretful about it all was Lady Bird Johnson, who carried Udall's banner to the four corners of the land, and had helped focus public attention on conservation and beautification as in no other Administration since Theodore Roosevelt's.

The Wirtz and Udall difficulties within the official family were probably no more severe than similar controversies in other Presidencies. But they were rasping notes in the orchestration of an orderly departure of one President and the orderly investiture of another. Wirtz issued his reorganization order against the President's wishes because he thought Johnson would have to swallow it. Udall simply got weary of the Presidential delay on his proposal and apparently believed Johnson would have to go along with it once it was announced publicly. Both were cut down for misjudging the man who was still their superior, lame duck or not. The complicating factor was that there was already an element of resentment and disagreement between the President and both.

Halfway between the two incidents, Johnson personally lectured the Cabinet against revolutionizing the government structure with major reorganizations or adopting new policies "which would be thus forced on the new Administration." To bind the hands of the Nixon Administration, he declared, "is neither desirable nor equitable."

The President said: "We have had five wonderful and productive years. Let's all take care that in this last month, we do not diminish our contribution by rash, eleventh-hour actions carrying consequences which have not been carefully considered at all levels of government, by all affected departments and by the President."

But the longer Richard Nixon delayed on announcing his Cabinet appointments, the more restive some of the Johnson Cabinet became.

At least two, Alan Boyd and Wilbur Cohen, told reporters they were thinking about going ahead with some administrative changes without waiting on the Republicans. And Cohen was happily readying his Congressional package, calling for expansion of Medicare and other programs. He met with Wilbur Mills, chairman of the House Ways and Means Committee, and persuaded him to introduce the Kiddiecare and Social Security bills. Cohen also wanted the Congress to overhaul the welfare system and establish national standards for welfare payments, in an effort to stem the migration of the poor from the rural South to the urban areas. Since Spiro T. Agnew had endorsed this idea as governor of Maryland, Cohen called this "the Agnew-Cohen Plan."

The first Nixon representatives to visit the White House after the election had little authority to do more than take a few notes and get a house plan.

The Johnson staff made it known that everyone was willing to help, but did not want to be pushy. Charlie Murphy said it had been his experience that new men often did not want as much help as old men wanted to give, perhaps because they thought most of it would be worthless advice. "Let them feel their way at their own pace," Murphy counseled.

The President made available to the President-elect an extensive suite of offices across Pennsylvania Avenue from the White

House, but while Nixon's aides made limited use of the space, Nixon preferred to keep his headquarters in the Hotel Pierre in New York City.

In November he was beginning a groping process, trying to fit square pegs into square holes in building a staff and a Cabinet. Aside from John Mitchell, who was to become his Attorney General, he professed to have no close aide during his first visit to Johnson on November 11.

Dean Rusk and Clark Clifford urged him to select his Secretaries of State and Defense promptly, and have them sitting in on departmental meetings at least by mid-December. "They will need every day to prepare themselves," Clifford said. Rusk also reminded him there were two hundred and fifty Presidential appointees in the State Department, all of whom would be resigning.

The real partisans in the Nixon camp obviously relished the prospect of numerous appointive positions in the government, but as a practical matter the Republicans discovered early that most slots would be difficult to fill.

With much fanfare a "talent search" was launched by mail. The thousands of letters that went out, seeking advice on prospects, and asking if the recipient himself might possibly be interested in government service, were the result of mailing lists built from a number of sources, including *Who's Who*.

"Mr. L. Johnson, 1600 Pennsylvania Ave., Washington, D.C." dutifully received his bid in the mail. He did not reply.

In some respects the Johnson-Nixon transfer of power was similar to the main street in any American city; the store fronts look respectable enough, but wait till you see the alley.

The trappings, the formalities, the nuts and bolts brought few problems. When Nixon finally named his Cabinet, their counterparts in the Johnson Administration gave a glittering reception for the newcomers. The briefing books were well prepared and departmental doors were opened to any and all Nixon appointees. Robert Murphy performed ably as Nixon's national security liaison until William Rogers and Melvin Laird were appointed to head the State and Defense Departments. On their first day together, Lady Bird Johnson and Pat Nixon got along well. "She is a nice, serious woman," was the comment later by the incumbent First Lady.

The two principals also hit it off when they got together twice in November and December. Nixon was frank about his shortage of trusted personnel waiting in the wings for Presidential assignments. Johnson was open handed, almost exuberant, in his desire to be helpful. Nixon seemed to know little about the actual operation of the White House, and if he had ever seen the living quarters on the second floor he did not show it. For a President who had bedroom conferences with his Vice President, this came as a surprise.

Most important of all, as Johnson said afterwards, "We're pretty much together on foreign policy."

For the Vice President-elect, Johnson had open arms, a bit of advice, and an unexpected public presentation.

Spiro Agnew came to the White House late one afternoon before Thanksgiving Day. The President was a few minutes late returning to the office after his nap, so he had Tom Johnson show the Maryland governor around the West Wing. Agnew seemed reserved and subdued; the attacks he received during the campaign had wounded him, and he showed it. "It's disgraceful what the Democrats did to him," Johnson told Hubert Humphrey earlier in the day. Humphrey, just returned from a post-election rest in the Virgin Islands, agreed it had been rather cruel.

In the President's Little Office, a cozy sitting room adjoining the Oval Office, Johnson showed Agnew his montage of inscribed photographs of previous Presidents and repeated a monologue he had spoken many times.

You think we've got hell. Think of what some of them went through. They said Hoover caused the economic collapse of the country, when he was not responsible at all. He was one of the best men of his time. They said Roosevelt was a dictator, and they spread all kinds of dirty stories about him. They said

Truman was an ignorant little haberdasher who couldn't even keep his business going in Kansas City. They said Eisenhower didn't know what was going on . . . that Sherman Adams ran everything . . . when really Eisenhower was one of the most brilliant men we had.

So Lyndon Johnson, whose tongue had slipped a time or two in his career and who was called a baby killer by some of America's leading intellectuals, tried the best he knew how to salve the feelings of the next Vice President, who had seen one slum and spoken in jest to an overweight Japanese.

When the press was called into the Oval Office to learn about their meeting, Agnew told them: "I primarily came to seek the counsel of a man I have always admired and respected."

Johnson took him to the East Room to a gathering of veterans' organizations where the President was to speak, and they stood side by side on the platform while the crowd applauded vigorously. "In January there will be a President who is a veteran and a Vice President who is a veteran," Johnson ad libbed, "and both the outgoing President and the outgoing Vice President will be working with them to try to pay due honor and see that justice is done to all the veterans of this country."

Johnson worked mightily to avoid any hint of criticism of his successor. Even during the widely publicized dispute following their first meeting when Nixon said he would share responsibility with the President on major foreign policy decisions, Johnson tried to calm the flare-up with a minimum of damage to their relationship.

In late November when Johnson issued a ringing call for continued progress in civil rights, during a speech to the National Urban League in New York, the press interpreted some of his remarks as criticism of Nixon.

Johnson was shocked when the *New York Times* said he had "indirectly challenged" Nixon to match his civil rights record and had engaged in "indirect criticism" of Nixon's economic policies. This was not the President's intent; the speech was a challenge to Negroes to keep working for equality and a promise that "I shall remain joined with you in fighting for that right to opportunity."

He talked of Negro unemployment, low income, and ghetto life, and declared: "So, it is true, we have come a long way. We had made a lot of verbal commitments. We have even changed a great many lives already for the better. But we are nowhere, nowhere in sight of where we must be before we can rest."

To interpret such comments as a poke at Nixon—as several commentators did—was astonishing to the White House.

Johnson's attitude toward the changing of the guard was expressed aptly in a speech to the prestigious Business Council in early December. He drew a word picture of an airliner flying through a storm, with "black, cold clouds rolling all around," and two hundred million passengers worrying whether the pilot has enough skill to bring it through safely.

"Some of us will claw at him and some of us will pull his ear and some of us will cuss him and some of us will tell him that he has a credibility gap and some of us will give him hell and some of us will knock him on the head and work on his co-pilot at the same time," Johnson related the fable, scarcely drawing a breath, and illustrating by clawing with his hand, pulling his ear, and slamming fist into hand.

Then, in a low and deliberate tone, he said: "If he goes down in that plane, we all go down with him . . . so if you ask me what you can do as a passenger in that plane, I say this: Sit there and try to find ways to help that pilot get that plane through those storms . . . and on the ground with a minimum of division."

The United States cannot long endure, he concluded, "the divisiveness that we have all over our nation."

Richard Nixon paid his second visit to the White House on December 12, ten minutes behind schedule because of the rush hour traffic in late afternoon. He and Johnson went straight to the Oval Office for two hours of talk about housekeeping, part of it concerning Johnson's needs in Texas as an ex-President and his plans for the Lyndon B. Johnson School of Public Affairs. By now

Nixon had assembled most of his staff, and the Johnson aides entertained their successors with cocktails in the White House Mess. It was stiffly formal for the two staffs at first, but after two or three drinks had flowed the conversations brightened.

Johnson and Nixon concluded their talks and went to the second floor to meet their wives. Ron Ziegler and I joined them there. We were filled in only sketchily for our news briefing; the Johnsons were in a hurry to attend a reception in their honor at the Kuwaiti Embassy. They said their goodbyes to the Nixons on the second floor, inviting their guests to wait there until Ziegler and I completed our briefing so the entire party could depart. Their daughter Tricia joined them, and for twenty minutes or so the soon-to-be First Family sat alone in the living quarters of the soon-to-depart First Family. I have often imagined them there, surrounded by the books, pictures, and keepsakes of one President and the ghosts of many others, perhaps a little overwhelmed by what they would soon inherit.

II · *Meanwhile, in the Alley . . .*

"The grace with which Lyndon Johnson is handing over the reins is admirable in every respect, but particularly in terms of the gargantuan anguish which it nobly conceals," wrote columnist Charles Bartlett, who surmised that leaving must be doubly hard for "this looming, pervasive force."

But Bartlett compared the agreeable atmosphere of the transition with "the placid slope of a rumbling volcano . . . the strains are there but they are held beneath the surface by the enormous control which Johnson characteristically exerts in crisis."

And so it was in those final weeks, as Johnson pushed and Nixon resisted, pitting declining muscle against gathering power.

Nixon had helped get the South Vietnamese to the negotiating table in Paris. He would help later in resolving the dispute there on the standing of the delegations, by intervening to persuade

President Thieu to accept Johnson's compromise on the shape of the table to be used.

But Thieu's elaborate overtures to the incoming Administration and the shadowy maneuverings of Mrs. Anna Chennault had left a bruise on the Johnson Administration. What Nixon told Saigon meant far more to them than Johnson's messages.

It was obvious that Nixon wanted every option open in foreign policy, a natural inclination.

Military arms talks with the Russians—postponed by the invasion of Czechoslovakia in August—could have begun in the period between the election and inauguration. The Russians were ready, but Nixon was not. He and Johnson could have attended a summit together—a rare and heartening show of unity before the world. But summit meeting aside, lower-level talks between the two countries could have begun. They did not, leaving those who opposed the arms race frustrated and waiting, for an indefinite period.

The nuclear nonproliferation treaty, a hallmark of the Johnson Administration, lay dormant for months, while two of the nonsigners—beleaguered Israel and Soviet-threatened West Germany, each quite capable of developing nuclear weapons—had ample excuse to dally while waiting on the United States.

America's one bit of leverage on Israel—the supersonic jet fighters which had been committed but not delivered—played out during the treaty delay, and Johnson ordered the State Department to go ahead and negotiate the trade.

On the domestic side, Johnson's most crucial decision concerned the income tax surcharge.

The law requires an outgoing President to submit a budget to the Congress, because only his Administration has the mechanism and the inordinate amount of time to conduct the hearings and prepare the appropriation requests.

So in late 1968 the President faced his customary problem: a budget nearing two hundred billion dollars, a chunk of mandatory increases such as Social Security improvements already voted, more demands from the military, more demands for the Great Society, demands in the Congress for cutbacks in spending, the economic danger of a large budget deficit, and the surtax—enacted to check inflation and balance the budget—due to expire in 1969.

With judicious trimming, there could be a small budget surplus without continuing the surtax. But that would harm domestic programs which deserved more funding, and deprive the space program of additional money.

Nixon had come out against the surtax in the campaign. With that in mind, a sensible course for Johnson seemed apparent, if painful. Congressmen Wilbur Mills of Ways and Means and George Mahon of Appropriations had told him Congress would never extend the tax unless Nixon wanted it. As Johnson expressed it to newsmen, "Congress won't increase taxes unless you whip them."

At one point the President mused: "The question is whether the outgoing President, who is up there singing his little swan song and saying goodbye, ought to start a fight over the tax bill by saying, 'I think we ought to have more taxes.' In comes the President-elect, saying, 'I don't think we ought to tax and tax and spend and spend.'"

If Nixon did not change his mind, Johnson decided, "it will please a lot of Republicans, and it will really hurt a lot of people."

In December, Johnson began the practice of inviting Nixon's newly designated Cabinet officers to the White House for private visits. When he was at the ranch over the New Year's holiday, Treasury Secretary-designate David Kennedy flew to Texas, and Johnson laid the tax problem on the line. The President said he would not ask the Congress to extend the surtax unless Nixon said he would not oppose the recommendation. He told Kennedy the tax was needed, and the Chicago banker agreed. Now the job was to sell Nixon.

On January 6, the President held his last breakfast meeting of the Democratic Congressional leaders. One of the old regulars was missing; Senator Russell Long had been unseated as whip by young Senator Edward Kennedy of Massachusetts. But the fare was the same as always, thankfully: baked eggs and scrambled eggs, juicy sausage patties, thick bacon, toast, and sweet rolls. We stuffed ourselves and worried about the poor folks who would suffer if the budget were cut.

"I don't want to recommend that the Democrats pass the tax if he won't ask his people to pass it," Johnson said of Nixon.

One by one, the leaders labeled it a hopeless cause. Why cut up the Democrats if the Republicans were going to be heroes by opposing high taxes?

Ted Kennedy "passed" the first time Johnson asked him his view. As the newest leader, he wanted to hear all of the arguments. The second time around, he expressed himself—in a rather rambling and inarticulate manner, but the implication was clear. He did not want to let Nixon off the hook. He hoped the President would find some middle way that the President-elect could support. If Democratic programs were going to be scuttled, he did not want Democrats to do the dirty work.

Johnson nodded and peered at him through his glasses. I thought it was a look of satisfaction. He had wanted someone to speak out for what he, the President, wanted to do. He still thought there was some jockeying room with Nixon.

After Kennedy's little speech, several of the other leaders opined that they, too, believed something might be worked out. Later in the day, Kennedy sent the President a note. He said he had had more time to reflect on the issue and wanted to clarify his position. He thought the surtax should be retained, and the President and the Democrats should fight for it.

Over the next few days, White House liberals stepped up their campaign with the President for a strong recommendation in the State of the Union message for retention of the surtax, thereby enabling a beefier budget. Liberals in the Congress were advocating a similar line. Johnson remained noncommittal; he even argued the other side. It was his usual method of operation—get everyone he could to urge what he wanted to do anyway, because then he might have the clout to bring it off.

Finally, word came from Nixon that he would go along. David

Kennedy and others close to the economic situation had persuaded him that the surtax was advisable until the new Administration had its chance to tackle the budget.

The President's State of the Union address to the Congress was scheduled for Tuesday night, January 14.

"Is there anything special you want me to tell the press this morning?" I asked him in his bedroom on the morning of January 13. He was propped up in bed, reading the newspapers.

"You can tell them you expect I will recommend the surtax in order to have a surplus in fiscal 1970," he said casually.

"Okay," I said.

The next evening, when Johnson made the formal recommendation to the Congress, the Nixon headquarters in New York issued a pre-prepared statement saying that the President-elect had always contended that the surtax should expire when budget and economic conditions permitted, which was a view shared by President Johnson. However, until the new Administration and the Congress could "ascertain the facts" that would justify abandoning the tax or reducing it, Nixon "will support President Johnson's recommendation that the surtax be continued."

The winter war on taxes was over, and lame duck Johnson had won a hard-earned victory.

Abe Fortas had fallen, and several other judicial appointments —including an appellate judgeship for White House aide Barefoot Sanders—had been held up by the Republicans until they died on the vine. And on the really important issues of international relations, Nixon held the hammer. But the budget was Johnson's and the Great Society banner would fly from the mainmast, Republican campaign promises notwithstanding.

III · "I Tried"

On November 22, the fifth anniversary of the Johnson Presidency, Major Hugh Robinson of the military staff carried a wreath to Arlington National Cemetery to place on John Kennedy's grave in behalf of the President. The Johnsons observed the anniversary by conducting, for the first time in the White House, a naturalization ceremony for new citizens.

Into the East Room they crowded, young and old, subdued by the grandeur of the occasion but proud and self-controlled. There was an eight-year-old girl from the Philippines and a seventy-two-year-old Chinese laundry worker, a beautician, a cab driver, a surgeon. The special guests for the ceremony included six members of the White House staff who were naturalized citizens. The room was set up as a court, for this was a legal proceeding transferred for one day to the house of Presidents.

It was an emotional morning. In an eloquent statement to the immigrants, Lilla Burt Cummings of the District of Columbia Bar Association reminded them that their new country "is something more than a nation—it is a vision—shimmering, bountiful, immeasurably spiritual—a vision of the perfectability of man and of the society he can create under freedom."

Despite all of America's troubles, she said, "still they come, by the hundreds of thousands, and still they come, bringing to us in these troubled times an historical perspective—the dream has not tarnished, the vision has not dimmed." She urged patience with America, "with this democracy as it reorders itself along new lines of vision. . . . It is the most creative, the most beautiful, even amid its convulsions, and the most worthy of reverence for it represents man in his highest aspiration."

Lyndon Johnson never doubted for a minute that his five years furthered the cause of man in his highest aspiration.

"It has been a marvelous period," he told a reporter on November 22, speaking of his own feelings about serving as President. "Perhaps we made a mistake in trying to go too far too fast, trying to do too much too soon, trying to correct the evils that have grown up over a century and to remake America overnight. I don't know. I hope not, for America's sake. But history will tell."

A major Johnson decision now was how to exit gracefully in terms of a final report to the Congress that had given him most of what he asked.

There were some around the President who wanted him to lay out a thorough program for the future—something for the Democratic majority to chew on, and an alternative to whatever Nixon proposed after January 20. Harry Truman had made his swan song a call for Democratic programs. Many liberals in Congress and in the Administration hoped Johnson would do the same. There was press speculation that Johnson would do just this; it was too great a temptation, according to this reasoning, for him not to stage one last grandstand play that would end his term with a proper bang.

Johnson chose instead to build his State of the Union report around national commitments as he saw them—nothing really dramatically new, nothing to tie the new Administration's hands too tightly, but a reminder to Richard Nixon and the country that the vision should not become tarnished, nor dimmed.

Long hours were spent in November and December with Budget Director Charles Zwick, various other officials, and White House aides led by Joe Califano and Larry Levinson. Agency ideas were in the hopper. Now was the time to scrape off the cream, and to make the budget fit the most compelling needs.

There were long trips for the President's girls. Mrs. Johnson went on a "last hurrah" tour to the Pacific Northwest to trumpet the cause of conservation. Luci and son Lyn made a quick visit to Honolulu to see Pat Nugent, on rest and recreation leave from Vietnam, and a short time later Lynda was off to Bangkok for a reunion with Major Chuck Robb.

For the President, there was only one trip of any length. On Friday the 13th of ·December he flew to El Paso for a final visit with one of his closest friends among foreign leaders, President Diaz Ordaz of Mexico. Together, they dedicated the Lopez Mateos Channel, symbolic of the agreement initiated by President Kennedy to restore a strip of Texas to Mexico. Standing on the bridge spanning the Rio Grande, they pushed a button that set off a dynamite blast to open the channel, but the water was so scarce that it was many minutes before a trickle ran down the concrete ditch. Afterward, there was a lengthy luncheon in the hot lobby of the Paso del Norte hotel, while American and Mexican photographers in the press room on the mezzanine resumed an argument over an encounter on the bridge when an overanxious Mexican got decked by a gringo for crowding him away from a picture. Thus the leaders pledged continued fidelity while the commoners fought as usual.

This was also the time for farewells in Washington, for nostalgia, for a good bit of sadness, and for anxiety over the future.

How would a man like Lyndon Johnson—a super-human dynamo on the Potomac for three decades—ever be able to adjust to a life of retirement on the Pedernales?

The news writers were posing that question to themselves every day, and their answers generally concluded that it would be impossible for him to do it. He would dabble in politics, he would run for office again himself, he would rip apart the Texas business scene and remake it in his own image, he would buy all of the land in the hill country.

These speculations had their obvious effect in the White House, but there was no way to stem the tide of stories about Johnson's future. "I'm going to do some reading, writing, and resting," he told reporters almost plaintively, but they did not believe him. One day he was reported dickering to buy one of the state's largest newspapers; the next he was solidifying his control over every bank within reach. No former assistant and no friend in Texas was given credit for any business deal on his own; Johnson was pictured in the background somewhere.

In the final days he did begin preparing for the inevitable. The Presidential library would be at the University of Texas in Austin; hundreds of thousands of documents and records had to be sorted, sealed, and moved from the White House. The university was also building a Lyndon B. Johnson School of Public Affairs; both the President and Mrs. Johnson were keenly interested in its shape and scope.

Johnson thought he might do some lecturing even before the opening of the school named for him. But he blew hot and cold on this chore.

"I'm not going to have a regular class," he told reporters. "I want to just exchange viewpoints with the youngsters. I hope to learn more than they do. I will probably get more out of them than they get out of me, because I may have been pretty well drained.

"But I want to go back, like Ponce de Leon, to the Fountain." His staff for Austin was pretty well set. Tom Johnson, my deputy, would head it. Bob Hardesty and Harry Middleton agreed to help him on his writings. Walt Rostow would be at the University of Texas, and available to help. Four of his most trusted longtime employees—Mildred Stegall, Willie Day Taylor, Mary Rather, and Dorothy Territo—were ready to go home with him. Bill Jorden would also come, leaving the Paris peace talks after the new American team had settled in sufficiently.

The rest of the White House people were beginning to scatter, in spirit if not in body. The lawyers were making plans to return to the law—Joe Califano, Charles Murphy, Harry McPherson, and DeVier Pierson in Washington, Ernie Goldstein in Paris, Larry Levinson in New York, Larry Temple in Austin. Barefoot Sanders was stranded on high center; his appointment to a judgeship in the District of Columbia would be sent to the Senate again in January, but there was a good chance Strom Thurmond and Richard Nixon would never let it come to a vote. (This is exactly what happened after January 20, and Sanders moved home to Dallas.) Jim Jones, newly married to a young and pretty attorney, would head for Tulsa and the law firm of Jones & Jones.

Legislative aide Mike Manatos hoped to continue to ply his trade on the Hill, representing private clients now. Fred Panzer, a research specialist whose duties included analyzing the public opinion polls (the President, naturally, called him his "poll cat"), would depart for the American Tobacco Institute. John Gonella and Chuck Roche of the legislative staff—Roche had been an original Kennedy campaigner in 1960—were looking for private business connections.

A few left early, thus avoiding the downhill struggle at the end.

Doug Cater was already hard at work writing his book, and Ben Wattenberg left for an identical venture. Sherwin Markman moved to a Washington law firm. John Roche's newspaper column was already in evidence. Will Sparks, a longtime writer for the President, departed for the New York financial world. George Reedy waited until after Christmas to return to private business.

Members of the National Security Council staff would soon be scattered to the winds. President Johnson sent Bill Bowdler to be ambassador to El Salvador and Nat Davis to be ambassador to Guatemala. Others were told that they would not be retained by Dr. Henry Kissinger in the new Administration and would return to the State Department, CIA, and other agencies from which they were borrowed. Bromley Smith, executive secretary of the NSC and operational manager of Walt Rostow's shop, got the news that he would be replaced, after serving in the post since Eisenhower's time.

One man with job security was Bill Hopkins, who had run the White House so competently for so long that he was immune. The same was true of Jiggs Fauver and his transportation office.

Others in the White House—secretaries, clerks, others who sometimes could survive a transition—had a jumpy Christmas season, wondering about their fate.

Nixon's incoming staff was admittedly short handed, so those without civil service protection still had a fifty-fifty chance of holding their jobs if they wanted them. Three of my seven secretaries remained—Connie Gerrard and Ann Garmon with the new press secretary, Ron Ziegler, and Sammie Bear with Vice President Agnew's office. A fourth, Jean Hundley, took a comparable job with another agency.

This was the pattern throughout the building. In the final analysis, very few government employees below the political level are tossed out in the street when the Presidency changes hands. Most have civil service ratings. Those who do not are usually in demand somewhere in the massive government if they want to stay. So President Nixon inherited a governmental apparatus that was predominantly Democratic, and there was very little he could do about it unless he desired to devote his entire time to the task.

The incoming President and his aides were quite considerate of Johnson's employees, but it was obvious they were already casting a wary eye at those believed to be top Democratic henchmen, or who had been openly partisan in the campaign. Even those with civil service protection were in line for removal by one means or another. Such are the rules of politics.

Johnson himself recommended that Nixon employ a strong loyalty test to those in policy-making roles. He urged Herbert Klein, the incoming communications director, to build a network of agency spokesmen loyal to Nixon and his policies—or suffer the consequences. Happily, some men in this group such as Bob McCloskey at the State Department and Dan Henkin at the Pentagon were able to weather the changeover. Others departed.

During his five years as President, Johnson discovered how simple it was for the man at the helm of government to be thwarted, boxed in, pushed or manipulated by underlings who might or might not have his interests at heart, or even share his views.

Free government cannot function as the will of one man, and the interchange of ideas within the executive branch certainly poses no threat to the Republic. Lyndon Johnson's predicament was that the political division within the Democratic Party was carried over into every facet of the Administration itself.

The war was part of it. The dovecote in the Senate Foreign Relations Committee was minuscule when compared with that in the executive agencies. Some assistant secretaries, public affairs officers, and finally a few who sat in the Cabinet itself were outspokenly anti-war. A good hostess could produce any number of Administration people willing to criticize the President at cocktail parties. Mixed with a liberal sprinkling of news media people, the evening could be delightful indeed.

Personality was part of it. Working for a President, especially a President who demands a great deal, can wear away the skin to the nerve ends. "He has been a good President, but—" was a rather common statement.

Political loyalties were a large part of it. Many Kennedy appointees simply never accepted Johnson, though grudgingly acknowledging his Great Society program. He was from the wrong part of the country and perhaps the wrong era. A Roosevelt populist and internationalist was all right in its place, but its place was not the post-John Kennedy era when bread and butter for "Molly and the kids" was not enough and when defending the world against Communism had died with John Foster Dulles. This oversimplifies their position, perhaps, but is close to the mark. Coupled with it for some of these people was a mixture of dislike, fear, and distrust of the man in the Oval Office; to them he was too overpowering, too self-oriented, too suspicious himself of the bureaucracy.

When the final split came with Robert Kennedy, there was no doubt about the loyalties of many in the Administration. They were Kennedy people, tried and tested. They had come into government on the wave of New Frontier optimism in 1961, and part of each of them died on November 22, 1963. A great many adapted and hitched their wagon to the Lyndon Johnson star, seeing in him the practical realization of their hopes for the nation. A great many others merely endured, waiting for the new leader from the Massachusetts shore.

It would be wrong to leave the impression that a disloyal government stood behind President Johnson or that the Administration was rife with unpatriotic and cynical hangers-on waiting for the opportunity to "do in" their leaders. There was, however, a decidedly anti-Johnson tinge to what was called the Johnson Administration, and it was no secret to anyone. How much it contributed to the troubled years of 1966–68 is conjectural and there is risk of overstating the case. But it is apparent that an Administration split along personality lines can be just as difficult for a President as one split along political lines, which Richard Nixon was destined to face.

It is small wonder that the people Johnson turned to were

those he had known for years and those whom he had learned to trust. The people he seemed to enjoy being with were employees, former employees like Margaret Mayer of the *Dallas Times Herald*, oldtime friends like the Bill Whites and the Bill Deasons, and relatively new but trusted friends like the Arthur Krims of New York City and Emmett and Marianne Means Reardon. There was also a small corterie from Capitol Hill, consisting mostly of members of the Texas delegation in the House of Representatives.

The President's close friends were by and large an intensely loyal group, receptive to his storehouse of tales and sympathetic to his problems. His social evenings were usually light hearted and heavily sprinkled with humor even when his duties were most onerous. He had the art of turning off a problem for a time and creating an interlude of pleasure and companionship when he could joke, tease, laugh, and talk until his heart's content, knowing that the "group" would keep his confidences. Sometimes after dinner there would be a movie in the White House theater—Mrs. Johnson and the girls loved films—but unless the plot caught the President's interest he was apt to doze off in his chair or retreat back upstairs for a rubdown and his night reading. The only film I ever knew him to like so much that he saw it more than once was the Spencer Tracy-Katharine Hepburn-Sidney Poitier heartwarmer, *Guess Who's Coming to Dinner*.

The loneliness of the Presidency may be an overworked cliche, but Lyndon Johnson did know loneliness. He was not happy when Mrs. Johnson was away and was like a caged lion if her absence was extended. His temper grew shorter and his hours at the office longer. Midnight dinners with whomever on the staff happened to be in the White House was the rule. The second floor of the Mansion could be an immensely barren place for a man alone. Sometimes the only companionship was provided by a little white dog named Yuki, which liked to sleep in the President's bed.

One evening in November, when Mrs. Johnson was on a trip, Jan and Barefoot Sanders invited Louann and Larry Temple and me to dinner at their house in the Virginia suburbs. Since my family was in Texas, I always took advantage of such opportunities. Tom Johnson was manning the night desk for the President and I told him I was slipping out to go to the Sanders'. An hour or so later a call came to Barefoot from the White House, asking if there were a couple of extra plates for Lyndon Johnson and Tom Johnson. They showed up shortly and Jan Sanders managed to divide the Mexican food sufficiently to take care of the surprise guests.

The President spent considerable time in Texas during his final weeks, as if he already yearned for the ranch even though the years on the Pedernales would stretch out soon enough and the glory of the White House would vanish even sooner. There was a long Thanksgiving weekend with Mrs. Johnson, the girls, and the grandchildren, then another weekend in mid-December. After Christmas it was back to the ranch for a week's work on the State of the Union message.

In Army-Secret Service parlance the LBJ Ranch was Volcano.* The reporters (and the staff) got a kick out of this, and in earlier days there was indeed a great deal of smoke and lava boiling forth when we were in Texas. Press visits to the ranch were common, and sometimes the news output in Texas was heavier than it was in Washington. But the last visits to the ranch were a study in Presidential silence. The day of spectaculars was ended.

Most of the travelling press had grown weary of Texas long before. Confinement to a hotel in Austin or San Antonio was no way to spend a week, and without plenty of work it could be sheer boredom. "Let's go down to the barber shop and watch the haircuts," was a typical comment. Newsmen who had developed friendships with local people fared much better, and during San Antonio's HemisFair in 1968 many brought their families down for the festivities, but the press in general never appreciated

* The White House, of course, was Crown, and Camp David was Cactus. For radio and code purposes the President was Volunteer, Mrs. Johnson was Victoria, Lynda was Velvet, and Luci was Venus. The staff had less glamorous pseudonyms. I inherited Welcome from Bill Moyers, Marvin Watson was Wisdom, Walt Rostow was Woodcutter, and Tom Johnson was the sonorous Whaleboat.

Johnson's lack of interest in resort areas for his working vacations. The President craved the home place, and only the home place.

"Work harder—the end is near," was the hand-printed sign Tom Johnson pinned above his desk in Washington.

But as the weeks narrowed down to a precious few, it became increasingly difficult to obey that admonition. The slowdown that began elsewhere in the government during the election period penetrated the White House from top to bottom, as one might expect. When the budget and the State of the Union were locked up, even those involved in these last-ditch labors were freed to contemplate their own futures. Busiest were those whose responsibilities concerned the move of materials and manpower to Texas, where after January 20 the Johnson Administration would turn its eyes to the past and leave the future to a fresher team.

Johnson's reflective moods were common now. "I have had great pleasure here," he said quietly to a group of columnists.

> I have seen a lot of my dreams come true. Of course, I have had some misfortunes and some disappointments. But I have nobody to blame. There is nothing of any consequence that I would change, as I look back. You say, 'He sure is a hard-headed, stubborn devil.' Well, that is the way I saw it and that is the way I see it now.
>
> But I have had the privilege of doing so many things that the average fellow can't do at all.

Johnson talked almost yearningly of how "nice" it would be to turn the office over to a new President. He always resented stories about his "tired Administration, but toward the end he confided to newsmen that Nixon would bring "fresh folks who want to come and stay instead of those who want to leave after eight years." And he talked of the vigor and "new ideas" of an incoming Administration.

About his plans for Texas, the President told the story of the man for whom he obtained a postmaster's appointment while he was a Congressman. Every time he visited his district, Johnson related, this postmaster told him he wanted to resign.

"I don't like to stomp around on these marble floors with my boots," was the explanation.

"Have you checked with your wife and buddies?" the Congressman asked.

"Yes."

"Are they for it?"

"They are against it."

"What did your mother say?"

"She said, 'You have the only job you ever had in your life where you can wear a necktie and now you are quitting it.'"

That was the way he felt, Johnson concluded. He wanted to go back where he did not have to wear a necktie.

One day I was having a farewell luncheon in the Fish Room for the three Australian newsmen stationed in Washington—Peter Barnett of the Australian Broadcasting Commission, Roy McCartney of the *Melbourne Herald*, and newcomer Bill Tipping of the *Melbourne Age*. The President, who loved Australia and Australians, dropped in for long reminiscences about his two Presidential visits to their country. On the latter trip—to attend the memorial service for his friend Prime Minister Holt—Johnson had invited Barnett and McCartney to accompany him as his guests, and it turned out to be a trip around the world.

Someday, the President told them, he wanted to go to Australia as a private citizen. If he were ever run out of the United States, he repeated an old pledge, he would head "down under" to live if they would have him.

When he had shaken hands and left the room, Tipping remarked sadly, "When he's gone it will be the end of an era in relations between our country and yours."

Presidential farewell appearances were the order of the day in the last few weeks. He posed for pictures with groups of White House employees—the police, the telephone operators, the mail clerks, the secretaries. For each there would be a group picture to remember him by.

A high point in emotion was the two hundredth and final State Dinner of the Administration, honoring Shaikh Sabah Al-Salim

Al-Sabah, Amir of Kuwait. White House social aide Bess Abell had recruited the same entertainers who had appeared at Johnson's first State Dinner, for President Antonio Segni of Italy in 1964. These were Robert Merrill, the operatic baritone, and the New Christy Minstrels in their green and white costumes. The guests ate pompano and pheasant, wild rice and braised celery. The Air Force Strolling Strings winded their way among the tables with nostalgic dinner music, and even a lengthy address by the Amir on the Palestinian refugee problem did little to bring a weighty note into the proceedings.

Afterward we crowded into the East Room to hear Merrill and the Minstrels. The opera star, who had once caused a mild scandal by singing "I've Got Plenty of Nothin'" at a White House dinner honoring British Prime Minister Harold Wilson whose country was experiencing a sterling shortage, would have offended no one in the Kuwaiti group this night if he had sung it again. But the Arab world's rich uncles heard instead another selection from Porgy and Bess, "It Ain't Necessarily So," sung by the poor Jewish boy from the streets of New York.

When the Minstrels took over, they sang—as did Merrill—the same songs they had sung at that first State Dinner long ago when the Great Society was young. "Follow the Drinking Gourd" was one, recalling the name for the Big Dipper in the days of the underground railroad when runaway slaves trudged northward. There was even a little testimonial from Minstrel Fats Johnson on a more contemporary theme: "Every time we go on campus someone asks why we don't sing protest songs. We don't sing them because we aren't protesting anything and because with all of its faults this is the best land in the world . . . and I get tired of people protesting against wars they never fought."

Then they sang "Green Green," which has a line: "I'm going away . . . to where the grass is greener still. . . ."

Old Cab Calloway was one of the guests and he told Margaret Mayer and my wife about his band's tour of Texas in the early 1930's. It had been humiliating to play in the Majestic Theater in Austin with the Negroes segregated in the balcony and to be run out of the city of Fort Worth. But a lot had happened since the 1930's, and after the entertainment when the guests were gathered in the foyer for dancing, Cab Calloway gave an impromptu performance with the Marine combo.

Arm in arm with the Texan President, he graveled out the 1964 campaign song with gusto: "Well, hello Lyndon . . . Golly gee, Lyndon . . . We have faith in thee, Lyndon. . . ." And a new ending: "You'll always be in our hearts, where you belong. . . ."

On December 16 the President, carrying Lyn Nugent, drove the short distance to the Ellipse near the Washington Monument to light the National Christmas Tree, a giant spruce from Utah. The weather was icy, and he was developing a cold equal in severity to his October infection.

On the seventeenth he drove to the Post Office Department for a farewell assembly of the postal workers. Postmaster General Watson had dug down in his own pocket to buy one hundred and twenty dollars worth of stamps—every issue since Johnson came to Congress in 1937. That night there were further tributes and gifts at the Federal-City Club near the White House at a reception sponsored by scores of Negro appointees and elected officials. Typically, Johnson took with him Preston Bruce, an assistant White House usher for many years and father-in-law of a Johnson judicial appointee (to Cardinal Spellman's funeral at St. Patrick's Johnson had taken his barber and good friend, Steve Martini). At the reception the President swapped quips with Supreme Court Justice Thurgood Marshall and ignored a sore throat to make a long, impassioned, and humorous speech about Negro progress and Negro friends.

The next morning I was called to the President's bedroom shortly after nine o'clock and found him dressing. His face was flushed. "Dr. Burkley says I should go to Bethesda," he said. "Tell the press I'm running a good fever and whatever else Dr. Burkley says you should tell them. Ride out there with me if you're not afraid of bugs."

So we departed for the naval hospital, with the doctor and Colonel Jim Cross, who had just returned from Vietnam and had dropped in to see Johnson. Riding the elevator to the third floor suite he had occupied several times before, Johnson told his medical escort: "Dr. Burkley thought you needed some business. You doctors don't have enough to do. What I really think is that he wanted me to get in here so he could enjoy his eggnog at home." The President, with temperature near one hundred and two degrees, was put to bed and promptly went to sleep.

Loyd Hackler and I set up a temporary press office at the hospital. Tom Johnson had been floored by pneumonia for several days, and a number of other White House people were afflicted with pre-Christmas miseries. The doctors told me to advise the press that Johnson had "flu-like symptoms," and I stuck dutifully to that line for a couple of days. Then I paid a call on the President, who got rid of that mishmash in a hurry. "I don't have flu-like symptoms," he snapped. "I've got the flu, the F-L-U."

The White House was a gloomy place during these days but not because of Johnson's flu, which we knew to be that and nothing more. In addition to the regular doldrums, Frank Borman, James Lovell, and Bill Anders were about to be launched by a Saturn rocket, spun out of orbit, and pointed toward the moon. The event sneaked up on us, as it apparently did the American people. It was almost inconceivable even to us that such an achievement was that close to realization, and the predominant feeling was one of apprehension. The NASA people were busily explaining everything that could go wrong with the space shot, and it all added up to three lost astronauts. The President was as much on edge as the rest of the world. I was staying at the White House now and had breakfast nearly every morning in the Mess with Dr. Ed Welsh, head of the Space Council. His matter-of-fact discussion of possible mishaps was bolstered by a calm confidence that the project would succeed, but the rest of us had plenty of doubts.

The President sat in a chair in his hospital room and watched the launch. Later he sent the three astronauts a message praising their courage and "the world's finest equipment." But he added that every step of the mission would be decided on the basis of safety.

There was another message, to the just-released crew of the Pueblo: "We are all aware of the ordeal through which you have passed, and we thank God it has ended."

And yet another, the armed forces at Christmastime:

It was your destiny to serve your nation in an hour of grave crisis. To you fell the hard duty of preserving freedom in the agony of war—during a restless time of doubt and division. . . . This will be my last Christmas message to you as your Commander in Chief. But I will remember you all the days of my life, as the patriots who manned the watchtowers in a time of peril, so that we might live as free men.

The President was home for Christmas, his second at the White House. The first four were spent at the ranch. On December 27, Apollo 8 splashed down in the Pacific, and Johnson promptly called the three wives of the astronauts. No prepared statement this time, just an expression of pride and thankfulness.

Later in the morning he was asked by the reporters how he felt about the period of waiting before the splashdown.

"I don't guess your blood pressure can get down completely normal until you see the astronauts come up out of that water, until they come on the carrier, until they are moved back home."

Walt Rostow informed the President that the Russian personnel manning their end of the teletype "hot line" in Moscow had asked for information on Apollo 8 during the voyage. The American technicians kept them posted throughout, using news reports in place of the encyclopedia passages normally transmitted to check the line.

Johnson relayed this development to the astronauts aboard the carrier. As for their accomplishment, he said: "We know that all the engineering marvels in the world could not take away one whit of our commitment and admiration for the three of you who were out there in the vastness of space. If I could have ex-

changed thoughts with you, I was going to ask you whether it felt
better coming down or going up. . . ."

On January 9, the astronauts were brought to the White House
for the traditional presentation of their NASA Distinguished
Service Medals by the President. There was little anyone could
add to the ocean of words that had described and lauded man's
first flight to the moon, his first escape from the gravity of earth,
but Johnson summed up his remarks with what he called "the
ultimate truth," that "there are few social or scientific or political
problems which cannot be solved by men, if they truly want to
solve them together."

Frank Borman stepped up and told Johnson: "Mr. President,
Jim Lovell has a picture of the ranch I think you would like to
have." The audience laughed when Lovell handed him a photograph of the earth taken from the moon.

The Johnson's farewells to the Congress began with a reception
in Longworth Office Building cafeteria, which smelled strongly
of old lettuce and salad dressing but was a bi-partisan love fest.
Curiously, the first new member of the House to shake his hand
was Allard Lowenstein of New York. In the snows of the previous
winter, it was Lowenstein the citizen who started the movement
to ditch old hawk Johnson in favor of a peace candidate.

The President saw Hubert Humphrey again after Humphrey
had gone to Norway for the funeral of Trigve Lie, onetime Secretary General of the United Nations. The big story about the trip
had been the stoning of the American Embassy in Oslo. It had
happened four hours before Humphrey arrived and the police
had not determined whether the vandals were anti-war demonstrators or not. Humphrey related that he talked to a number of
Norwegian young people at the funeral and saw no signs of anti-
Americanism, but the U.S. Information Service would never be
able to sell that story. The stoning of the embassy was big news,
and as Humphrey told it, "NBC read Reuters and cabled their
man in Oslo: 'Should we send crew to cover Humphrey riot?' "

"What are you going to do after January 20?" Johnson asked
his Vice President.

"Go to Cleveland on the twenty-first and make a speech, for pay," Humphrey responded.

On January 14 the President held his one hundred and eighteenth, and last, Tuesday luncheon in the Family Dining Room. The regulars were all there, except for General Wheeler, who was out of the country and was represented by General McConnell of the Air Force.

"Is there any feeling among the Joint Chiefs that the bombing should be resumed?" the President asked McConnell.

"Not at this time," the general replied.

That was about the extent of the business transacted.

In the pre-Clifford days, Bob McNamara had always been attentive to the historic serving plates used at the Mansion. It was his habit to study the plate, then pick it up and read the label on the back. I picked up the habit and today noted that the serving plates were Benjamin Harrison 1892, with a black rim circling an eagle and the national motto.

Dean Rusk volunteered to serve the sherry, aided by McConnell. "I've got to serve from the left," the Secretary corrected himself when he almost poured from the wrong side. "I have to get ready for civil life."

When the waiters brought in the lamb chops and baked eggplant, the President noted that the eggplant was steaming hot as usual.

"Dean, I want to warn you before you burn your tongue," he said to Rusk. "This is the last time you'll have to eat this. I know it's the last time I'm going to eat it."

That night Johnson made what the press called his "sentimental journey" to the House Chamber to deliver the State of the Union message in person. No President had done it that way since John Adams. Johnson had had brief doubts that he should make a personal appearance, but everyone around him was opposed to a bland and anti-climactic message delivered to the Congress and read by a clerk.

A year before, he had gone to this chamber half-convinced that he should end his State of the Union message with a statement of retirement after his term was completed. He had had me draft this portion of the speech in secrecy, and I had gone to the extreme of having Tom Johnson type a clean copy rather than widen the small circle who knew he was considering withdrawal. Believing the statement was in his pocket, where I had seen him put it, I had waited expectantly in the rear of the chamber for the bombshell. It did not come; he had left the statement behind at the White House rather than be tempted. He had decided this wasn't the time or place. On March 31 he finally took the step he had been debating with himself since early autumn. And the search for a graceful way to quit was over.

Tonight I stood at the back of the chamber and heard wave after wave of applause as the President walked down the aisle and mounted the rostrum. This was high drama ("Great theater in the very best sense of that word," said Senator Charles Percy afterward). He was smiling in that close-mouthed way of his, and when he nodded from side to side the applause and cheers rose a few decibels. Finally he began. His tone was neither brash nor apologetic as he spelled out briefly the goals of his Administration, at home and abroad. He said the nation had found a "new confidence" in meeting some of the challenges of the past five years, but acknowledged also that there was "turbulence and doubt" in meeting others. Throughout this time, he said, "I have been sustained by my faith in representative democracy."

He spoke of America's commitment to the betterment of life. "Breaking those promises would be a tragedy for our country." He ticked off only a few recommendations: Wilbur Cohen's Kiddiecare, increased Social Security, more money for housing, more money for the model cities program, more "teeth" in the fair housing and voting rights programs, expanded job training.

As for Vietnam, he said the prospects for peace were better than at any time since the war effort was stepped up in 1965. There was still hard fighting ahead, and the nation owed its enduring gratitude to its men at the front. Because of our commitment, the free nations of Asia were now sure that we cared about them.

He hoped the Senate would act promptly on the nuclear non-proliferation treaty and that arms talks with the Soviet Union could be resumed. The Israeli-Arab hostility would be another powder keg left to his successor, but he hoped for an early settlement.

Fifty-one times during the forty-five minute speech he was interrupted by applause, and his audience saved the loudest cheers for the personal comments that came near the end. This was when he spoke of his first love, the Congress, and pointed to the gallery where he had served as a doorkeeper in his first year in Washington, thirty-eight years before.

He called for national unity and for support of President Nixon, who "will need your understanding, just as I did." Of Nixon he went on to say, "The burdens he will bear will be borne for all of us."

Then, in a hushed chamber, he spoke his epilogue: "I hope it may be said, a hundred years from now, that by working together we helped to make our country more just—more just for all its people—as well as to insure the blessings of liberty for our posterity. I believe it will be said that we tried."

The audience did not seem to understand he had finished, but as he closed his speech book the shouts and cheers from both Democrats and Republicans erupted, and when he began to make his way to the door of the chamber dozens of hands went out to him and some of the more sentimental Congressmen began to sing "Auld Lang Syne" but were drowned out in the tumult.

In the gallery Lady Bird Johnson wiped her eyes but claimed later it was because Lyn Nugent had swung his baby bottle around, and she was afraid he would drop it over the rail and conk a Congressman. She said she was laughing, not crying. The press took this as a small credibility gap.

The President was relieved that it was over, elated by the reaction, pleased that his finale had been successful. There was brief panic when he discovered he had left his wristwatch on the rostrum; but Jim Jones retrieved it. So the President returned in a quiet motorcade to the White House with everything he took with him, leaving only an ocean of good will on both sides of the aisle, something that he had sometimes failed to generate in five hectic years. The Republicans decided not to have their customary post-State of the Union press conference to denounce the Democratic President.

It was one of those rare moments in American history when nearly everybody likes a President, or at least masks his dislike. It is easy, of course, to respect a man at the end of his career. Only a few days would be needed for the old divisions to reappear, and President Nixon would get his taste of that, but for the moment all was serene in the cold Washington winter.

"In his farewell to politics, to the Hill and to the Presidency last night, Johnson added a graceful finale to five of the most rancorous years in our history," wrote Haynes Johnson of the *Washington Star*.

The epitaphs were flowing freely in the nation's press. Charles Roberts of *Newsweek* summed up the Administration with these words:

> He leaves office a man whose epitaph will someday defy the confines of even a Texas-size tombstone: the most militant civil-rights advocate ever to occupy the White House, reviled by Negro militants; a Southerner scorned by Southerners as a turncoat; a liberal despised by liberals despite the fact he achieved most of what they sought for thirty years; a friend of education—rejected by intellectuals; a compromiser who could not compromise a war ten thousand miles away; a consensus-seeker who in the clutch abandoned his consensus rather than his convictions; a power-hungry partisan politician who, in the end, shunned power and partisanship to achieve national unity.

And Max Frankel, in the *New York Times*, pointed out that young protestors were wearing lapel buttons proclaiming, with hostile intent but obvious ambiguity, that "L.B.J. will go down in history." Frankel concluded: "It is fair only to guess that Lyndon Baines Johnson was a man of such ferocious appetite and intensity and a President who did so much while trying for still so much more, that he will, as the buttons said, go down in history."

At the President's last Cabinet meeting he was presented with his chair, purchased by the Cabinet officers, to take back to Texas. There was a series of praise and appreciation, and perhaps the most eloquent tribute came from Russ Wiggins, onetime editor of the *Washington Post* and now U.S. Ambassador to the United Nations. "It is seldom that within the electoral span of a single Administration do we plant and harvest," he said. "Usually the results are deferred until after that Administration has been succeeded by others. We are really orchardists and not grain growers. Crop maturity is long deferred. I feel confident, Mr. President, that when the fruits of your policies are gathered in, Americans are going to say how great the harvest has been."

Johnson took the occasion to say nice things about as many of his staff as he could think of. Then Mrs. Johnson came in, and he asked her to say goodbye to the Cabinet.

"It has been a high excitement to have been associated with people like you," he said. "It has been a great adventure. I have loved it, every hour of it, and I have learned a lot, I think . . . I hope. I am just so proud of you, everyone, and so glad my country has had your services and that I have had you as friends. Several words I have cut out of my vocabulary. Among them are 'last' and 'goodbye.' So I will look forward to seeing all of you."

It appeared that the meeting would end on that relatively saddening note, but the President chose not to permit it. Remembering that he had not said a word of praise for DeVier Pierson, he remarked: "I didn't mention the best lawyer in the White House. I commend him to any of you who may be investigated in the next few months."

On Sunday I appeared on *Meet the Press* for my swan song. I was pleased that Larry Spivak had assembled a first-rate panel—Ray Scherer, Pete Lisagor, Tom Wicker, and Hugh Sidey. Since I was now virtually an historic figure rather than a live press secretary, it was the most gentle jousting I had ever received.

They seemed to be more interested in getting it across to the new Administration that the press bites when it isn't fed.

This left-handed question from Lisagor: "Mr. Christian . . . isn't the President likely to get a reputation for being secretive and devious, if he leaves an ill-informed spokesman at the mercy of the White House press? You attended those Tuesday luncheons. You knew the substance of great affairs. Do you think that a press secretary . . . perhaps the new one coming in . . . ought to be as informed as you were?"

It was difficult for me to suppress a grin as I assured the panel I agreed.

Hugh Sidey asked me in his nicest Iowa tone of voice: "Have you ever directly lied, Mr. Christian?"

"I have not," I answered firmly.

"You have not done that," Sidey responded, and it sounded to me as if he said it with conviction. As they say, I felt warm all over. At long last, I was believed!

On Johnson's last Sunday in the White House the Marine Corps band played a new tune for him on the South Lawn: "The Pedernales River March." It will never replace "The Stars and Stripes Forever," but it seemed fitting enough as the young men in red coats belted it out while the President and his family stood smiling on the Truman Balcony. That night Walt Rostow did a virtuoso performance of the march on the White House piano, leading me to believe he may have been the secret composer.

On Monday morning Johnson worked hastily on last-minute matters, then was hustled into his morning coat by Ken Gaddis to greet Richard Nixon when he arrived at 10:30 a.m. The President had assigned Leonard Marks, director of the U.S. Information Agency, to coordinate the inaugural events from his standpoint, and he had been briefed down to the final minute of his waning Presidency.

Mrs. Johnson prowled the White House, drinking in the last sights of familiar nooks and crannies and saying goodbye to the Mansion staff. My wife and I ran into her on the third floor, where she was touring the guest bedrooms and the solarium for the last time. "I'm just saying goodbye to a wonderful, wonderful place," she murmured.

In the press office my three remaining girls—Evelyn Furgerson, Ann Garmon, and Connie Gerrard—were buried in press releases. Last minute actions by the outgoing President, including a string of Medals of Freedom, had to be announced. It was nearly noon when the final handout from the Johnson White House was dropped in the press room.

The last minutes were traumatic, to say the least. There was a general rushing around from office to office to say the inevitable goodbyes, and some of us were still packing tag-end Johnson materials that morning. The girls were giving way to their emotions as the realization began to strike home that it was all over, and somehow the hard years didn't seem so bad.

At 11:05 a.m. Leonard Marks ushered the two Presidents and Senator Dirksen into the black Presidential limousine for the drive to the Capitol through the gray and icy morning. From that point on it became Richard Nixon's day.

As I started to climb into the press pool car for the motorcade, Glen Phillips walked up to tell me goodbye. He had cut his ties with the University of Texas to help me in the press office during the final year, and of all the people I knew, he hated to leave the most.

"Where are you going?" I asked him.

"Back to my apartment to watch the tube, I guess," he said. "After that, I don't know."

He walked reluctantly out the gate onto Pennsylvania Avenue and was lost in the crowd of spectators.

For Johnson after the inaugural ceremony there was a luncheon for the closest of the close friends at the Bethesda home of Clark and Marnie Clifford. There were a few from the Senate—Henry Jackson, Birch Bayh, and Gale McGee, among them. Jake Pickle, the President's home district Congressman and longtime colleague, was there. Only some of the Cabinet members were on hand, and

Henry Fowler, the faithful former Treasury Secretary who had rejoined the banking world. We ate ham and drank bloody marys and told each other goodbye until there was little else to say.

Outside, the crowd pressed around the house. Whenever Johnson or one of his family appeared at the front door, they cheered. "Tell the press," Averell Harriman said to me, "that Marnie Clifford regrets she has but one lawn to give to her country."

At Andrews Air Force Base the band played "Hail to the Chief," although he wasn't the Chief any longer, and a frost-bitten crowd of old friends shook the Johnsons' hands until they finally got aboard the plane.

At 3:43 p.m., Boeing 707, No. 26000 departed for Texas. It was difficult to believe that for this flight it was no longer Air Force One.

Index

ABC (American Broadcasting Company), 60, 133, 196, 197, 208, 213

Abell, Bess, 15, 264

Abrams, General Creighton, 33, 34, 48, 53, 70, 71, 82–92, 101, 102, 104, 106, 112, 113, 118, 120

Adams, Sherman, 246

Agnew, Spiro T., 156, 161, 243, 245, 246, 257

Agronsky, Martin, 145

Albert, Carl, 25, 37, 105

Alsop, Joe, 202

Apple, R. W., Jr., 128, 129, 217

Arends, Leslie, 105

Associated Press (AP), 7, 23, 50, 61, 62, 72, 98, 126, 130, 183, 184, 186, 191, 200, 216, 220, 230

Ball, George, 75, 78, 115, 158, 165

Baltimore Sun, 6, 192, 194, 221

Bartlett, Charles, 202, 248

Baskin, Bob, 194, 220

Beech, Keyes, 109

Boggs, Hale, 25, 105

Borman, Frank, 266, 268

Boyd, Alan, 239, 243

Brinkley, David, 195

Buchwald, Art, 231

Bundy, McGeorge, 11, 50, 51, 53, 54, 218

Bundy, William, 50, 54

Bunker, Ambassador Ellsworth, 23, 33, 34, 48, 53–55, 57, 59, 61, 63, 64, 70, 82, 84, 88, 95–102, 104, 109, 113, 114, 131, 132, 134, 138, 218

Burkley, Admiral George, 15, 265, 266

Califano, Joe, 8, 13, 14, 16, 18, 71, 75, 165, 235, 238, 239, 254, 256

Calloway, Cab, 264, 265

Cambodia, 33, 79, 87, 114, 119, 137, 140

Carpenter, Liz, 15, 73, 100, 230

Cater, Douglass, 11, 14, 165, 185, 239, 257

CBS (Columbia Broadcasting Company), 57, 67, 76, 92, 135, 136, 145, 173, 197, 201, 209, 212–214

Chancellor, John, 196

Chapman, General Leonard, 54

Chennault, Mrs. Anna, 93, 94, 109, 110, 249

Chicago Daily News, 109, 135, 193, 201

Chicago Tribune, 194

Christian George, 8, 14, 16, 17, 19, 20, 24–26, 29–32, 35, 36, 38, 41, 42, 48–50, 52, 53, 55, 56, 59–61, 65, 68–72, 82, 85–89, 91, 92, 102, 110, 123, 125, 126, 129, 131, 136, 137, 139, 142, 151, 158, 169, 172, 173, 179–181, 183, 186, 191, 196, 199–203, 206–216, 218–225, 228–230, 248, 252, 260, 261, 263, 265, 266, 270, 273, 276

Christian, Jo Anne, 142, 264, 274

Christian Science Monitor, 6, 199

Christopher, Warren, 238

Clark, Ramsey, 16, 72, 154, 164, 239

Clifford, Clark, 48, 51–58, 64,

67, 70, 73, 75–79, 82, 85, 95, 101, 102, 110, 112–116, 127, 129, 132–137, 144, 145, 174, 198, 238, 244, 275
Clifford, Marnie, 275, 276
Cohen, Wilbur, 164, 239, 240, 243, 270
Congressional Record, 6
Connally, Governor John B., 166, 177, 208
Cook, Judge Marlow, 172
Cooke, Archbishop Terence, 167
Cormier, Frank, 191, 220, 221
Cornell, Douglas, 72, 184
Cronkite, Walter, 197, 212, 213
Cross, Colonel Jim, 11, 265
Cunningham, Walter, 27, 176

Dallas News, 194, 220
Dallas Times Herald, 260
Daniel, Margaret, 38–40
Daniel, Price, 208, 220, 221
Deakin, Jim, 201, 202
Debré, Michel, 23, 26, 27
De Gaulle, Charles, 21, 27, 98
Dewey, Governor Tom, 166, 168
Dirksen, Senator Everett, 31, 62, 105, 123, 124, 176, 275
DMZ, 33, 34, 60, 65, 82, 83, 86, 87, 101, 104, 112, 118, 119, 132, 133, 151
Dobrynin, Anatoly, 142, 143
Drummond, Roscoe, 202

Eisele, Donn, 27, 176
Eisenhower, President Dwight, 30, 40, 41, 110, 131, 152, 155, 170, 187, 191, 197, 206, 246, 257
Eisenhower, Mrs. Dwight, 93
Ellington, Governor Buford, 59, 236, 238
Evans, Cliff, 199

Face the Nation, 67, 135
Fauver, Jiggs, 20, 173, 257

Fehmer, Marie, 15, 43, 97
Fleming, Bob, 30, 200
Ford, Gerald, 37, 105, 156
Fortas, Abe, 21, 55, 252
Fowler, Henry, 144, 276
Frankel, Max, 222, 272
Freeman, Orville, 22, 37, 164, 177, 217, 239
Fulbright, Senator J. William, 31, 145

Gaddis, Ken, 15, 100, 274
Gaither, Jim, 13, 235
Garmon, Ann, 257, 275
Gerrard, Connie, 191, 257, 275
Ginsburgh, Brigadier General Bob, 85, 86
Glassboro, New Jersey, 141, 144, 160
Goldberg, Arthur, 218, 223, 224
Goldstein, Ernest, 14–16, 256
Gonella, John, 17, 256
Gorton, John, 61
Goulding, Phil, 211–213

Hackler, Loyd, 35, 72, 100, 105, 106, 125, 191, 211, 225, 226, 266
Hanoi, 32–34, 48, 50–55, 57, 58, 60, 63–65, 69, 70, 73, 74, 76, 79, 82, 83, 89, 91, 94–96, 101, 104, 106, 109–111, 114, 115, 117, 118, 122, 132, 133, 136, 137, 152, 153
Hardesty, Bob, 14, 36, 47, 256
Harlow, Bryce, 128, 129
Harriman, Averell, 32, 53–55, 57, 58, 63, 64, 70, 73, 83, 95, 96, 112, 136, 152, 276
Harvan, 32, 33, 53, 79, 82, 86
Helms, Dick, 48, 52, 56, 57, 85, 102
Hill, Clint, 163
Ho Chi Minh, 32, 96, 119, 121, 152
Holt, Harold, 224, 263

Hoover, President Herbert, 11, 41, 170, 245
Hopkins, Bill, 11, 257
Horner, Garnett (Jack), 124, 193, 226
Humphrey, Hubert, 11, 21, 22, 26, 31, 37, 42, 44–46, 51, 59–61, 63, 67, 74, 75, 77–81, 89, 94, 102, 104, 105, 107–109, 111, 118, 133, 147–153, 156–159, 161, 164–168, 170, 171, 174–178, 180, 181, 195, 196, 233, 234, 238, 245, 268, 269
Humphrey, Muriel, 148
Huntley, Chet, 197
Huong, Prime Minister, 96

Inouye, Senator Dan, 156
Issues and Answers, 133

Jackson, Senator Henry, 275
Jacobsen, Jake, 11
Jenkins, Walter, 11, 12
Johnson, Mrs. Lady Bird, 8, 9, 15, 19, 30, 35, 56, 66, 71, 73, 83, 96, 100, 107, 121, 122, 150, 153, 161, 176, 179, 215, 216, 229, 230, 242, 245, 254, 255, 260, 261, 271, 273–275
Johnson, Lyndon, 10–16, 19, 20, 23, 25, 32–37, 44–68, 70–77, 79–83, 92, 94–105, 108–134, 136–138, 142–167, 179–183, 185–193, 196–206, 208–210, 213–234, 239, 240, 243–256, 258–263, 268, 273–277
  morning habits of, 5–9
  telephone habits of, 17
  aptitude for administration, 18
  and nuclear weapons treaty, 21, 22, 24, 26–31, 43
  visits President Truman, 38–40
  signs farm bill, 42
  and gun control bill, 24, 43, 69
  calls General Abrams to Washington, 84–91
  announces bombing halt of North Vietnam, 106, 107
  and Pueblo incident, 139, 140
  meets with Kosygin, 141
  makes speeches on Humphrey's behalf, 168–178
  dispute with Wirtz, 235–238
  differences with Udall, 241, 242
  sent to Bethesda Naval Hospital, 265–267
  delivers last State of Union message, 269–272
Johnson, Tom, 8, 17, 19, 30–32, 35, 38, 41, 42, 48, 52, 55, 56, 72, 73, 85, 88, 102, 125, 163, 169, 179, 191, 199, 224, 245, 256, 261, 262, 266, 270
Jones, Jim, 8, 14, 19, 30, 34, 42, 47, 73, 86, 88, 98, 172, 256, 271
Jorden, William, 62, 256

Kalb, Marvin, 57, 76
Kaplow, Herb, 182
Katzenbach, Nicholas, 78
Kennedy, David, 250–252
Kennedy, Senator Edward, 45, 250, 251
Kennedy, Mrs. Jacqueline, 65
Kennedy, President John F., 10, 15, 41, 52, 76, 81, 140, 148, 152, 154, 170, 185, 188, 191, 197, 205, 206, 230, 239, 252, 254, 256, 259
Kennedy, Senator Robert F., 44, 118, 154, 160, 161, 164, 218, 241, 259
Khrushchev, Nikita, 76, 142
Kilpatrick, Carroll, 28, 193, 224
Kissinger, Dr. Henry, 257
Klein, Herbert, 123, 211, 258
Knebel, Fletcher, 184
Knoll, Erwin, 219, 225
Kosygin, Chairman, 34, 137, 141–146, 160, 202

Kraft, Joe, 202
Krim, Arthur, 82, 260
Krock, Arthur, 185
Ky, Nguyen Cao, 64, 89, 96, 97, 101, 132, 134, 136

Laird, Melvin, 75, 244
Laise, Carol, 131
Lam, Pham Dang, 95, 96
Lawrence, Bill, 208
LeMay, General Curtis, 74, 161, 168
Levinson, Larry, 13, 16, 17, 24, 254, 256
Lewine, Fran, 50, 73
Lincoln, Abraham, 52, 120, 170
Lippmann, Walter, 202
Lisagor, Peter, 135, 193, 273, 274
Loan, Ngo Minh, 53
Lodge, Henry Cabot, 122, 125, 131, 217–219
Long, Senator Russell, 25, 250
Lovell, James, 266, 268

Macy, John, 209
Maguire, Charles, 14, 59, 169
Manatos, Mike, 11, 14, 17, 256
Manning, Bob, 173
Mansfield, Senator Mike, 22, 25, 26, 31, 105, 123
Markman, Sherwin, 257
Marks, Leonard, 223, 274, 275
Marshall, Thurgood, 265
Mayer, Margaret, 260, 264
McBride, Rosemary, 191, 212
McCafferty, Art, 5, 7
McCarthy, Senator Eugene, 31, 44, 45, 118, 153, 154, 158, 167
McClendon, Sarah, 201, 231
McCloskey, Bob, 65, 69, 70, 211, 258
McConnell, General J. P., 54, 269
McCormack, John, 25, 26, 42, 65, 105
McGaffin, Bill, 201, 219

McGovern, Senator George, 31, 45, 118
McNamara, Robert, 56, 77, 115, 116, 141, 144, 213, 214, 217, 269
McPherson, Harry, 14–17, 22, 26, 28, 35, 37, 42, 73, 85, 88, 89, 95, 100, 256
Means, Marianne, 202, 260
Medici, Giuseppe, 23, 27, 28
Meet the Press, 198, 273
Middleton, Harry, 14, 36, 47, 256
Mills, Wilbur, 243, 250
Minneapolis Tribune, 184
Mitchell, John, 244
Momyer, General William W., 71
Monroney, Senator Mike, 181
Moorer, Admiral Thomas, 54
Morse, Wayne, 31, 181
Moyers, Bill, 11–14, 20, 208
Murphy, Charles S., 14, 233, 234, 243, 256
Murphy, Robert D., 125, 127, 129, 130, 145, 146, 244
Muskie, Edmund, 45, 61, 156, 157, 161, 165, 170, 171, 175–177, 181

NASA, 22, 68, 209, 266, 268
National Liberation Front (NLF), 32, 58, 69, 70, 95, 96, 106, 109, 111, 114, 132, 134, 135, 138
National Security Council, 15, 28, 60, 102, 108, 142, 143, 148, 257
NBC (National Broadcasting Company), 6, 11, 17, 49, 106, 182, 195, 196, 201, 213, 268
Newsday, 12
Newsweek, 182, 203, 216, 227, 272
New York Times, The, 6, 57, 62, 128, 146, 185, 186, 192, 193, 207, 217–219, 222, 246, 272

New Yorker, The, 214, 215
Nitze, Paul, 78
Nixon, Mrs. Pat, 122, 245
Nixon, President-elect Richard, 21, 29, 31, 46, 51, 59–61, 63, 72, 74, 75, 77, 79–81, 93, 94, 102, 104, 105, 108–111, 121–131, 137, 138, 144–147, 154–156, 161, 163–169, 174-176, 180, 182, 187, 198, 211, 227, 234, 239, 243–252, 254, 256–259, 271, 272, 274, 275
Nixon, Tricia, 248
North Korea, 119, 137–141
North Vietnam, 27, 32–34, 51, 53, 58, 60, 61, 63, 67, 70, 73, 74, 76–80, 82, 83, 86, 87, 99–101, 106, 108, 109, 111, 112, 116–119, 128, 133–135, 138, 141, 149–151, 153, 212
Nugent, Luci, 35, 37–40, 43, 71, 100, 107, 176, 254
Nugent, Lyn, 27, 35, 36, 40, 43, 71, 107, 175, 254, 265, 271
Nugent, Pat, 71, 254

O'Brien, Larry, 11, 164, 165
Okamoto, Yoichi, 26, 98
Okun, Arthur M., 179
Onassis, Aristotle, 65
Ordaz, President Diaz, 254

Pachios, Harold, 224, 225
Palmer, General Bruce, 54
Paris peace talks, 24, 34, 69, 79, 84, 89, 95, 109, 131, 135, 136, 141, 152, 183, 256
Park, President Chung Hee, 139, 140
Pearson, Lester, 223, 224
Peden, Katherine, 171, 172
Perkins, Carl, 171, 172
Phillips, Glen, 200, 275
Phong, Nguyen Xuan, 138
Pickle, Jake, 275
Pierpont, Bob, 173, 201

Pierson, DeVier, 14, 22, 35, 37, 42, 73, 242, 256, 273
Pueblo, 137–141, 229, 267

Rather, Dan, 92, 209, 212–215
Rather, Mary, 15, 256
Rayburn, Sam, 40, 65, 154, 178
Reasoner, Harry, 197
Reedy, George, 11, 20, 208, 257
Reuters, 183, 194, 268
Robb, Major Chuck, 73, 254
Robb, Lucinda, 73, 100
Robb, Lynda Bird Johnson, 35, 56, 73, 100, 153, 229, 254
Roberts, Chalmers, 136, 202
Roche, Chuck, 11, 17, 256
Roche, John, 11, 17, 257
Roosevelt, President Franklin, 40, 41, 90, 102, 103, 170, 191, 245
Roosevelt, Theodore, 170, 242
Rostow, Walt, 8, 13, 15, 17, 18, 28, 32, 47, 48, 52, 54, 56, 59, 60, 62, 66, 77, 79, 82, 85, 88, 89, 95, 99–102, 110–112, 120, 129, 138, 142, 208, 211, 212, 256, 257, 267, 274
Rovere, Richard, 214, 215
Rowan, Steve, 136
Rusk, Dean, 32–34, 48, 51–60, 70, 73, 76, 77, 79, 82–89, 91, 95, 101, 102, 106, 110, 114–116, 119, 122, 125, 127, 129, 130, 133, 137, 139, 140, 143, 144, 158, 227, 244, 269
Rusk, Virginia, 116
Russell, Senator Richard, 54, 55, 145

Saigon, 23, 24, 29, 32, 48, 51, 53–55, 57–61, 63, 64, 67, 70–72, 77–79, 83, 84, 87–89, 94–97, 99–101, 109–111, 113, 114, 122, 124, 131–138, 158, 189, 212, 217, 218, 249
St. Louis Post-Dispatch, 94, 201, 220

Salinger, Pierre, 20
Sanders, Barefoot, 14, 16, 105, 252, 256, 260, 261
Scherer, Ray, 17, 182, 273
Schirra, Walter, 27, 176
Schneider, Wunebald, 48
Sidney, Hugh, 219, 273, 274
Sihanouk, Prince, 137, 140, 141
Smith, Al, 167, 175
Smith, C. R., 16, 239
Smith, Merriman, 184, 191, 200, 220, 221
Smothers Brothers, 171
South Vietnam, 23, 24, 32, 33, 63, 64, 67, 70, 78, 80, 81, 86, 88, 89, 91, 93, 95, 101, 105, 106, 111, 115, 117, 119, 128, 131–135, 138, 150–152, 154, 176, 212, 214, 217
Spivak, Lawrence, 198, 273
Staggers, Harley, 171, 173
Stennis, Senator John, 145
Stern, Carl, 49, 201
Stevenson, Adlai, 157
Stewart, Michael, 23, 27

Tass, 194
Taylor, Maxwell, 48, 52, 56, 82, 85
Temple, Larry, 8, 14, 16, 36, 71, 85, 256, 260
Thieu, President Nguyen Van, 23, 54, 55, 57–59, 61, 63, 64, 67, 70, 82, 84, 88–91, 95–101, 106, 109–115, 122, 124, 132–134, 138, 249
Tho, Le Duc, 52, 54
Thomas, Helen, 73, 99, 229
Truesdell, Norman, 47–49
Truman, Mrs. Bess, 30, 38–40
Truman, President Harry, 19, 30, 32, 34, 36, 38–41, 131, 152, 154, 157, 162, 168, 191, 205, 246, 254
Twain, Mark, 7, 55

Udall, Stewart, 240–242
United Press International (UPI), 7, 28, 98, 99, 125, 126, 183, 184, 191, 200, 220, 229, 230

Valenti, Jack, 9, 11, 177
Vance, Cyrus, 32, 53–55, 57, 58, 63, 70, 73, 75, 91, 95, 136, 138, 152, 217
Viet Cong, 33, 58, 78, 84, 100, 101, 111, 116, 154

Wallace, George, 46, 60, 61, 74, 102, 104, 105, 161, 164, 168, 169, 234
Wall Street Journal, 6
Washington Daily News, 192
Washington Post, 6, 7, 28, 74, 115, 124, 136, 186, 192, 193, 200, 202, 224, 235, 273
Washington Star, 95, 124, 158, 192, 193, 202, 226, 272
Watson, Marvin, 11–14, 16, 220, 221, 239, 265
Weaver, Robert, 239
Webb, Jim, 68, 209
Welsh, Dr. Edward, 165, 266
Westmoreland, General William C., 54, 86, 116, 118, 120, 217, 218
Wheeler, General Earle, 48, 51–53, 56, 76, 82, 85, 87, 102, 116, 118–121, 269
White, William S. (Bill), 186, 260
Wirtz, Alvin, 40
Wirtz, Willard, 71, 164, 235–239, 242

Yarborough, Senator Ralph, 166, 177
Youngblood, Rufus, 163

Ziegler, Ron, 123, 125, 126, 131, 248, 257
Zwick, Charles, 211, 234, 254